John Timms.

D0768694

SUFFERING

WHAT THE
BIBLE SAYS
ABOUT

SUFFERING

by

Willie W. White

College Press Publishing Company, Joplin, Missouri

Library of Congress Catalog Card Number: 84-71392
International Standard Book Number: 0-89900-096-7

Table of Contents

viii

Preface

In the back of a lonely wilderness a solitary shepherd walked with his sheep. At a mount called Horeb he was startled by a strange sight: a bush burned with fire without being consumed. As the wondering shepherd drew near to behold this remarkable sight, a divine voice called, "Moses, Moses, . . . put off thy shoes from off thy feet, for the place whereon thou standest is holy ground" (Exod. 3:4-5).

To presume to write concerning the problem of suffering is to walk on holy ground. It is ground where all have trod and it has been watered with tears and stained by the bloody footprints of the suffering ones.

The author approaches this awesome task with the profound realization that the problem of suffering is far beyond our fullest comprehension and that there are no easy answers. No amount of money can buy the answer. No philosopher can teach it. The God Who gave us being is the only One Who can tell us. I know of but one place to go to discover that divine answer: The Holy Bible. Hence the title of this volume, *What the Bible Says about Suffering.*

"What the Bible Says about Suffering" is not intended as a profound treatise for the scholar, but as a common-sense answer for the common man.

"What the Bible Says about Suffering" is written for the young husband and wife who are sitting in the hospital room, with aching throats and burning eyes, as they watch their only son losing his battle with leukemia.

It is written for those in the twilight years who are waiting in the nursing home, forgotten and alone.

It is written for the man who has just opened his pay envelope and found a "pink slip." How can he go home and tell his wife that there will be no money for the rent, the groceries, and their little one's surgery?

It is written for the widowed mother who has collapsed in her chair, clutching in her hand the piece of paper bearing the message which begins, "We regret to inform you . . ."

It is written for the heart-broken father who is entering the police morgue to identify the body of his boy who was driving under the influence of liquor.

It is written for the young wife who sits staring blankly into the telephone receiver as the voice of her best friend trails away: "I think I should tell you that your husband is having an affair with another woman."

It is written for the man who is bending low over the hospital bed to say "good-bye" to the one who has been his faithful and loving companion for more than fifty years.

It is written for the young person who is torn between the opportunity of a week in Christian camp and the invitation to attend a party where he knows there will be liquor and drugs and sex.

"What the Bible Says about Suffering" is not written from an ivory tower. It is one thing to explain suffering. It is quite another to suffer. How easy it is to sit in an easy chair and philosophize about suffering.

"What the Bible Says about Suffering" is written for the common man by a common man. It is written for the suffering by one who has known suffering. It is written for the lonely by one who has walked the vale of loneliness. It is written for the needy by one who, as a lad, knew the pinch of poverty. It is written with a hand reaching out to those who are in need of understanding and companionship.

The writer pleads guilty to being over-simplistic, but takes comfort in the knowledge that the Man of Nazareth spoke in such a way that common people heard Him gladly. I pray that common people may hear this treatise gladly and be comforted and blessed.

Willie W. White
April, 1984

Chapter One

PERFECT - THROUGH SUFFERINGS

One of the greatest evidences of God's love for His children is that He permits them to suffer—and gives them the grace to see it through. "But no one has ever suffered as I have suffered." Don't you believe it! Jesus did—and He was made perfect through sufferings.

> For it became him, for whom are all things, and through whom are all things, in bringing many sons unto glory, to make the author of their salvation perfect through sufferings (Heb. 2:10).

Can this be possible: Jesus Christ, the Son of God, the Saviour of men, the One Who made all things and for Whom all things were made, the Author of our salvation, "made perfect through sufferings?" Was He not divine? Was He not always perfect? Wherein was His imperfection, His weakness, His sin? Who was able to respond when He issued the challenge, "Which one of you convicteth me of sin?" (John 8:46). Does the author of the Hebrew letter contradict himself when he declares that Jesus was "without sin" (Heb. 4:15), and that He was "holy, guileless, undefiled, separated from sinners, and made higher than the heavens" (Heb. 7:26)? What can it mean: "Perfect through sufferings?"

In commenting on this dilemma, the splendid Greek scholar, A.T. Robertson, observes, "If one recoils from the idea of God making Christ perfect, he should bear in mind that it is the humanity of Jesus that is under discussion."[1] Note carefully the picture of the Son which is drawn in the preceding verses. He is superior to the angels and more to

---

1. A.T. Robertson, *Word Pictures in the New Testament* (Nashville, Tenn., 1933), vol. 5, p. 347.

be heeded, yet for those brief years in which He was subjected to human limitations He was made "a little lower than the angels" (v. 9). Our Lord was qualified to be the Savior of men only by suffering as a man.

Those who knew the language in which the author wrote did not share our problems of understanding the word "perfect." It is the Greek word *Teleiosai* (first aorist active infinite of *teleioō*). The outstanding Greek authority Thayer defines the word as "wanting nothing necessary to completeness . . . to bring the end (goal) proposed." The word might well be translated "finished," "completed," or "done." It contains the thought of fulfilling the purpose for which a thing is made, completed for a task. His sufferings completed the process of His training. "By means of sufferings" God perfected His Son in His human life for His task as Redeemer and Savior. Without suffering there can be no completion of the plan of God.

The writer enlarges upon this wonderful theme in Hebrews 5, where, in verses 8 and 9, he declares, "Though He was a Son, yet learned obedience by the things which he suffered; and having been made perfect, he became unto all them that obey him the author of eternal salvation." Our salvation is perfected through His perfection! Thank you, Lord!

Tetelestai

"Perfect"—what a wonderful and meaningful word! And how its meaning is enhanced when we discover that this was next to the last word to fall from the lips of our Lord as He offered Himself for our sins on the cross of Calvary: "It is finished" (John 19:30). This phrase, in the original, is the one word *tetelestai* - finished, completed, done! Note

2

carefully that our Lord does not say, "I am finished," but "It is finished."

What was finished at Calvary? Obviously, the earthly life of God's Son was finished. His exile was over. He has accomplished the task which the Father has given Him to do. He is now ready to commit His spirit into the hands of the loving Father and to go back home.

What was finished? The old law, with its "shalts" and its "shalt nots," for "He hath taken it out of the way, nailing it to the cross" (Col. 2:14). Since this be true, let us stand fast and be not entangled again in a yoke of bondage.

But, more wonderful than all of this, God's plan for redeeming lost humanity is finished. The eternal, all-powerful Creator is now free to love His rebellious and sinful children into His eternal Kingdom without violating His holy justice. The Son, Who knew no sin, has been made to be sin on our behalf; that we might become the righteousness of God in Him (II Cor. 5:21). Heaven's gate is now opened wide to redeemed humanity, and we rejoice with joy unspeakable and full of glory—*tetelestai!*

How grateful we should be for our Savior's "finished work" on Calvary! How we should worship and adore Him for it! How His atonement should lead us to fall down before Him in faith and love and surrender! Perhaps our appreciation of this marvelous gift would be greatly enhanced if we could but grasp the depth of meaning in the word "It is finished."

F. W. Borham, in "A Handful of Stars," points out that *tetelestai* (it is finished) was a word which might be used by a farmer. When there was born to his flock or herd a beautiful little animal in which no flaw or imperfection could be found, he might look with delight upon that new little arrival and fondly murmur, "tetelestai"—perfect!

3

This, the sixth word from the cross, was also a priestly word. When some worshiper, with a deep sense of love and gratitude for his Maker, brought the very best of his flock as an offering to God, the priest, who all too frequently witnessed the blind and defective and inferior brought for sacrifice, might look with appreciation upon the offering of gratitude and love and declare, "tetelestai."

It was an artist's word, this word which was wrung from the lips of the suffering Savior. When the artist, sculptor, or artisan had completed his task, and could see no way in which his work might be improved, he might look with pride upon his masterpiece and declare, "tetelestai, tetelestai."

But, more wonderful than all of these, is the fact that this was also a legal word. When a debtor completed payment of his indebtedness the banker would take the note and write across it the one word tetelestai—paid in full. Our debt is paid. Sin's penalty is cancelled. "Jehovah hath laid on him the iniquity of us all" (Isa. 53:6). It is finished - completed —done!

> "It is finished,"
> "It is finished,"
> My salvation full and free;
> Jesus paid the debt for sinners,
> When He died on Calvary.
> —*Ellis L. Carnett*

In His Steps

The God-man of Galilee was perfected through sufferings to provide our salvation, and how grateful we should be, but does the story end at Calvary? Is no response to come from the redeemed? Ought not love respond to love and sacrifice to sacrifice? Where is the loving and faithful wife who devotes her life to her home, demonstrating her utmost devotion to her husband by her constant labor of love, and then demand that her husband love her? No, it doesn't work that way. Love responds to love, spontaneously and gladly. What a tragedy it is that the only one of God's creatures which does not invariably respond to love is man.

It was many years ago that I read the story of the taming of a Bengal tiger. With the passing of the years details are hazy, but I would like to share the story with you as I recall it: There was a time that it was thought that a Bengal tiger could not be tamed; it was simply too wild and ferocious. An animal trainer in New York City declared, "I can tame a Bengal tiger," but all who heard laughed and opined that it could not be done. Wealthy men, hearing of the trainer's remarks, wagered large sums of money as to whether the trainer could make good his boast.

In a remote jungle a tiger was captured and caged. The cage was wrapped in heavy canvas, secured by cables, and shipped to New York City. Those who had made the wager came to watch the unveiling. As the cables were loosed and the canvas unwrapped, the ferocious beast threw the weight of his massive body time and time again against the bars of his cage in a vain attempt to reach those he thought to be his tormentors. The trainer took a piece of meat on a heavy oak handle and thrust it through the bars of the cage. With one sweep of that great paw the meat was stripped from the wood and the handle splintered to shreds. Spectators turned away saying, "A Bengal tiger cannot be tamed."

Day after day the trainer ministered to the needs of this beautiful and savage animal, patiently displaying the love which was on his heart for all of God's creatures.

5

The day of testing arrived at last, the day on which the bets were to be paid, one way or the other. Witnesses were on hand to observe as the animal lover took a cube of steak in his fingers and proferred it through the bars of the cage. The Bengal tiger walked over and received it as gently as a kitten. How tragic that with mankind love does not invariably respond to love.

The One Who bore a cross for us has invited us to suffer with Him. In Matthew 16:24 we hear that compelling challenge, "If any man would come after me, let him deny himself, and take up his cross, and follow me." And how have we responded? Has our attitude cried out, "a cross for Jesus, but none for me . . . a cross for remission, but none to bear?"

> Must Jesus bear the cross alone,
> And all the world go free?
> No; there's a cross for every one,
> And there's a cross for me.[2]

Peter, the "Big Fisherman," was called from his nets to discipleship. He lived with Jesus for three and one-half years. He was one of the three who was nearest the Master. He had professed to love Jesus more than any of the other disciples. He had proudly declared that if all others should forsake he would remain true. Then, one dark night, about a fire of coals in a courtyard, while his Master underwent the mockery of a trial, he thrice denied that he even knew the Man of Galilee. The suffering Christ turned and looked intently at him, and Peter went out and wept bitterly. How grateful we should be that this is not the last we hear of Peter. There were but a few dark days which passed until, along the shores of blue Galilee, the denier met the One he had denied . . . and Peter became "the rock."

---

2. Thomas Shepherd, "Must Jesus Bear the Cross Alone?"

Dawn was breaking over the sea called Galilee when I stepped out upon the balcony of our hotel in Tiberias and looked out over those peaceful waters. We were hosting our annual Holy Land tour, and I treasured these few precious moments before entering into the duties of the day. Purple mists were arising from the waters, faintly touched by the blush of dawn, and I stood there in awe, realizing that I was again looking upon a scene which my Lord frequently witnessed so many years ago, and that I would be privileged that day to once more "walk where Jesus walked."

As I looked out reverently over blue Galilee I saw through the mist a little fishing boat and a lone fisherman, and I wondered . . . was this his occupation? Had he fished all night? Had he been successful? Were there a loving wife and children waiting for him to come home to his kosher breakfast of fruits and vegetables and eggs and cheeses and pickles and raw fish? . . . and I thought of another dawn by Galilee, nineteen and one-half centuries ago . . .

The breaking of day revealed seven men in a fishing boat. Galilee had been their home. Here they had labored at their chosen tasks until one day a solitary figure on the seashore had called, "Come, follow me," and they had left all to follow. For three and one-half years they had followed. They were His closest friends. They ate with Him. They walked with Him. They marveled at His miraculous works. They treasured the words of wisdom which fell from His lips. There was much that they did not understand, but their paramount desire was to become like Him. Surely it was He Who would redeem His people and restore the golden age to Israel . . . but strange things had happened . . .

Their Leader had been captured as He knelt in prayer in a lonely olive orchard outside a city wall. He was brought

7

into the city, mocked, persecuted, tried, and condemned. They had followed at a distance as He carried a Roman cross to a hill called Calvary, and there they had witnessed the death of their Messiah. Their hopes were buried with that dead body in the cold stone tomb of Joseph of Arimathea.

But with the dawning of the third day there came a ray of hope. Women who had been early at the tomb hurried to them with the breath-taking announcement that the tomb was empty, that they had seen the living Lord, and that they were directed to go and tell His disciples *and Peter* that He would go before them into Galilee and that they would see Him there. "And Peter"—how wonderful! The one who had professed to love the Master above all others, and the one who had been first to deny Him, is especially mentioned by the living Christ.

And so they have come with haste to Galilee, but the Master was not awaiting them. Was it in deep discouragement that Simon Peter declared, "I go a fishing?" Was he ready so soon to return to his old occupation and to his former manner of life? Was he surrendering to doubts and despair? How great can be the influence of a single individual. There were six others to declare, "We also come with thee."

It is in John 21 that we read this beautiful account of that glorious dawn by Galilee. Seven discouraged men entered into the boat; they toiled all night; and that night they took nothing. How strange! These men were professional fishermen, yet they fished all night without success. But how wonderful to note that a lone figure stood on the shore while they fished. Surely there can be no more beautiful picture of God than this: a God who would be partner with man! A God Who rejoices with us in our victories and sorrows with us in our defeats! A God Who stands on the shore while we fish!

And when day was breaking, Jesus spoke: "Children, have ye aught to eat?" Why wait until daybreak to speak? It would not have been so important the night before. They have now reached the end of their endurance, ready to admit their own failure. How often, in His love and wisdom, He waits until morning to speak.

One of the most beautifully significant portions of the story is that He fills their nets with fish. Why? Could it be because He desires them to be successful? Could it be that He wants to teach them to listen to His direction and to depend fully on Him? When they are ready to listen to His advice the fish begin to come.

And then He called them to breakfast. When they got out on land they saw a fire of coals, and fish, and bread. How tragic had they been left with the fish! Oftimes we are so busy with the fish that we miss the fellowship.

It was following this heavenly breakfast on the shore of Galilee that Peter experienced the purging and the peace of forgiveness and was restored to full discipleship. Singling out the one who had denied, the compassionate Christ asks, "Peter, son of John, lovest thou me?" Three times He repeats the question and three times Peter responds, "Yes, Lord." Around a fire in a courtyard, he had thrice denied. Now, around the breakfast fire, he thrice professes his love. And the sympathetic Saviour, unwilling to lay the base sin of denial on Peter, responds, "Feed my lambs . . . tend my sheep . . . feed my sheep." How that thrills my soul and encourages my heart, for behind Peter I come creeping along, praying for forgiveness.

"And Peter" discovered the exhilaration of restoration to discipleship—no longer the weak and vacillating fisherman, but Peter "the rock."

It was Peter who took the lead on Pentecost, as the church was established. It was Peter who was first to carry the gospel of redeeming grace to the gentiles. It was Peter who became a pillar of the church in Jerusalem. After Peter met the risen Christ and experienced the purging of forgiveness he never wavered. He knew what it was to suffer with Christ and not be ashamed. As he wrote to the saints who were being scattered through persecution, he reminded them, "Christ also suffered for you, leaving you an example, that ye should follow his steps" (I Peter 2:2). If Christ suffered for us, and if we are to follow His steps, we are obligated to face up to the question, "What did Christ suffer, and as I follow Him what suffering may I expect?"

1. The suffering of physical pain.

Very few of us will ever be called upon to face pain which would begin to approach that of crucifixion. The most painful death ever devised by sinful humanity was this "death of the stake." It was a death which was reserved for the vilest of criminals and for the runaway slaves. The suffering begs description. Roman crucifixion began with the stake of scourging—a stake driven low into the ground, where the criminal's hands were bound and the taut flesh of the back laid bare to the cat-of-nine-tails: leather thongs which were frequently tipped with nails or pieces of bone or metal. At the first blow the blood spurted and the bones of the back were laid bare. The flailing continued until the back was a raw mass of bloody pulp. Strong men frequently died under the scourge.

10

If the sufferer survived the scourge, the cross (or cross-bar) was placed upon the lacerated back and the criminal was compelled to bear the cross to the place of execution. Upon arriving at this dread spot, the criminal was stripped naked, his clothing becoming the property of his executioners. The arms were tied to the cross bar, nails driven through the hands, and the cross elevated until the victim's feet were a foot or two above the ground. The feet were then crossed and a long spike pinned them to the upright beam. In this agonizing position the sufferer was exposed to the heat and the insects and the taunts and jeers of the passers-by.

The pain and trauma of crucifixion is extremely difficult for us to comprehend. The laceration of the scourge—the piercing of the spikes—the striving to lift the body by pushing upward on the spikes driven through the feet, as the victim struggles for a breath of air—the mockery and the shame—the crawling insects—the cramping muscles—and, finally, merciful unconsciousness. Strong men, at times, lived from three to five days on the cross.

. . . and this is the death our Lord elected to die for us! God help us to welcome any suffering which brings us any nearer the side of the suffering Savior!

2. The suffering of sin.

The physical pain of the crucifixion was intense indeed, but there was a suffering in the light of which His suffering of pain paled into insignificance: the suffering of sin. Our first reaction might well be to recoil and to object, "But He was the Son of God. He was pure and undefiled. It would be impossible for the Holy Jesus to know the suffering of

11

sin." Consider well the reply of the apostle Paul in II Cor. 5:21: "Him who knew no sin he made to be sin on our behalf; that we might become the righteousness of God in him." As the Savior offered the perfect sacrifice for sin, He gathered up in Himself the sins of all mankind and covered them with His own precious blood.

Name off, one by one, all of the sins that you have ever committed. On the cross of Calvary the Lamb of God became that. Did you ever take that which was not rightfully yours? Then on Calvary the honest Jesus became a thief. Did you curse? Then, as He took your place, the holy Jesus blasphemed the name of His Father. Was yours the sin of drunkenness? Then the sober Jesus became a drunkard. Did you hate your brother? Then the loving Jesus hated His brethren. Were you guilty of fornication? Then the pure Jesus became an adulterer. And for those guilty of murder the Prince of Life became guilty of His brother's blood. Think of gathering all of the sins of humanity into one great heap. What a seething mass of wickedness! Yet this was the burden of the Redeemer as He became sin on our behalf, that we might become the righteousness of God in Him. What condescension! What love! What mercy! What amazing grace!

What was it that caused Jesus to die upon the cross in six hours, when strong men had been known to live under this agony for as long as five days? Was He a weakling, this Galilean? Was His body so weak that it could no longer withstand the rigors of the crucifixion? Not the Jesus Whom I have known and served these many years. The Carpenter of Nazareth dwelt in a body that was physically strong. That perfect body had to be extremely strong to endure what He endured. After difficult days and sleepless nights, His body weakened by the loss of blood, He went out, bearing a cross which Roman custom had made to weigh three hundred pounds. He was a man among men, yet He died in six hours. Why? Was it not His guilt? The weight of your sin and mine was upon Him. It was necessary that the Father forsake Him as He became sin, and in six hours it broke His heart. And it may well be that this is no figure of speech, for the divine record declares that after He had expired the soldiers pierced His side with a spear and that there came forth blood and water. The physician tells me that this might indicate a ruptured heart. Jesus did not die of the physical pain alone. The great loving heart of the Savior broke as He carried our sins to Calvary and offered the perfect sacrifice for their remission.

> Have you read the story of the cross,
> Where Jesus bled and died?
> Where your debt was paid by the precious blood
> That flowed from His wounded side—
>
> He died of a broken heart for you;
> He died of a broken heart,
> Oh wondrous love! It was for you
> He died of a broken heart.[3]

Dear one, are you laboring under the suffering of sin? Look to the One Who became sin on your behalf, that you might become the righteousness of God in Him.

3. The suffering of poverty.

It is the lot of many of our world's population to experience the suffering which may come through extreme poverty. At

---

3. T. Dennis, "The Broken Heart."

the time of this writing the nations of the world have fallen back from the proud economic progress we thought we were attaining to economic failure for many. There are those in our once affluent society who are experiencing the pinch of poverty and are not just sure how to cope. The author resides in a state which is largely dependent upon the timber industry to sustain its economy. In this time of recession logging woods are silent, sawmills are closed, building has largely ceased, and families are hurting.

Who among us has not seen those heart-rending pictures which have recently come to us from the mission field? Diseased bodies, caused by malnutrition . . . little children with bloated bellies and sunken eyes . . . distraught mothers, holding in their arms the wasted bodies of their babes who have died because there was no sustenance . . . and we feel a sense of shame that we have complained because all of our wants were not fulfilled.

If you are ever prone to complain over your lack of this world's goods, consider well the financial status of the Carpenter of Nazareth. It was a Jewish scribe who approached the Master one day with a noble resolution: "Teacher, I will follow thee whithersoever thou goest." How remarkable! This one who was recognized as a teacher among God's chosen addresses the Galilean as "teacher" and offers himself as a willing follower. What a wonderful opportunity for the Master to add a man of status to the little band of disciples. But Jesus, knowing the hearts of men, saw something in this man's heart which might well prevent full allegiance, yet He did not rebuke nor condemn but, so very gently, He put the test: "The foxes have holes, and the birds of the heaven have nests; but the Son of man hath not where to lay his head" (Matt. 8:20). Here the curtain

14

falls on the little drama. We hear no more of this enthusiastic scribe. Perhaps the price was too great.

The Son of God, Who owned all things by right of creation, willingly relinquished title to them all. Those things which He utilized during His earthly sojourn were borrowed things:

He Who was the Bread of Life borrowed His sustenance. The eighth chapter of the book of Luke catalogues a little band of women who ministered to them of their substance.

On a grassy plain by a lakeside, He borrowed a small lad's lunch to feed the multitude.

He borrowed a boat to use as a podium from which to address the throngs on the shore.

He borrowed a humble beast of burden upon which to ride into His throne city.

He borrowed an upper room in which to eat a farewell meal with His dearest friends.

He borrowed a lonely garden in which to agonize in prayer.

He died not owning six feet of ground in which to be buried and His lifeless body was tenderly lain in a tomb which was borrowed from Joseph of Arimathea. At death He had nothing to divide but a seamless robe.

Dear friend, if poverty should ever be your lot, remember that there is One Who understands all about it. "For ye know the grace of our Lord Jesus Christ, that, though he was rich, yet for your sakes he became poor, that ye, through his poverty might become rich" (II Cor. 8:9).

4. The suffering of misunderstanding and loneliness.

It is not easy to be misunderstood—and it hurts to be lonely. Jesus experienced both.

15

The multitude had found one who could fill their stomachs. He had taken a lad's lunch of five biscuits and two little fish and before their wondering gaze had blessed and broke and distributed that pitifully small lunch among about five thousand men until they were all filled. Surely one such as this would make a fine leader and provider, and so they came to Capernaum, seeking Jesus. When they found Him they were met with the rebuke, "Ye seek me, not because ye saw signs, but because ye ate of the loaves and were filled." To these curious and vacillating seekers the Master Teacher presents Himself as the Bread of Life, concluding with the declaration that "no man can come unto me, except it be given unto him of the Father" (cf. John 6:1ff.).

These would-be disciples were more interested in the god of the belly than the God of Galilee and so they declared it a "hard saying," and many of them went away to walk with Him no more. Jesus turned to the little band which remained and put to them one of the most pathetic questions to ever fall from His lips: "Would ye also go away?" How the Master must have longed for understanding and companionship, and how heartening must have been Peter's response, "Lord, to whom shall we go? thou hast the words of eternal life."

But surely His family would understand Him. There were brothers who had shared the humble carpenter cottage in Nazareth. Doubtless they had joined Him in play and in toil. They had witnessed His manner of life. Perhaps they had heard of these strange events which had surrounded His birth and the miracles of His early ministry, but John informs us that His brethren mocked Him, implying that He was a fame-seeker and that He should go where He could be seen of men. Then John adds succinctly, "For even his brethren

16

did not believe on him" (John 7:5). Oh, to be understood by those we love!

The Man of Sorrows knew to the fullest what it meant to be alone. How many long nights He devoted to prayer, alone save for His Heavenly Father. It is Matthew who tells us that following the feeding of the five thousand He sent the disciples across the sea while He went up into the mountain to pray, and when even was come, He was there alone (Matt. 14:23).

It was during His last night upon earth that He ate a farewell supper with His little band of friends, and when they had reclined at table He said, "With desire I have desired to eat this passover with you before I suffer" (Luke 22:15). With His own agony just at hand, He spoke words of comfort and instruction, then, when they had sung a hymn, they went out to a lonely olive orchard on the slope of the mount of Olives. Arriving in the garden called Gethsemane, He took with Him the three who had been closest to Him (how He longed for someone to share this bitter hour with Him) but even they could not share fully in His agony. He went on alone. He was parted from them about a stone's cast and kneeled down and prayed—alone.

It was when He had won this agonizing victory in the garden that He was captured by the religionists and the Roman oppressors, a great multitude with swords and staves, coming to capture a lone man! The nearer our Lord came to the cross, the fewer friends He had. One of His closest friends had betrayed Him, another had denied Him, and now they all forsook Him and fled. The Galilean went to the place of trial, the stake of scourging, and the hill called Golgotha—alone.

17

It was alone the Saviour prayed
In dark Gethsemane;
Alone He drained the bitter cup
And suffered there for me.

Alone, alone, He bore it all alone;
He gave Himself to save His own,
He suffered, bled and died
Alone, alone.[4]

If you would follow in the steps of this lone Galilean there will come times that you, too, will know loneliness. May God help us to welcome any loneliness which brings us any nearer the side of the lonely Jesus. But, my friend, you are never completely alone, for He Who is faithful has promised to be with you, and you can say with Him in your hour of deepest grief, "I am not alone, because the Father is with me" (John 16:32).

5. The suffering of the loss of loved ones.

All of us who have lived long have experienced the debilitating loss of loved ones: a life-companion, father or mother, son or daughter, grandparents or grandchildren. Their passing left an aching void and a broken heart. The Great Sufferer has been there—and He understands.

The ministry of Jesus of Nazareth was introduced by His cousin, John the Baptist: that rough, zealous, courageous evangel, the one clad in camel's hair and subsisting on locusts and wild honey. John was God's man. He never wavered or apologized for the message God had given him to deliver. He was no respecter of persons. One day he stood before a proud and haughty king, denounced his sin, and paid with his life for his faithfulness and fortitude. And so they came and told Jesus: His fore-runner, the one

4. Ben H. Price, "Alone."

who was to go before Him in the spirit and power of Elijah, His cousin, was dead. Jesus had lost a loved one.

On the southern slope of the mount of Olives nestles the quiet little village of Bethany. How precious to Jesus was this little town. How frequently He paused here for rest and refreshment. Here in Bethany lived a family that Jesus loved. There was Mary, the quiet, thoughtful one, the one who delighted to sit at the feet of the master teacher. There was Martha, the busy, mothering one, the one who took pride in her cooking and care of the house. And then there was brother Lazarus, one who was beloved by the Master.

One day a messenger brought disturbing tidings: Lazarus was desperately ill. The response of Jesus was amazing. When He heard that His friend was sick He remained two days in the place where He was. It was in this setting that He uttered that profound and basic truth as to one of the divine purposes in suffering and sorrow: "This sickness is not unto death, but for the glory of God, that the Son of God may be glorified thereby" (John 11:4).

One of the most beautiful and revealing events in the ministry of our Lord occurred when He came to minister to the grieving family of Lazarus. Before He called forth the body of His friend from the confines of that cold stone tomb He spoke words of comfort and assurance to the grieving sisters. When the loving Jesus saw the weeping of Mary and her friends His heart was moved with compassion, and the divine record states, so simply and beautifully, "Jesus wept." This, the shortest verse in the Bible, ought not be quoted lightly nor thoughtlessly. Rather, it is a verse which should be regarded with reverence and awe: "Jesus wept." He had no tears for His own grief, but they fell freely over the grief of others.

19

Does Jesus care when I've said "goodbye"
To the dearest on earth to me,
And my sad heart aches Till it nearly breaks,
Is it aught to Him? does He see?

O yes, He cares, I know He cares,
His heart is touched with my grief;
When the days are weary, The long nights dreary,
I know my Saviour cares.[5]

The Fellowship of His Suffering

The paramount goal of the apostle was that he might know Christ, and the power of His resurrection, and the fellowship of His suffering (Phil. 3:10). Earlier in this letter to his beloved church Paul has declared that "to you *it hath been granted* in the behalf of Christ, not only to believe on him, but also to suffer on his behalf" (Phil. 1:29. Italics are the author's). How strange! Who among us *desires* to suffer? Is it not our nature to shun suffering and to feel that something has "gone wrong" when we suffer? But here the inspired apostle declares that "it has been granted" us to suffer. Those early disciples had captured this truth, and it enabled them to depart from the religious council where they had been beaten for their testimony, "rejoicing that they were counted worthy to suffer dishonor for the Name" (Acts 5:41). One of our greatest fears ought be that we will not be found worthy to suffer for Him.

"Christ also suffered for you, leaving you an example, that ye should follow his steps" (I Peter 2:21). He has not asked us to take a single step which He has not taken before us. He knew the suffering of pain, the suffering of sin, the

---

5. Frank E. Graeff, "Does Jesus Care?"

suffering of poverty, the suffering of misunderstanding, the suffering of loneliness, and the suffering of the loss of loved ones. If we are to know the fellowship of His suffering will we not endure these same sufferings with Him and rejoice that we are counted worthy to suffer?

C.S. Lewis, in "The Problem of Pain," quotes from George MacDonald's *Unspoken Sermons:* "The Son of God suffered unto the death, not that men might not suffer, but that their sufferings might be like His."[6]

The body of preacher Paul was battered and scarred. That old warrior of the cross had suffered for Jesus as we never shall. As he concludes the letter to his dear friends of Galatia, he makes the request, "Henceforth let no man trouble me; for I bear branded in my body the marks of Jesus" (Gal. 6:17).

There is an ancient legend which portrays St. Peter standing at the gate of heaven to examine those who petition to enter the pearly white city. And what is he looking for? Perfect church attendance records? Medals for meritorious service? The treasurer's statements of tithes and offerings paid? A roster of church offices held? No, none of these things. He is examining heaven's candidates for *scars.*

> Hast thou no scar?
>> No hidden scar on foot, or side, or hand,
>> I hear thee sung as mighty in the land;
> I hear them hail thy bright ascendant star,
> Hast thou no scar?
>
> Hast thou no wound?
>> Yet I was wounded by the archers, spent,
>> Leaned me against a tree to die; and rent
> By ravening beasts that compassed Me, I swooned:

---

6. C.S. Lewis, *The Problem of Pain* (New York: MacMillan Publishing Co., 1962), flyleaf.

No wound? No scar?
   Yet, as the Master shall the servant be,
   And pierced are the feet that follow Me;
   But thine are whole; can he have followed far
   Who has no wound nor scar?[7]

Apostle Peter, writing to the sufferers of the Dispersion, reminds them that after they have suffered a little while the God of all grace would himself perfect, establish and strengthen them (cf. I Peter 5:10).

The Son of God was made perfect through sufferings—so are His disciples!

* * * * *

Since penning the foregoing lines, the one who has been my loving and faithful partner for forty-eight years has gone home with Jesus. From girlhood she had walked closely with her Lord and she knew Him well. It was last Wednesday evening, and we were walking closely together as we had walked so oft before. The pathway led through the shadowed valley, but we feared no evil, for with us was the Divine Presence.

As we walked together we approached the Father's home, and He Who knows what is best for His children opened wide the door and called, "Come home." Reluctantly (not for her sake, but for the sake of the lonely ones left behind) she answered the bidding of that gracious voice and is now waiting in that beautiful home where there is no more sickness, sorrow, pain, or death.

Dear God, it is lonely! But I wonder . . . am I now more qualified to share with you who walk the vale of suffering and sorrow? Have I found answers which I had not known theretofore? As heart-ache joins heartache, as grief reaches

---

7. Amy Carmichael, "Hast Thou No Scar?"

out to touch grief, and as tears mingle with tears, am I better able to see more clearly through the mist of His wise design? Is it true that we can see further through a tear than through a telescope? Can I now suffer more deeply with those who are in pain, share more fully with those in sorrow, and say more honestly to those who are hurting, "I know, dear friend, I know?"

> Not now, but in the coming years,
> It may be in the better land,
> We'll read the meaning of our tears,
> And there, some time, we'll understand.
>
> Then trust in God thro' all the days;
> Fear not, for He doth hold thy hand;
> Though dark thy way, still sing and praise,
> Some time, sometime, we'll understand.[8]

May He Who does all things well grant us the grace to understand that we, too, may become perfect through suffering.

---

8. Maxwell N. Cornelius, "Some Time We'll Understand."

Chapter Two

WHEN SUFFERING COMES

It was the late James Earl Ladd I., a giant of a man, mentally, spiritually, and physically ("five feet, seventeen and a half in his stocking feet," as he was wont to put it), who recounted the following oriental legend.

A grieving mother of India approached the Gua-ta-ma Buddha, to petition him to restore her dead child. Buddha promised that he would restore the little one if the mother would but bring him a few grains of rice from a home that had never known trouble. With a light heart, she optimistically set out upon her quest. Days lengthened into weeks; weeks into months; months into years. At long last she returned to admit her failure: not a home was found where trouble had never entered![1]

Eliphaz, a "friend" of Job, offered the sufferer some very faulty advice, but, in his first discourse, he made the profound observation that "Man is born unto trouble, as the sparks fly upward" (Job 5:7). Albert Schweitzer, that great humanitarian of many talents and gigantic intellect, reminded us that the world is "mysteriously full of suffering." The gentle Buddha, after years of meditation on the deep issues of life, reached the conclusion that existence and suffering are one.

Suffering is a universal problem, and the one of Christian faith is not immune. The apostle Paul kept the record straight as he declared, "All that would live godly in Christ Jesus shall suffer persecution" (II Tim. 3:12). Jesus promised that those who would dare to follow Him would know suffering— and happiness. He begins that marvelous Sermon on the

---

1. James Earl Ladd, *As Much As In Me Is* (Portland, Ore.: Beattie and Company, 1951), p. 149.

Mount with the list of the happy people (the Greek word translated "blessed" means "happy"). How strange to our ears, in our affluency and our comfort: "Happy are they that mourn . . . Happy are they that have been persecuted . . . Happy are you when men shall reproach you and persecute you . . . (Matt. 5:3-12). How contrary to our standards of well-being and success!

When we find ourselves in the crucible of suffering and, in our agony, feel that no one has ever suffered as we suffer, we would do well to listen to philosopher Socrates as he observes, "If all our misfortune were laid in one common heap, where everyone must take an equal portion, most people would be content to take their own and depart."

Where is the home where trouble has never entered? Where is the life which has never been touched by suffering? The dark hand of sorrow and pain has been laid upon us all and, out of darkness, we cry out for the answer.

Suffering comes. Suffering comes to all. And suffering comes under many guises.

Guises of Suffering

1. The suffering of sickness and pain.

This is the suffering which C.S. Lewis so aptly describes as "The Problem of Pain."[2] The story of sickness and pain is as old as the story of sin. With the coming of sin came the penalty of pain: pain in child-bearing, grievous toil, physical infirmity, death. Who among us is immune to sickness, trauma, and disease?

_____

2. C.S. Lewis, *The Problem of Pain* (New York: Macmillan Publishing Co., 1962).

25

2. Suffering caused by poverty.

Poverty, of itself, does not bring suffering, but extreme poverty may lead to malnutrition, to disease, and to death. How difficult it is for us in our land of plenty to realize that thousands of children will go to bed hungry tonight, and that one-third of our world's population is starving.

3. The suffering of loneliness.

One of the saddest verses in the Bible was uttered by King David, as he took refuge in a cave from those who sought his life: "Look on my right hand, and see; For there is no man that knoweth me: Refuge hath failed me; No man careth for my soul" (Psalm 142:4). God's man had given in to loneliness. It is not necessary to be abandoned in a cave to experience the pangs of loneliness. There are "lonely people in the city," and they are hurting.

4. The suffering of being misunderstood.

Yes, it hurts when our words and actions are misunderstood. How often we attempt to speak words of comfort or strive to be helpful, only to be rejected by the intended recipient. At times those whom we would bless lash out and the lash leaves its mark.

5. Suffering in the family circle.

Our current philosophy of materialism, the "new morality," and situation ethics have invaded our homes and are taking their toll. One-half of our marriages now end in divorce. Many other couples are enduring instead of enjoying their home and family relationship. The generation gap is still

26

far too wide. There are prodigal sons, prodigal daughters, and prodigal parents. Many despair of a happy and united home.

6. The suffering of temptation.

If you question that there is suffering in the temptation experience, consider well the wrestling of the apostle: "not what I would, that I do practice; but what I hate, that I do. . . . Wretched man that I am! who shall deliver me out of the body of this death?" (Rom. 7:15, 24).

As the writer of the Hebrew letter recounts the sufferings of the fathers of the faith, he reminds us that "they were stoned, they were sawn asunder, they were tempted, they were slain with the sword" (Heb. 11:37). Here, in the midst of the catalogue of extreme physical suffering and death is the statement, "They were tempted." He who has never experienced suffering in his struggle with temptation has never really faced temptation.

7. The suffering of bereavement.

None of us who has lived long has escaped the pain of the loss of a loved one: a beloved companion, a caring father, a loving mother, a dear child or grandparent, and the parting has left an aching void which is never quite completely healed. There is a pain which far surpasses the physical in the heart cry of David as he learns of the tragic and needless death of the son whom he loved so very dearly: "O my son Absalom, my son, my son Absalom! would I had died for thee, O Absalom, my son, my son!" (II Sam. 18:33).

What Causes Suffering?

When suffering lays its painful hand upon us, or when we delve deeply into the pain problem, we come eventually

27

to the inevitable "why?" What, after all, is the basic cause of suffering? Throughout the ages men have agonized and groped for the answer, and many of their conclusions are pitifully inadequate.

1. The whim of a capricious God?

There are many who blame God for everything bad that happens. Even the language of our insurance policies suggests this concept. Floods, hurricanes, and hail storms are referred to as "acts of God." Is God a stern old man who sits "up there," holding in his hands the puppet strings? Does he pull the strings and put his creatures through those painful gyrations for his own amusement? If this be true, where is the freedom of will? The Scripture teaches both the sovereignty of God and the free will of man. In the very beginning God formed man in His image. He was a perfect being, but a free moral agent. His was the power to choose good or evil. Would you have it otherwise? Would you be no different to the animal? Would you avoid the struggle which builds character and brings the thrill of victory? How we ought to thank and praise Him for the power of choice.

2. To discipline and direct us?

One of the heart-rending experiences that is the common lot of ministers is that of being called into a home where a little one has died and, at times, it is the only child. How often the grieving parents will punish themselves with the suggestion that God "took the baby" to teach them a lesson or to punish them for some misdeed or for some short-coming, such as their failure to attend church or to give to the Lord's work. The trouble with this answer is that it just isn't true.

It is not Biblical, nor is it reasonable. God does not resort to such cruel tactics to accomplish His will. He may use such tragedies to build lives which are stronger and more dependent upon Him, but He does not orchestrate the suffering process in order to discipline or to direct.

3. Punishment for sin?

Whenever tragedy strikes there are always those who wonder what they have done to deserve such a fate. The "friends" of Job were convinced that his extreme suffering was caused by his sin and endeavored to extract from him a confession of his guilt. The Greek word *poine*, from which we derive the English word "pain" means punishment. The concept that tragedy and pain come as punishment for our sin is a popular concept, but it is not a scriptural concept.

It is true that suffering came into the world as a result of sin and we are all touched by its "fall out." It is also true that some of our suffering is caused directly by sin. A father commits adultery and disease is transmitted to his wife and children. A chain smoker may develop emphysema. The drunkard may contract cirrhosis of the liver. The glutton may get the gout. A person under the influence of alcohol or other drugs may drive his car into a throng of people, causing untold suffering and death.

C.S. Lewis has pointed out, in his inimitable way, that when men become wicked they will hurt one another, and that this may account for four-fifths of the suffering of men. He continues, brilliantly and logically, "It is men, not God, who have produced racks, whips, prisons, slavery, guns, bayonets, and bombs; it is by human avarice or human stupidity, not by the churlishness of nature, that we have poverty and overwork."[3]

Jesus and His disciples once came upon one who was blind from his birth. "Rabbi," asked His disciples, "Who sinned, this man or his parents, that he should be born blind?" In their thinking, surely someone had sinned, and the result was evident in sightless eyes. And He Who is the Light of the world set the record straight as He replied, "Neither did this man sin, nor his parents: but that the works of God should be made manifest in him" (John 9:1-3).

Again, there were those who told the Master of the Galileans whose blood Pilate had mingled with their sacrifices. Apparently these informers were wondering what sins had been committed that merited such extreme punishment. He Whose wisdom so far surpasses ours replied, "Think ye that these Galilaeans were sinners above all the Galilaeans, because they have suffered these things? I tell you, Nay: but except ye repent, ye shall all in like manner perish. Or those eighteen, upon whom the tower in Siloam fell, and killed them, think ye that they were offenders above all the men that dwell in Jerusalem? I tell you, Nay; but, except ye repent, ye shall all likewise perish" (Luke 13:2-5).

If suffering is an indication of God's wrath, and comes as punishment for man's sins, there are many who are getting by too cheaply!

4. Satan?

It is altogether possible that many of life's griefs and misfortunes which we commonly attribute to God or to "fate"

---

3. Lewis, *op. cit.*, p. 89.

may be caused by our common adversary, the devil. The Scripture frequently associates disease with Satan. In the epic of Job, Satan taunts God with, "Skin for skin, yea, all that a man hath will he give for his life. But put forth thy hand now, and touch his bone and his flesh, and he will renounce thee to thy face. And Jehovah said unto Satan, Behold, he is in thy hand; only spare his life. So Satan went forth from the presence of Jehovah, and smote Job with sore boils from the sole of his foot unto his crown" (Job 2:4-7).

In a Jewish synagogue, the Master looked one day with compassion on a woman who had been bowed in her infirmity for 18 years. The Great Physician laid His hands upon her and straightened her deformed body, then justified this sabbath-day miracle by asking His hypocritical antagonists, "Ought not this woman, being a daughter of Abraham, *whom Satan had bound*, lo, these eighteen years, to have been loosed from this bond on the day of the sabbath?" (Luke 13:16. Italics are the author's).

As Paul instructed the Corinthians to remove the sinful man from their fellowship, that the body might be kept pure, he makes this interesting comment, "Deliver such a one unto Satan for the destruction of the flesh . . ." (I Cor. 5:5). Perhaps there may be times that our loving Father may see fit to give Satan limited authority over our bodies in order to accomplish His wise design.

5. Natural law?

Our God is a God of order and design. He has established certain principles through which He "upholds all things by the word of His power" (Heb. 1:3). Is not much of the

31

pain and anguish and misfortune of this life brought about by the violation of natural law? It is not that God *causes* everything that occurs, but He does *permit* it.

Let us look again at the problem posed by the death of the babe. Instead of believing that God "took" the baby to punish them, the parents might well consider questions such as these: Was the little one not strong enough to adapt to life outside the mother's womb? Was the doctor's knowledge and skill inadequate to meet the situation? Was the illness not detected in time to be adequately treated, or was it a mysterious illness for which medical science has not yet found an answer?

Think again of the man who looks upon his business failure as wrought by the hand of God. Might not the failure have been caused by the depressed economy, a dishonest business partner, or the failure of his debtors to pay up?

Or the driver who rounds the curve at an unreasonable speed and his car crashes the guard rail and plunges into the abyss. It is not an "act of God"; it is the simple operation of a law of physics. God did not cause; God did permit . . . But why?

Why Doesn't God Prevent Suffering?

And so we come, full-circle, to the perennial question: Why does a loving and caring God permit suffering? Is He not in control of His creation? Is He not the Omnipotent One? Does He take delight in the suffering of His creatures? Is He powerless to prevent suffering, or doesn't He care?" Such questions have caused some to conclude that if there be a God He can not be both powerful and good. If He were all-powerful, could He not prevent suffering? If He were good, would He be willing for His children to suffer?

Thus, as we struggle through our maze of questions, we come finally to the most common (and the most difficult) question of all: "Why do the *innocent* suffer? Why does God make no distinction between the good and the bad? If we but had sufficient faith, would we not avoid the misfortunes of life?" May the all-wise God grant us the grace to think this problem through so carefully that we will be enabled to visualize what would result if people of faith were immune to suffering.

1. An undependable universe.

It has pleased the Creator to operate this universe by *order* rather than by *whim*. Picture what would result if God spared His children all misfortune —

A man of great Christian faith is mountain climbing. Bone-weary, he becomes careless and slips over the precipice. Because he is a man of faith, God reaches down and pulls him back to safety or wafts him gently to the earth below.

A drunken driver rounds a curve and meets, head-on, a bus loaded with Christian young people, on their way to youth camp. To spare His children, God touches the steering wheel and moves the careening car back to a position of safety.

A minister and wife return home late at night and are confronted by a thug in the act of robbing their home. He turns his gun on them and pulls the trigger. Because they trust implicitly in God and are effective in His service, God raises an invisible shield or turns the bullets to paper, and they suffer no harm . . .

What an unpredictable and undependable universe! Sometimes the law of gravity would operate, sometimes it would not. Sometimes objects would be hard, sometimes they

33

would be soft. Sometimes time would move on schedule, sometimes it would be erratic. God would be kept busy with these special adjustments instead of operating the world according to those general laws which we must learn to respect on the penalty of pain or death.

All of this is not to say that God *can not* intervene, nor that He never chooses to do so, but His interventions are the exception, not the rule. That to which we object is the premise that God *always* intervenes when His children are endangered, and that when He does not that there is either something wrong with God or with them. God has chosen to run His universe in an orderly fashion. We live in a universe with fixed laws, and the believer is subject to these laws as surely as is the unbeliever.

2. Petted and spoiled children.

The child who is given everything he desires, or who pouts and begs until he gets his own way, becomes a spoiled brat. He is disliked and shunned and when he is thrown upon his own is unable to cope. Without discipline the children of God become spoiled and ineffective and miss those experiences of life which may be used as building blocks of Christian character. C.S. Lewis expands this idea extremely well as he observes:

> We want, in fact, not so much a Father in Heaven as a grandfather in heaven—a senile benevolence who, as they say, "liked to see young people enjoying themselves," and whose plan for the universe was simply that it might be truly said at the end of each day, "a good time was had by all."[4]

---

4. Lewis, *ibid.*, p. 40.

The God Who knows what is best for His children has granted the gift of pain. It is a divine gift, but it is a gift that no one wants. How needful pain is. Without it how could we detect danger? Leprosy, or Hansen's disease, is one of the most cruel of diseases, not so much because of the pain, but because it serves as an anaesthetic, numbing the extremeties of the body so that they are insensitive to pain. Without the danger detector of pain, the diseased one suffers burns, cuts, and bruises until the flesh is mutilated and destroyed.

Philip Yancey quotes Dr. Paul Brand, of Carville, Louisiana, as saying, "Thank God for inventing pain! I don't think He could have done a better job. It's beautiful."[5] C.S. Lewis underscores this thought as he points out that "God whispers to us in our pleasure, speaks in our conscience, but shouts in our pain, it is his megaphone to rouse a deaf world."[6] How would we ever know pleasure had we not experienced pain?

God never promised that His people would be immune to all pain and misfortune. He promised something better: His presence, His love, His grace, and the strength to see it through. As one observant soul was heard to remark, "He makes it to rain on the just and the unjust alike, but He gives His child an umbrella."

3. Christianity would lose its essence.

The call of Christ has always been the call of the difficult. He never envisioned a cult of the comfortable. "And he said unto all, if any man would come after me, let him deny

5. Philip Yancey, *Where is God When it Hurts?*, (Grand Rapids, Mich.: Zondervan Publishing House, 1977), p. 23.

6. Lewis, *op. cit.*, p. 93.

himself, and take up his cross daily, and follow me" (Luke 9:23). How utterly impossible to carry a cross and never know suffering. From whence this concept that Christianity is always the easy, pleasant way? It is the difficult way, the hill-climbing way, the suffering way. It is the way that demands your utmost and drains your life-blood, but it has in the very heart of it that which we all seek: satisfaction, sufficiency, service, salvation, and significance to life.

E. Stanley Jones relates a view expressed by a Christian gentleman at a Round Table Conference in India: "I have found that if you follow Christ, three things will happen to you: First, you will be delivered from all fears. Second, you will be absurdly happy. Third, you will have trouble."[7]

Philip Yancey summarizes it well in one choice little paragraph:

> In a sense, it would be easier for God to step in, to have faith for us, to help us in extraordinary ways. But He has chosen to stand before us, loving arms extended, while He asks us to walk, to participate in our own soul-making. That process involves pain.[8]

If the all-wise Father had planned it otherwise, if Christians escaped all trouble, men would throng the church, embracing Christianity as a talisman or a life insurance policy, avoid the struggle which prepares man for life and for heaven, and miss the very essence of our Christian faith.

How Shall We Meet Suffering?

Since suffering is the common lot of the human race, and since we, each one, shall enter into the suffering experience, it behooves us to think carefully as to how we shall

---

7. E. Stanley Jones, *Christ and Human Suffering,* (New York-Nashville: Abingdon-Cokesbury Press, 1933), p. 118.
8. Yancey, *op. cit.,* p. 76.

meet it. Responses to the problem of suffering are varied, but they are usually sincere responses, for when we enter the arena of suffering we are apt to lay aside the speculative and the superficial.

How frequently we need to be reminded that the important thing is not what happens to us but how we react to that which is happening. What happens *in* us is far more important than what happens *to* us. Why men suffer is important, but how they meet suffering is more important. It is our response to suffering that displays the stuff out of which we are made and determines our character and our destiny.

The following catalogue is not intended to be exhaustive, but, as we see the varied responses of the suffering, and as we analyze our own responses, these appear most obvious.

1. Deny it.

Some meet suffering by denying its reality. This is the answer of Christian Science: "Suffering is an illusion of the mind . . . all that is reality is the Eternal Mind which can harbor no evil and we are a part of that Mind, therefore sin and suffering and death are unreal and exist only in the mortal mind." But this response is unrealistic and does not meet the test of human experience.

In his marvelous sermon on The Blood Atonement, James Earl Ladd pens this graphic illustration:

> A few years ago a little boy went out to go swimming. It was a little bit cold, and he stayed in the water too long. He was weakened and enervated. On the way home he passed by an apple orchard where there were some green apples. Now mind you, he was in a bad condition to begin with. Then he climbed over the fence and ate fourteen green apples. Immediately, from the standpoint of bureaucracy,

37

there was a great upset in the department of interior, and while he was doubled over rubbing the cramps out of his stomach muscles a very good, sweet, gracious and lovely lady, like they have in story books, came by and said: "Little boy, what is wrong?"

He told her he had a "tummy" ache. She smiled sweetly and proceeded to disabuse him of his hallucination.

She said, "God is good; God is love, and pain is an error of the mortal mind, and you are simply laboring under an illusion that you are experiencing pain."

The boy looked up at her for a minute, felt of his "tummy," and said, "Lady, it's all right for you to talk that way, but I've got inside information."[9]

We know the reality of suffering, for we have experienced suffering.

A member of the aforementioned cult once asked a friend, "How is George doing?" "Not so good; he's sick," was the reply. "No, no! you mean he thinks he is sick," the friend corrected. A few weeks later the two met again. "How is George getting along?" the friend asked. "You know," he replied, "it's the craziest thing. George is lying up there at the funeral home—he thinks he is dead!"

The response of denial is unrealistic and it does not meet the test of experience. The suffering of Jesus and His disciples was not a figment of the imagination. If suffering is not a reality, then the cross of Christ is a cruel hoax and a grotesque travesty.

2. Panic.

There are some fearful souls who panic when trouble comes. Under the pressure of pain and loss they "go all to

---

9. Ladd, *op. cit.*, pp. 63, 64.

pieces." They can't handle it. They remind us of the old service cliche, "When in trouble or in doubt, run in circles, scream and shout." The one who panics in suffering is worse than useless to himself and to others.

I wonder if this is what happened to Judas. He had sold his Master for thirty pieces of silver and, under the cover of darkness, he had betrayed the Son of Man with a kiss. But morning came and the traitor saw the One he had sold delivered to the Roman governor that the sentence of death might be pronounced. Was it too late to avert the tragedy? Could he undo the terrible wrong he had committed? In deep remorse he brought back those few paltry coins to the religionists who had purchased the body of the Son of God and cried out, "I have sinned in that I have betrayed innocent blood." Could it be that he panicked at the response, "What is that to us? see thou to it?" Whether or not this was the prompting emotion, the end of the story is the lifeless body of the treasurer dangling from the end of a rope.

Judas was a part of the problem, not a part of the solution. The answer of panic to suffering is no answer at all.

3. Hide from it.

The suffering process is never pleasant. None of us desires to suffer, so many make an effort to escape it. We are a "nation on wheels." More than 21 million Americans change residence every year. Some try to escape problem situations by moving to a new area, only to find the same kind of people and the same kind of problems that they left behind. If the problems and the problem responses are within us, we carry them wherever we go.

With alcohol so readily available, there are many who attempt to escape from problems by hiding in a bottle. Suffering, sorrow, and tragedy strike and they resort to an alcoholic stupor where, for a short while, they are enabled to forget, only to awaken to find the problem still there and themselves less able to cope. This is no small problem in our "land of the free." At least ten million adult Americans are problem drinkers and we are bequeathing this heritage to our children. More than three-fourths of our children will become drunk before they have completed High School. Deaths directly related to alcohol now range in excess of 200,000 every year. Only cancer and heart and vascular disease surpass that number as a cause of death. The bottle is not an adequate hiding place.

Others, in the depth of the despair which suffering has brought, endeavor to escape by removing their lives from this vale of suffering. One of the most vivid recollections of the Great Depression is that of business tycoons, when learning that those things upon which they had depended were wiped away, leaping to their deaths from their office windows. Today, in most states, suicide ranks as the ninth or tenth cause of death.

Again, this response is not limited to adults. The suicide rate among young people has tripled since 1955, and an estimated 5,000 youths, between ages 15 and 24, commit suicide each year. Within the next hour 64 American children will attempt suicide. Suicide is now the number two killer of teen-agers in the United States. May God forgive us for our failure to teach our children how to meet suffering!

Say what you will, the solution to the suffering problem is not to be found in a change of scenery, or in the bottom of a bottle, or in suicide.

4. Cynicism.

There are many disillusioned souls who would meet suffering by anticipating it. Their attitude cries out, "I knew it was coming. It always happens to me." The cynic wrings what little comfort he can out of the fact that he was aware that suffering would be his lot. What a miserable way to find comfort! The response of the cynic resolves nothing; rather, it underscores the reality of pain and misfortune. It brings despair to the sufferer and depression to those with whom he comes in contact.

5. Stoicism.

E. Stanley Jones tells of an Indian tribe in South America in which as soon as a child is born the father greets it with these words: "You are born into a world of trouble. Shut your mouth, be quiet and bear it."[10] Such a response is not limited to Indians in South America. The response of the stoic is that suffering shall come, therefore harden yourself to meet it. This attitude finds arrogant expression in the familiar words of William Ernest Henley—

> Out of the night that covers me,
>   Black as the pit from pole to pole,
> I thank whatever gods may be
>   For my unconquerable soul. . . .
>
> It matter not how strait the gate,
>   How charged with punishment the scroll,
> I am the master of my fate:
>   I am the captain of my soul.[11]

---

10. Jones, *op. cit.*, pp. 44-45.
11. William Ernest Henley, "Invictus."

How sad, with the sea so vast and the storm so wild, that man must captain his own frail craft. How much more comforting and sustaining to have a Captain who knows the sea and is capable and willing to guide us through the storm to the security of the harbor. This assurance finds fine expression in the response of Dorothea Day to "Invictus":

> I have no fear, though strait the gate,
>   He cleared from punishment the scroll.
> Christ is the Master of my fate,
>   Christ is the Captain of my soul.[12]

The writer once spoke to an older lady, urging her to accept Jesus as her Lord and Saviour. Her response: "No, I will not, and if I have to go to Hell, I can take it." The answer of the stoic is about as far removed from the Christian solution as it can possibly be.

6. Become embittered.

One of the most popular (and most tragic) ways to meet suffering is the way of rebellion. This is the way that cries out, "Why did God do this to me? It isn't fair. If there be a God, he is not a just God." And so the suffering eats like a canker sore. The suffering one becomes embittered, withdrawn, and useless to himself and to his fellowman. His is a miserable existence and he becomes a disperser of gloom to all who are touched by his life.

7. Surrender.

Among the most common answers to the suffering problem is that of surrender. The sufferer exerts no effort to

---

12. From "My Captain," by Dorothea Day.

understand or to cope, and becomes a helpless invalid, and that needlessly. He becomes a hypochondriac, wallowing in the sea of despondency, snatching what crumbs of comfort he may from the sympathy he extracts from others. Every thought, word, and deed calls attention to himself. His eyes have been closed to the joys and the opportunities of this life. A miserable existence—a life unlived—and a premature death!

8. Use it.

On occasion, we encounter one of those great souls who recognize suffering for what it is: a gift from God, an integral part of the life process, and something to be used for the good of man and the glory of God, and so they accept it, are blessed, and become a blessing.

On a grassy plain by a sparkling sea, the compassionate Christ fed about 5,000 hungering disciples. When they had eaten and were filled, the Miracle-worker instructed His disciples, "Gather up the broken pieces which remain over, that nothing be lost" (John 6:12). *Christianity is the one way of life which throws nothing away!* It is not necessary that we relegate any of life's experience to the trash heap. If we will but have it so, we can take them all and build them into a life that is strong and useful and pleasing to Him Who is its Author.

This is the way that our Example met suffering. He made no attempt to deny it or to avoid it. He knew full well what awaited Him in the last week of His ministry, yet He "stedfastly set his face to go to Jerusalem" (Luke 9:51). The rigors of the Gethsemane and the Golgotha experiences were at hand, yet He went to meet them with a song. Our Lord did not suffer to spare us from all suffering, but to

43

WHAT THE BIBLE SAYS ABOUT SUFFERING

teach us how to bear suffering and how to *use* it to the glory of God.

Are there times that all about you seem to be naught but "broken pieces?" Don't throw them away. Gather them all together, that nothing be lost. Use them to your good and to God's glory.

9. Commit all to God.

The apostle Peter, who knew from dear experience what it meant to "suffer as a Christian," wrote words of comfort and instruction to fellow-sufferers. As he approached the climax of this beautiful treatise, he reaches the highest of conclusions as to how suffering should be met: "Wherefore let them also that suffer according to the will of God commit their souls in well-doing unto a faithful Creator" (1 Peter 4:19). As he continues to speak of the glory which awaits the victor, he admonishes, "Casting all your anxiety upon him, because he careth for you" (1 Peter 5:7). This precious little admonition is the basis for that beautiful chorus which we sang so many years ago in Christian youth camp:

> He careth for you;
> He careth for you.
> Through sunshine or shadow
> He careth for you.

Then how can we meet suffering without God?

Many of you are familiar with the name of Harry Lauder, the Scottish humorist of yesteryear. All are not aware of the tragedy which he used to make his life a blessing to many. Mr. Lauder lost his only son in the First World War. When his friends spoke with admiration of the way in which he had borne this tremendous loss, Lauder replied, "When

44

a man has been hit as I have been, there are only three
ways open to him—drink, despair, or God; and I am looking to God for the consolation and courage I now need."

Chapter Three

WHY DON'T THEY TAKE THE NET DOWN?

A happy little family group was traveling the narrow, winding highway between Portland and Seaside, Oregon. A giant Douglas Fir tree, a monarch of the forest which had stood sentinel above the winding road for many decades, crashed upon the highway, striking the speeding automobile and hurtling five lives into eternity. If the tree had fallen a moment earlier, the driver could have stopped the car. If one second later, the car would have been safely by. But no; it was timed to a fraction of a second to strike a speeding automobile and kill five people. Why? If there is a God in heaven, a God Who created and sustains His universe, a God Who "upholds all things by the word of His power," could He not have stayed the fall of this giant of the forest?

On Christmas Day a beautiful and vivacious young wife and mother died of cancer, leaving a loving husband and two fine little boys. She was a radiant and active Christian leader, loved and respected by all who knew her. Her family and her church needed her very much. Hundreds of Christians prayed fervently for her healing, but her life was not spared. Why?

Two happy little boys contracted the dread disease, leukemia. One was from a family which had little time for the things of God. This lad was treated and the disease placed in remission. He is alive and well today. The second boy was a minister's son, an intellectual genius, a happy little Christian. Thousands prayed earnestly for his recovery. For three years he suffered more intensely than any child should have to suffer, then he went home with Jesus. Why?

What is your answer, my friend, to the incompleteness and the injustices of this life? Hardship and starvation on one hand; ease and plenty on the other. For some it has been dungeons and slavery; for others, liberty and freedom. Thousands have been slain; murderers have gone free. Socrates drinks the hemlock; his murderers are at ease in Athens. Paul goes to the block; Nero lives on in luxury. Disciples of the Nazarene are clothed in the skins of wild animals, to be torn to bits by the dogs, or are rolled in pitch and set ablaze to light the gardens of a mad emperor; the emperor lives on in comfort and in regal splendor. Why?

Witness the brilliant young poet, Shelley, dying at the age of 30; Raphael at 37; Lord Byron in his 30's. Consider the poets who never lived to pen a sonnet, the artists who never produced a painting, the statesmen who never came to office, the preachers who never stood in the pulpit. Why?

The perfect body of a young Galilean was spiked to a Roman cross. He was thirty-three years of age. His ministry of teaching, preaching, and healing had spanned but three and one-half years. He was rejected by those He came to save. And now the God Whom He had loved and trusted and Whom He had served so faithfully is turning away while His Son bears the burden of the sins of mankind. All of the pathos and agony of a hurting world is caught up in those few words which are wrung from the lips of the suffering Saviour: "My God, why?"

These are not easy questions, and there are no easy answers. As Leslie Weatherhead so cogently observes, "A God whose ways could all be comprehended by so insignificant a creature as man, would be inadequate for such a universe as this."[1]

---

1. Leslie D. Weatherhead, *Why Do Men Suffer?* (New York, Nashville: Abingdon Press, 1936), p. 9.

The question which is brought to ministers of the gospel far more than all others is *WHY?* "Why did this happen to me? I believe in God. I read the Bible. I attend church. I pray. I try to help others. I strive to do God's will . . . and now see what has happened to me: sickness—pain—sorrow loss—bereavement—WHY? Why did God let this happen *TO ME?*" . . . and I freely confess that there are many times that I must reply, "I don't know why, but this I do know: somewhere in the shadows stands God, keeping watch over His own, that there is a divine purpose in suffering, and that someday we shall understand."

A dear little lady was watching her first game of tennis. Noticing how frequently the ball went into the net, she turned to a friend who stood nearby and inquired, "Why don't they take the net down?" How many of us play the game of life like that: unable to see the purpose or the blessing in the obstacle before us, we cry out, "Take the net down. Take the net down!"

The One Who gave us being has a purpose in suffering; not that He *causes* suffering, but that He *uses* it to our good and His glory. The divine purpose is revealed in a beautiful, ancient book which we call the Holy Bible. *What does the Bible say as to the divine purpose in suffering?* May we consider well the divine answer.

1. Suffering may glorify God.

The apostle Peter, writing to early Christians who had been scattered by persecution, admonishes them, "Let none of you suffer as a murderer, or a thief . . . but if a man suffer as a Christian, let him not be ashamed; but let him glorify God in this name" (I Peter 4:15-16).

In the hamlet of Bethany lived a family who Jesus loved; Martha and Mary and Lazarus. When word came to Jesus of the sickness of beloved Lazarus, He declared, "This sickness is not unto death, but *for the glory of God*" (John 11:4. Italics are the author's.). It was four days later that Jesus and His disciples came to Bethany and the Lord of life called the body of His friend from the confines of the cold stone tomb. The narrative continues, "Many therefore of the Jews, who came to Mary and beheld that which he did, believed on him" (John 11:45). Lazarus suffered; God was glorified. Some of God's greatest preachers never stood in the pulpit!

It was midnight. The first two Christian missionaries sat on the cold dirt floor of the inner prison in Philippi. Their feet were locked in the stocks and their backs streaming blood. What had they done to deserve such treatment? Nothing, except that they loved their Lord and the souls of their fellowmen so much that they couldn't keep quiet about the salvation which is found only in Jesus Christ.

How would we have reacted had we been in the position of Paul and Silas: unjustly criticized and condemned, the object of mob violence, and undergoing intense physical pain? Would we have cried out against the "injustice of God," protested our innocence, and wondered if God really loved us? Not Paul and Silas! Their feet and hands were bound, but their lips were not sealed, so they were "praying and singing hymns unto God." Their sufferings became songs. E. Stanley Jones writes beautifully of this prison experience:

> Did song ever come out of the heart of deeper injustice and did it thereby ever have deeper meaning? They went higher and higher in their notes of praise until they struck such high notes that God had to bring in the earthquake for a bass![2]

---

2. E. Stanley Jones, *Christ and Human Suffering* (New York, Nashville: Abingdon-Cokesbury Press, 1933), pp. 86-87.

The quaking earth shook the prison-house so that all of the doors were opened and everyone's bands were loosed. The fearful jailor, whose suicide was interrupted by Paul, fell down before the missionaries, crying out, "What must I do to be saved?" In response to the divine directive, this penitent believer and his family were baptized into Christ— and a church was born in Philippi. Years later, the missionary who was so deeply wronged in that Philippian jail wrote a letter to this young church. It is a letter which is included in the heart of our New Testament Scripture—a letter which has brought faith and comfort and encouragement to many aching hearts. Two faithful missionaries used their suffering— and God was glorified!

2. Suffering may make us Christlike.

The saints in Rome are reminded that they are "fore-ordained to be conformed to the image of his Son" (Rom. 8:29). Paul's heart desire is that he might know Christ, and the power of His resurrection, and the fellowship of His sufferings (Phil. 3:10). Peter reminds us that Christ's suffering for us leaves an example, that we should follow in His steps (I Peter 2:21). Christ being what He is, if His disciples are what they should be, they are bound to know suffering as a result of following Christ.

Ignatius, Bishop of Antioch in the early second century, was on his way to martyrdom in Rome. From the city of Smyrna he wrote to the church in Rome, urging them to do nothing to prevent his martyrdom and displaying his faith and his understanding of the purpose of suffering in these immortal words:

> Now I begin to be a disciple. I care for nothing, of visible or invisible things, so that I may but win Christ. Let fire and

the cross, let the companies of wild beasts, let breaking of bones and tearing of limbs, let the grinding of the whole body, and all the malice of the devil, come upon me; be it so, only may I win Christ Jesus![3]

As the heroic martyr was about to be thrown to the wild beasts, and was brought to a point where he could hear the roaring of the lions, he cried out, "I am the wheat of Christ: I am going to be ground with the teeth of wild beasts, that I may be found pure bread."[4]

Saints became like the Saviour through sacrifice: "Now I begin to be a disiple!" May our caring God grant us the grace to welcome any suffering which makes us more like the Master.

3. Suffering may increase our faith.

How prone we are when suffering comes to permit faith to run low. The punster has well pointed out that frequently our greatest need is that of a "faith lift." How much we need to be reminded that "after ye have suffered for a little while" God Himself shall "perfect, establish, strengthen you" (I Peter 5:10).

Who is there among us who has never passed through the Valley of Doubt? Honest doubt need not be a bad thing. Doubts faced honestly and thoughtfully can result in the increasing and the strengthening of our faith. There may be a marked contrast between doubt and disbelief. Doubt may be searching for the light, but disbelief is being content with the darkness. At times God may place us on our backs to cause us to look up.

3. William Byron Forbush, D.D., *Fox's Book of Martyrs* (Philadelphia, Pa., Universal Book House, 1926), pp. 7, 8.
4. *Ibid.*

Consider Thomas, the one who yet today stands as the symbol of doubt. Thomas was a disciple. He lived for more than three years with the Master, as did the others. He heard the words of wisdom which fell from His lips. He observed that spotless life. He witnessed raging storms stilled, multitudes fed with a lad's lunch, sightless eyes opened, twisted limbs straightened, outcast lepers cleansed, demon-possessed freed, even the dead restored to life and health. But then, one dark morning, Thomas saw his miracle-worker nailed to a cross—and Thomas surrendered to his doubts. Just where Thomas spent those two long days we are not told, but John informs us that when the risen Lord appeared to the disciples on the third day that Thomas was not with them. How sad! Here is a disciple who had "quit going to church," and what a blessing he missed!

The other disciples were not ready to give up on the doubter. The record declares that they found him and said to him, "Thomas, we have seen the Lord." But Thomas replied, in effect, "Oh, no. You haven't seen my Lord. I saw them lift Him up upon a tree. I saw them drive great spikes through His hands and feet. I saw them thrust a spear into His side. Unless I can put my finger into the print of the nails, and put my hand into His side, I will not believe."

Eight days passed and the disciples were gathered together and this time Thomas was with them. He had "come back to church." And Jesus came with that familiar greeting, "Peace be unto you." Then, singling out the doubter, the compassionate Christ called out to Thomas, "Thomas, come here. Thomas, put your finger in the nail-prints. Thomas, put your hand into my side. Thomas, be not faithless, but believing." And the one who had so recently been the doubter cried out, "My Lord and my God" (cf. John

52

20:19-29). Never again do we hear of Thomas giving way to his doubts. Tradition tells us that he died the painful death of a martyr rather than relinquish one iota of his faith. Suffering may increase our faith, if we will but have it so.

4. Suffering may purify our lives.

The psalmist, who had suffered greatly, reached the startling conclusion that it was good that he had been afflicted, for before his affliction he went astray, but now he observed God's word (Psalm 119:67, 71).

Jesus declared "Blessed are they that mourn" because He well knew that out of suffering may come the awareness of some of life's truest values. In his book "The Prophet," Gibran explains it thus: "Your pain is the breaking of the shell which encloses your understanding. Even as the stone of the fruit must break that its heart may stand in the sun, so must you know pain."

One who has never suffered will never fully experience understanding. Some of our most important discoveries are made in the crucible of suffering, and it is often during those moments of pain and desperation that we glimpse life in a new perspective and grow toward the likeness of the stature of the fulness of Christ.

The purging of suffering is not a pleasant process, but the end result may be a life that is at peace and on right terms with its Maker. God used Peter to reveal this blessed truth as he admonishes his hearers to arm themselves with the mind of Christ, "for he that hath suffered in the flesh hath ceased from sin" (I Peter 4:1).

Most of us have, at some time, admired the beauty of the water lily. Passing by a dirty, brackish pond, we have marveled at the contrasting green of the lily pads upon the dirty water

53

and have reveled in the beauty of the creamy white flower which these plants bear. Reaching down through the muck and the mire, those slender stems draw nourishment from the mud below, to bring sustenance to a beautiful flower. Have you not seen lives like that? The environment is not the best. There is very little there that is beautiful and desirable but, out of the darkness and the oppression, there emerges a life which is beautiful to behold—a life which brings enjoyment and peace to those who pass by. It is possible that lives be made as beautiful and pure as the lily through suffering and misfortune.

5. Suffering may make and keep us humble.

God seldom uses a life which is completely unbroken. It is true that He wants a whole heart, but that He will accept a broken one. Many of God's greatest saints have been those who have been brought low before the cross through their suffering. Saul of Tarsus was once a proud and haughty Pharisee, but God called him a "chosen vessel." When God called Ananias to reach out a hand of love and fellowship to Saul, Ananias objected that he had heard of the evil that Saul had done to the saints at Jerusalem, and that now he was on a mission to capture followers of the Way, but the Lord, Who knows the hearts of men and the potential that is there, replied, "Go thy way: for he is a chosen vessel unto me . . . for I will show him how many things he must suffer for my name's sake" (Acts 9:15-16). God can use some mighty unlikely vessels when they are given freely to Him.

On the Damascus way, Saul the persecutor met the risen Christ and became a new creature in Him. He was honored by "visions and revelations." He declared that he was caught

54

up into paradise, and heard things which were not lawful to utter. What an opportunity to glory and boast of this experience but, lest he be "exalted overmuch," God gave him a thorn in the flesh to keep him humble. What this thorn was is left to conjecture. Some have surmised that it was poor eyesight. We are not sure, but we know that some physical infirmity was granted that this apostle to the Gentile might be kept humble and usable for God.

God can not use some people because they are too great. May He grant us the grace to transform suffering into genuine humility, that we might be small enough to be used of Him.

6. Suffering may teach us patience.

How strange to be able to associate rejoicing with tribulation, yet we are directed in Romans 5:3 to "rejoice in our tribulations: knowing that tribulation worketh stedfastness." Someone has suggested that "When God sends me some tribulation, I think He wants me to tribulate!" Patience is not an easy virtue to attain. We are an impatient people: we want what we want when we want it. In our impatience, we cry out," God, give me patience—right now!" Perhaps we need tribulation as our teacher, knowing that "the proving of your faith worketh patience." May the patient God "let patience have its perfect work, that ye may be perfect and entire, lacking in nothing;" (James 1:3-4).

Nestled in the heart of the seven "graces" which Peter would have us attain, appears the word "patience," and then the writer concludes, "if these things are yours and abound, they make you to be not idle nor unfruitful unto the knowledge of our Lord Jesus Christ" (II Peter 1:5-8). For the epitome of patience we look to Him "who, when he was reviled, reviled not again; when he suffered threatened not; but committed himself to him that judgeth righteously" (I Peter 2:23).

Jesus made no effort to withhold from His disciples the knowledge of those things which they would suffer because they were His. During His last week of ministry with them He warned of the trouble to come and added, "They shall lay their hands on you, and shall persecute you, delivering you up to the synagogues and prisons, bringing you before kings and governors for my name's sake. It shall turn out unto you for a testimony" (Luke 21:12-13). As they patiently endured, they would be afforded the opportunity to witness to their faith and glorify their God.

As their Master continues to warn them that they would be delivered up even by those who were dearest to them, and that they would be hated of all men and that some would be put to death, He concludes, "In your patience ye shall win your souls" (Luke 2:19). Patience in suffering brings the victory in this life and prepares the suffering one for a home in heaven.

Those to whom this world is most deeply indebted are individuals who have learned patience by following in His steps. David Livingstone, that outstanding nineteenth century missionary and explorer of Africa, was granted the grace to wave good-bye to his wife and children and then, for twenty years, to bury himself in the heart of that dark continent; ever pressing on, his body wracked by pain and disease, facing the terrors of the jungle, the wild beasts, the snakes, the savages, until that triumphant morning when faithful black boys found the body of their "great master" on his knees by his cot. Livingstone explained his life of patient, sacrificial service by asking, "Would you like me to tell you what supported me through all the years of exile? It was this, 'Lo, I am with you always, even unto the end of the world.' " After the victor had gone to claim the crown, this was found among the last entries in his diary:

> " 'Lo, I am with you always, even unto the end of the world.' It is the word of a gentleman of the most strict and sacred honor, so there's an end of it."

May we follow in their train by learning patience through suffering.

7. Suffering may teach us gratitude.

An invalid was reported to have exulted, "Oh, I am so happy today: the doctor says that I may lie on my other side!" How often our ingratitude has been rebuked by the radiant and grateful spirit of those who are experiencing more intense suffering than we shall ever know. Saul of Tarsus, who became the great apostle to the Gentiles, suffered greatly for his faith. In II Corinthians, Chapter 11, he catalogues his apostolic labors and sufferings: five times he received forty stripes save one—thrice he was beaten with rods—once he was stoned—thrice he suffered shipwreck— a night and a day in the deep—in all manner of perils— hungry, thirsty, cold and naked—and, pressing upon him daily, anxiety for the churches—yet, through it all, he could testify, "If I must needs glory, I will glory of the things that concern my weakness" (II Cor. 11:30).

Regardless of pain and hardship, there is always that for which we should be profoundly grateful. A dear old lady testified, "Yes, it's pretty hard to get along with only two teeth, one upper and one lower, but, thank goodness, they meet!"

Without the experience of suffering it would be impossible to experience abounding gratitude and joy. The most cheerful, the most patient, and the most grateful have learned their lesson in the School of Affliction.

8. Suffering may lead us to the place of prayer.

James, speaking from the depths of his own experience, shares with us the precious panacea for suffering as he urges, so succinctly, "Is any among you suffering? let him pray" (James 5:13). Prayer has always brought surcease to suffering saints. Our Friend and Example always faced suffering with prayer. Before the greatest ordeals of His life He devoted entire nights to prayer. That night in which He was betrayed He prayed in a garden. In His intense agony on Calvary He prayed. Stephen, the first Christian martyr, as the stones fell upon his defenseless body, prayed. Paul's "thorn in the flesh" led him directly to the Throne Room in prayer.

The problem is that when we are called upon to endure pain and suffering we don't feel much like praying. When it is hardest to pray we need to pray the hardest. We can often do more than pray, but not until we have prayed. We never learn how to really pray until there is nothing left for us to do.

He Who knows what is best for His children never taught us to pray that we might avoid all misfortune, nor that all pain and hardship be removed from us, but that, through it all, our trust would be placed in Him. Somewhere amidst the suffering and the anxiety and the doubt, we must find the hand of God and grasp it tightly. There is a purging and a strengthening in suffering when it brings us low before the throne.

I was raised in the beautiful hills of Oregon. From my youth, I have greatly enjoyed the hunting and the fishing that our area so generously affords. I have an only son and, in this regard, he has followed in his father's steps. Throughout the years we have spent many enjoyable days on the lakes and along the streams.

On one mid-winter day, when Bill was just a little lad, I decided to take him steelhead fishing. It was a typical winter day in Oregon and, as the day wore on, we got wet and cold and miserable. The fish were not at all cooperative, so we reluctantly made the decision to go home. As I reeled in my lure, I became aware of some activity on the end of my line. It was not lively enough to be a steelhead and, as I brought it nearer the shore, we could see that it was just a big sucker.

In the thinking of a small boy, a sucker was better than nothing at all, so little Bill determined to land the fish. Seizing the gaff hook, he climbed out on a limb and reached down with the gaff. In his excitement, he slipped and tumbled into the murky waters below. He came up gasping and sputtering in the icy water. I shall always remember the look on my son's face: not fear or dismay, but he looked up with all of the confidence in the world, knowing that his dad was there and that he could count on him for rescue.

Oh, my friend, when you are struggling in the cold, dark current, unable to see it through in your own power and ability, if you will but look up, you will see the face of the One Who is able and willing to save. God grant that your suffering may lead you to the place of prayer.

9. Suffering may make us sympathetic and helpful.

One of the most beautiful of the divine purposes in suffering is outlined in these precious words to the saints in Corinth:

Blessed be the God and Father of our Lord Jesus Christ, the Father of mercies and God of all comfort; who comforteth us in all our affliction, that we may be able to comfort them that are in any affliction, through the comfort wherewith we ourselves are comforted of God (II Cor. 1:3-4).

Those who have passed through, or yet reside in, the Vale of Suffering should be able to sympathize with others in their hardships and infirmities. "Compassion" is an interesting word. It comes to us from the two Latin words meaning "to suffer with." We identify with the sufferer. In the words of Shakespeare, "He jests at scars who never felt a wound." We can never be really sympathetic toward others until we have been in the place where we needed sympathy. There was a time when I, as a minister, said to bereaved ones, "I know; I know." But I didn't know. It was only when I entered into the company of the bereaved that I could say it truthfully: "I know, dear friend, I know."

Bill Gold, writing in the Washington Post at the Thanksgiving season, remarked, "I think that one of the things I'm most grateful for on Thanksgiving Day is that, when the Lord was deciding who would need help at this season and who would be in a position to give help, He permitted me to be among the givers."

"Comfort ye, comfort ye my people, saith your God" (Isa. 40:1).

10. Suffering may prepare us for home.

It may well be that John, the beloved, was the only apostle to die a natural death. He lived a long and fruitful life. He knew toil, hardship, persecution, and exile, but his faith never wavered; he remained true to his Lord to the very end. John, the aged, was in the isle called Patmos, for the

60

word of God and the testimony of Jesus. He was in the Spirit on the Lord's Day, when the curtain of the centuries was drawn aside and John was permitted to look down through the corridor of the years, to see those things which God has prepared for those who love and serve Him.

One of the thrilling visions granted to John on Patmos was that of the sealing of the 144,000, twelve-thousand out of each of the tribes of Israel. After these things he beheld a great multitude which no man could number, standing before the throne, arrayed in white robes and palms in their hands. "John," asked one of the elders, "who are these that are arrayed in the white robes?" John humbly responded, "My lord, thou knowest." How thrilling the explanation of the heavenly messenger: "These are they that have come out of the great tribulation, and they washed their robes, and made them white in the blood of the Lamb" (Rev. 7:14). "Coming out" of tribulation can equip us for a home in heaven.

There is no virtue per se in enduring tribulation. It is only when the tribulation leads us to "wash our robes," and refines us, and makes us usable, and leads us to place our trust in the Saviour and to become more like Him, that we are equipped to spend eternity in His presence. Paul reminds the saints at Rome that if they suffer with Him they may also be glorified with Him (Rom. 8:17). It sounds very much as though he is saying, "No cross - no crown." Longing for the crown, we do not weary of the cross, knowing that "Our light affliction, which is for the moment, worketh for us more and more exceedingly an eternal weight of glory" (II Cor. 4:17).

Walter Scott, the brilliant author of an earlier day, was toiling at his desk throughout the long hours of the night.

61

The writer was so weak and weary and ill that he penned a phrase, lay aside his pen, and went home with God. It is said that the last three words that Scott ever wrote were these: "In the morning." Beautiful! Here we toil in the night. Here we suffer in the night. We endure through the long hours of the night, but rest and peace and joy and blessing come in the morning. In the moonlight age of the Old Testament, the Psalmist grasped this tremendous truth and cried out, "Weeping may tarry for the night, but joy cometh in the morning" (Psalm 30:5).

Doug Oldham, the big man with the golden voice, presents a tremendous testimony in sermon and song. In his beautiful album, "Doug Oldham Live," he shares the thrilling story of Richard Wurmbrandt, that courageous soldier of the cross who was a prisoner of the communists for seventeen years. Three of those dark years were spent in solitary confinement. It was mid-winter, and the captives were being held underground in a cold stone cell. A drunken, sadistic guard at times came in and caused the prisoners to lie face down on the stone floor while he walked on their backs with his hob-nailed boots.

One dark night Wurmbrandt was again being tortured. It seemed that the pain and agony were almost more than he could bear and that he would surely have to recant. As he lay there in his suffering, he heard a fellow-prisoner whisper, "Wurmbrandt!" Slowly and painfully he turned his head and attempted to look through glazed eyes at his fellow-sufferer. "Wurmbrandt," exulted the prisoner, "I've just written a great new song about Jesus!" And Wurmbrandt thought, "If someone enduring such agony can write a song about Jesus, surely I can hold on until morning."

WHY DON'T THEY TAKE THE NET DOWN?

If you've knelt beside the rubble of an aching, broken heart,
When the things you gave your life to fell apart;
You're not the first to be acquainted with sorrow, grief or
    pain,
But the Master promised sunshine after rain.

To invest your seed of trust in God in mountains you can't
    move,
You risk your life on things you can-not prove,
But to give the things you can-not keep for what you can-not
    lose
Is the way to find the joy God has for you.

Hold on my child, Joy comes in the morning,
Weeping only lasts for the night;
Hold on my child, Joy comes in the morning,
The darkest hour means dawn is just in sight.[5]

---

5. William & Gloria Gaither, "Joy Comes in the Morning" (Alexandria, Indiana:
Alexandria House, 1974).

Chapter Four

IT'S HOT IN THE FURNACE

Some six hundred years before the birth of Christ, a proud and haughty king ruled the province of Babylon. King Nebuchadnezzar had captured Jerusalem and had taken some of the finest of the youth of Israel to be his attendants. The Book of Daniel relates the thrilling story of the faith of four of these young men: Daniel, Shadrach, Meshack, and Abednego. It was Daniel who was used of God in interpreting the king's dream and, in spite of the king's acknowledgement to Daniel that "Your God is the God of gods, and the Lord of kings," he soon turned back to his polytheistic religion and the worship of his idols.

In the plain of Dura, King Nebuchadnezzar erected a huge image of gold, approximately nine feet wide and ninety feet tall, and commanded all of his subjects to fall down and worship the golden image. There were three captive boys who were subjects of a Higher Power. Shadrach, Meshach, and Abednego remembered that the Creator had commanded Israel that they should have no other gods before Him; that they should make no graven image, nor bow down before any idol. Their God had priority.

When the three God-fearing youths were brought before him, Nebuchadnezzar issued the edict: Fall down and worship the image, or be cast into the midst of a fiery furnace. The boys needed no time to think it over. Immediately they made their decision and response: "Our God whom we serve is able to deliver us from the burning fiery furnace . . . but if not . . . we will not serve thy gods, nor worship the golden image which thou hast set up" (Dan. 3:17-18). What faith! Their "if not" gives these Jewish lads a place among the Christian martyrs.

Perhaps the writer of the Hebrew letter had these young heroes in mind when, in his catalogue of the faithful, he speaks of those who, by faith, quenched the power of fire (Heb. 11:34). Three young captives in a foreign land were possessed by a whole-hearted belief in God, and were determined to put Him first, regardless of the consequences. They believed that their God was able to deliver, but if He did not choose to do so, His purpose would be served even by their deaths. How infinitely better to die with God's approval than to live without it!

In his fury, the king commanded that the furnace be heated seven times its normal heat and that strong men of his army should bind the young men and cast them into the furnace. They were bound in their own clothing and thrown into the midst of the furnace, a furnace which was emitting so much heat that those who brought them to the place of execution were slain by the intensity of the fire. As the king witnessed this barbaric spectacle, he beheld a strange sight: four men loose, walking in the midst of the fire and the aspect of the fourth was like "a son of the gods."

Who was the fourth man in the furnace? Nebuchadnezzar declared that God "sent his angel." Is it so difficult to believe that this "angel" is Malachi's "messenger of the covenant" —the Rock that followed Israel in the wilderness, of which Paul declares "and the rock was Christ" (I Cor. 10:4)—the Son of God Who was always concerned over His people, and Who, when the fulness of time came, was made flesh and dwelt among us? Regardless of our opinion as to the identity of this fourth man, he was sent by God to honor the faith of His children. When God puts a man in the furnace He goes there with him. How much better to be with God in trouble than out of trouble without Him!

How difficult, and how unnecessary, it is to go through the fire without the fourth man! There come those times in life that we are tested by fire. Fires of affliction and trial and temptation are the common lot of us all. How blessed is the one who has learned to lean hard on the promise, "I will in no wise fail thee, neither will I in any wise forsake thee" (Heb. 13:5).

> How firm a foundation, ye saints of the Lord,
> Is laid for your faith in His excellent Word!
> What more can He say than to you He hath said,
> To you who for refuge to Jesus have fled?
>
> When thro' fiery trials thy pathway shall lie,
> My grace, all-sufficient, shall be thy supply;
> *The flames shall not hurt thee,* I only design
> Thy dross to consume, and thy gold to refine.[1]

At the place of the furnace the triumph was witnessed as three young men came forth out of the midst of the fire, their bodies whole, their hair unsinged, their clothing unscorched, and no smell of fire upon them. What a beautiful fulfillment of the promise that God had made through the prophet Isaiah:

> Fear not, for I have redeemed thee; I have called thee by thy name, thou art mine. When thou passest through the waters, I will be with thee; and through the rivers, they shall not overflow thee: when thou walkest through the fire, thou shalt not be burned, neither shall the flame kindle upon thee (Isa. 43:1-2).

These three heroes lost nothing in the fire save the bonds which had bound them. Trouble and suffering may be the means by which God consumes our bonds and purifies our souls. The heathen king's verdict as he witnessed the power

---

1. "How Firm a Foundation," author unknown, (italics are the author's).

of God was that "there is no other God that is able to deliver after this sort."

> He is able to deliver thee;
> He is able to deliver thee;
> Tho' by sin opprest, Go to Him for rest:
> Our God is able to deliver thee.
> — W. A. Ogden

Fiery furnaces are not limited to the time of king Nebuchadnezzar. Those who would follow Christ are privileged to suffer with Him. Paul, who suffered greatly for his faith, reminds the saints at Philippi, "Because to you it hath been granted in the behalf of Christ, not only to believe on him, but also to suffer in his behalf" (Phil. 1:29). Jesus warned His disciples, "If they persecute me, they will also persecute you" (John 15:20). Apostle Paul reminded young Timothy that "all that would live godly in Christ Jesus shall suffer persecution" (II Tim. 3:12). Why is it that a loving God permits His children to pass through the furnace?

1. In the furnace, God chooses His people.

Isaiah lived and prophesied during a time of intense suffering. Because of their sin and rebellion, Israel and Judah were taken captive by Assyria and their once proud cities were destroyed. God spoke to these captive people through prophets, admonishing and encouraging them and enabling them to look toward the birth and the reign of the Prince of Peace. This was the setting for God's tremendous declaration through Isaiah, "I have refined thee, but not as silver; I have chosen thee in the furnace of affliction" (Isa. 48:10). Some of God's greatest saints were discovered in the furnace. How truly it has been said that "God gets His best soldiers from the Highlands of affliction."

67

God chose some mighty unlikely people to accomplish His purpose. One such was a man named Gideon. His family was the poorest in Manasseh and, according to Gideon's evaluation, he was least in his father's house. Because of Israel's sin and rebellion, God had delivered them into the hand of Midian, who despoiled the land. In the midst of this trying situation, young Gideon was beating out wheat in a winepress, to hide it from the Midianites, when he unexpectedly became host to a heavenly visitor.

"Jehovah is with thee, thou mighty man of valor," was the angel's greeting."

Gideon's response was that which suffering ones have made throughout the ages: "If God is with us, why then is all this befallen us?"

But God saw the potential in Gideon, looked upon him, and said, "Go in thy might and save Israel . . . Surely I will be with thee, and thou shalt smite the Midianites as one man." And we all remember Gideon: Gideon and his sign of the fleece—Gideon reducing the size of his army that God might receive the glory—Gideon who threw off the yoke of the oppressor and wrought the victory for God (cf. Judg. 6, 8).

God did not use Gideon for want of something better, God chose Gideon in the furnace of affliction. Such God used then, and such God uses today.

It may well be that suffering is a mark of divine favor, for "whom the Lord loveth he chasteneth" (Heb. 12:6). It was Paul's highest desire to know Christ and the fellowship of His suffering. How we ought welcome any suffering which brings us any nearer the suffering Saviour.

Jesus never promised His disciples a rose garden. His call was the call of the difficult—cross-bearing, persecution, loneliness, poverty, and wearisome toil—but He did promise them that from it all there would come significant blessings. As the Master Teacher sat on the hillside and began that matchless sermon which we call the Sermon on the Mount, He listed the happy mourners, concluding with "Blessed are they that have been persecuted for righteousness' sake: for theirs is the kingdom of heaven" (Matt. 5:10). His people are blessed by becoming involved in something that is meaningful and that outlasts earthly life.

Dietrich Bonhoffer, the Christian martyr of Nazi Germany, once said, "Life has to involve commitment, for we are made to give ourselves to high causes. Never pity the man who is persecuted for his commitment, but feel sorry for the man whose life was never worth persecuting."

In the furnace of affliction there are encountered those friendly obstacles which make us strong and help us to grow and put us in the company of those whom God has chosen for Himself and for His glad service.

For every hill I've had to climb,
For every stone that bruised my feet,
For all the blood and sweat and grime,
For blinding storm and burning heat,
My heart sings but a grateful song—
    These were the things that
        made me strong.

For all the heartaches and the tears,
For all the anguish and the pain,
For gloomy days and fruitless years,
And for the hopes that lived in vain,
I do give thanks; for now I know
    These were the things that
        helped me grow.

69

'Tis not the softer things of life,
Which stimulates man's will to strive,
But bleak adversity and strife
Do most to keep man's will alive.
O'er rose-strewn paths the weaklings creep,
    But brave hearts dare
        to climb the steep![2]

2. In the furnace, God tries His children's faith.

Peter writes to the "sojourners of the Dispersion." The foretold persecution of the saints is at hand. They have begun to experience participation in the sufferings of Christ, and Peter admonishes, "Think it not strange concerning the fiery trial among you, which cometh upon you to prove you" (I Peter 4:12). The furnace can be a place of testing and a place of strengthening. God doesn't put His people through the fire until they are fireproof.

Those early Christian martyrs discovered the worth of the furnace. Their faith was found to be more precious than gold and enabled them to endure a death which glorified their Redeemer. Beneath the city of Rome is the labyrinth of catacombs, the prayer rooms of the early Christians under persecution—and their cemeteries. Untold thousands of the bodies of the saints were here laid to rest. As we walk those dark corridors, lined with row upon row of crypts, we come occasionally to much larger vaults, beautifully embellished and inscribed. In response to our question, the guide replies, "These are the tombs of the martyrs." Their faith found fruition in the yielding up of life for their Master.

Here, on the cold grey wall of the catacomb, is an inscription which I shall always remember and cherish. It is

---

2. "Friendly Obstacles," author unknown.

the engraving of a large anchor (the Christian's "anchor of the soul") and, beneath the anchor, the fish. The sign of the fish predates the sign of the cross, for the Greek word for "fish" contains the first letters of five words which were most precious to His followers (Jesus—Christ—God—Son —Saviour). To the right of the engraving there are three interlocking circles: the symbol of the communion or eucharist, which was frequently celebrated in these subterranean passages before the break of day. Above it all there is the circle which represents the everlasting God Who has promised, "I will in no wise fail thee, neither will I in any wise forsake thee" (Heb. 13:5). This was the assurance that enabled the martyrs to march to their deaths with a song on their lips and a faith in their hearts.

Another of the moving experiences as we visit Rome is our pilgrimage to the Mamertine prison, where tradition says that Paul was imprisoned. It is a dark, dank dungeon, beneath an ancient building. Here, in this black cavern, our little band of pilgrims lift their voice in song: "Faith of our fathers, living still, in spite of dungeon, fire, or sword," bow our heads and thank the all-wise God Who tries His children's faith through the fire.

Elk hunters of the Pacific Northwest know the meaning of rough weather. It was a bitter-cold November day in the Wallowa Mountains of Northeastern Oregon, and a blizzard was fast approaching. I stood upon the brink of a precipice, looking down into a mighty gorge. The Minam River hurried noisily along more than a mile below, on its journey to join the Wallowa and the Snake rivers, thence to the Columbia and on to the mighty Pacific. A howling, biting wind, sharp as though honed on an iceberg, hurled flakes of snow and pellets of sleet into my face.

71

Suddenly, cutting sharply through the gale, came the piercing scream of an eagle. Looking high into the heavens, I saw him hanging there, wings spread wide, facing the scudding clouds, defying the stormy blast, permitting his set wings to carry him ever higher above the storm. It is only in a resisting medium that a bird can fly. I bless God for that day in which I discovered that it is the set of the wings that determines how high you rise in the storm. There is now added meaning to me in Exodus 19:4, "I bare you on eagles' wings, and brought you unto myself."

3. In the furnace, God receives glory.

Peter knew what it was to suffer for the faith, and how these sufferings can be used to the glory of God. How incredible that he should admonish his hearers to "rejoice" as they partake of the sufferings of Christ, and that those are "blessed" who are reproached for His name. He continues his admonition that none should suffer as an evil-doer, but "If a man suffer as a Christian, let him not be ashamed; but let him *glorify God* in this name" (I Peter 4:16. Italics are the author's).

It was vacillating Peter who boasted so proudly, "If all shall be offended in thee, I will never be offended . . . Even if I must die with thee, yet will I not deny thee" (Matt. 26:33, 35). Peter here professed love and loyalty above that of all other disciples, but the testing time came. In the garden Peter witnessed the capture of his Master, and he followed behind as they brought Him into the court of the high priest.

About the fire in the courtyard, Peter failed the test. The one who had pledged his faithfulness so ardently thrice denied his Lord, cursing and swearing and protesting, "I

know not the man." Jesus turned on Peter the look of pity-
ing love, and Peter went out and wept bitterly.

Now, in response to the invitation of the resurrected
Christ, the disciples have met with their Master on the shore
of Galilee. Here they breakfasted with Him and enjoyed
the sweet fellowship of days gone by. Following the meal,
Jesus called Peter aside and thrice inquired as to his love.
Three times, around another fire, Peter had denied. Now
three times, about the fire on the seashore, Peter declares
his love and is restored to full discipleship.

It is following this tender scene of the restoration of the
penitent one that the loving and forgiving Saviour revealed
to Peter that which awaited him:

> Verily, verily, I say unto thee, When thou wast young,
> thou girded thyself, and walkedst whither thou wouldest:
> but when thou shalt be old, thou shalt stretch forth thy
> hands, and another shall gird thee, and carry thee whither
> thou wouldest not. Now this he spake, signifying *by what*
> *manner of death he should glorify God* (John 21:18-19.
> Italics are the author's.).

The only satisfactory answer to these two verses is that
Peter was to die the death of a martyr. The universal testimony of the early church writers is that Peter was martyred.
Tradition says that Peter was crucified, and that as he approached his cross he requested to be crucified head downward, declaring that he was not worthy to be crucified in
the same position as was his Master.

Throughout the years men have looked upon the service
and the sacrifice of Peter—and have glorified God.

No great work for God or man was ever wrought without someone suffering. Carlyle pointed out that even the
writing of a great book "is some man's life-blood."

Following the catalogue of the faithful in the eleventh chapter of the Hebrew letter, the writer reminds us that chastening may result in our good and in God's glory, that all chastening seems grievous, but that afterward it yields fruit (Heb. 12:11). The plow may have to dig deeply to break up the hardened soil. God may have to plow deep furrows in the souls of those He would use to His glory. The farmer doesn't waste his time plowing the sand hills or the rock piles. If the plowshare bites deeply, remember that there is something there that He deems worth cultivating, and that the crop may glorify your Maker.

One of the seven selected by the early Jerusalem church to serve the widows' tables was a man named Stephen. Stephen was "a man full of faith and of the Holy Spirit," and he was a preaching deacon. Jealous religionists brought him before the royal court of the Jews, where he preached that beautiful sermon recorded in the seventh chapter of Acts. As he rebuked them for their stubborness and their sin, they turned upon him. Stephen was ready to give his life for his faith, but he was not forsaken. He declared, "I see the heavens opened, and the Son of man standing on the right hand of God" (Acts 7:56). We read elsewhere of the Son being seated on the right hand of God, but here He is standing. Could it be that there was something so grand and thrilling about the death of the first martyr that the Son of God sprang to His feet to hold out His arms and say, "Welcome home, Stephen"?

These religionists, unwilling to accept the testimony of the martyr, cast him out of the city and stoned him. The witnesses, who were required to cast the first stones, laid their garments at the feet of a little, bigoted, blood-thirsty Jew named Saul. Saul, who became Paul, the apostle to

74

the Gentiles, never forgot Stephen. Years later, he also knew the meaning of mob violence and, as he stood on the castle stairs in Jerusalem and addressed the blood-thirsty mob, he remembered Stephen and declared, "I also was standing by, and consenting" (Acts 22:20). Had Stephen not died, Saul might not have lived. Stephen suffered—Paul was won—the gospel came to Gentiles—and God received glory.

4. In the furnace, the lives of His saints are refined, made usable, and equipped for heaven.

There is no birth without a pang, nor do we grow into the measure of the stature of the fulness of Christ without suffering. The good, the pure, and the beautiful are born in the furnace of affliction. At the very heart of the pain and suffering may be found the blessing we need. He who would have nothing to do with thorns must never attempt to pick roses.

One of the interesting experiences as one participates in a guided tour of Egypt is that of visiting the perfume shops. The climate along the Nile is ideal for producing strikingly beautiful and fragrant roses. As the visitors are seated in a circle in the little shop, the proprietor passes among them and smears each hand or arm with the essence of the various fragrances before making his sales pitch. The tourists may then purchase small bottles of the pure essence which they may bring home and, cutting the essence with many parts of alcohol, may utilize the quality product as gifts for friends. It is all very interesting, but always remember that the rose must be crushed to yield its sweetest perfume.

It is an exhilarating experience to stand upon a mountain top, with the vista of the handiwork of God stretched out before you, but there is no high mountain without a deep valley beside it—and if you don't climb the mountain, you can't see the view.

It was your author's blessed privilege to serve for many years in the field of new church evangelism. What a thrill and what a challenge to go into a needy community and seek out a few precious souls who are so dedicated to their Lord that they are willing to spend and be spent that there might be a congregation of born-again children of God in their community.

One such church-planting experience was in a beautiful town in Central Oregon. The nucleus was formed, a temporary place of meeting secured, and a search launched for a building site. The acreage which God made available to us was the outstandingly beautiful site of a former nursery: a haven of trees and shrubs and flowers, known in the community as "God's Three Acres."

Concerned and committed men of our baby congregation remodeled the residence on the property into a chapel, built a steeple, erected a sign, and worship services were begun. The guest house was appropriated by our outstanding group of young people as their place of meeting.

The church was established, the first minister was called, and the organizing evangelist moved on. Many months later, it was my privilege to again visit the young church. I walked slowly over the grounds of God's Three Acres and was smitten with an acute case of nostalgia, as I thought of the dedication of both young and old which had made it all possible. As I entered the little guest house and thought of the wonderful and sacrificial ministry of these young people, I saw on the wall a poster which spoke so eloquently of the secret of the success of this youth group. The words which spoke to me that day, and that have been precious and

76

challenging to me throughout the intervening years, are these: "If you won't climb the mountain, you can't see the view."

To appreciate the sunlight it is necessary to endure the darkness. The nights are dark in the forest, and as one passes through those long hours of the night it seems that just before the stars begin to dim and the grey dawn appears that the old saying is surely true: "The darkest hour is just before the dawning." It is a moving experience to sit by a campfire and, in the dark hour which precedes the dawning, to hear the clear and beautiful song of the birds as they anticipate the day. As Elihu endeavored to comfort suffering Job, he reminded him of his Maker, "Who giveth songs in the night" (Job 35:10).

One of the awesome sights of the author's boyhood was to pause at the village blacksmith shop and observe the old-time blacksmith at work at forge and anvil. The forge was heated white-hot with the hand-bellows; the metal thrust into the heart of the extreme heat, then withdrawn and placed in a trough of water. Time after time, the process was repeated: the white-hot heat, then the chill of the water, until the metal was tempered and made usable. God has a forge—a place of extremities—and His most beautiful and effective saints have passed through it.

Beauty may emerge from affliction. A gem cannot be polished without friction, nor can a child of God be perfected without adversity. There are beaches along the beautiful Oregon coast that are covered with stones (one is known as Agate Beach). To those of us who are laymen in the world of stone, the rocks appear as just ordinary stones, but the "rock hound" selects from among them and places them in the tumbler or under his saw, and there emerges an object

77

of breath-taking beauty. Polishing is not a pleasant process for the object being polished, but it is necessary for every stone that becomes a gem. We admire the finished product, but we shrink from the process. Even the diamond must endure a great deal of cutting before it shows its brilliancy.

A crucible is defined as a vessel for melting metals or minerals. God has such a crucible—a place where the precious metal is tested and refined. As Job wrestles with the problem of suffering, he cries out with a deep insight, "When he hath tried me, I shall come forth as gold" (Job 23:10). God would have no furnaces if there were no gold to be separated from the dross.

Zechariah was one of the Old Testament prophets through whom God spoke to captive Israel. The prophet was faithful in delivering the message of God, pointing out that they were suffering oppression because they had disobeyed God. As the curtain of the centuries was drawn aside, the prophet was enabled to see the coming of the King, the return of Judah and Israel to the Land of Promise, and a fountain opened for cleansing. It is at this point that Jehovah warns that only one-third of the people shall be left in the land, but that He would "bring the third part into the fire, and will refine them as silver is refined, and will try them as gold is tried. They shall call on my name, and I will hear them: I will say, It is my people; and they shall say, "Jehovah is my God" (Zech. 13:9).

Long ago, I read a beautiful story of how the craftsman of old refined silver. The silver-bearing ore was placed in a large vat while an intense fire was kindled beneath. As the heat penetrated the ore, the silver began to be released and to run free. The refiner stood, looking down into the vat, until just the right moment—the moment that he could see the reflection of his face in the silver—then the heat was turned off. Wonderful! Perhaps the Master Refiner is just waiting until He can see the reflection of His face in us before we are freed from the heat.

He sat by a fire of seven-fold heat,
    As He watched by the precious ore,
And closer He bent with a searching gaze
    As He heated it more and more.

He knew He had ore that could stand the test,
    And He wanted the finest gold
To mould a crown for the King to wear,
    Set with gems with a price untold.

So He laid our gold in the burning fire,
    Though we fain would have said Him, "Nay,"
And He watched the dross that we had not seen,
    And it melted and passed away.

And the gold grew brighter and yet more bright,
    But our eyes were so dim with tears,
We saw but the fire—not the Master's hand,
    And questioned with anxious fears.

Yet our gold shown out with a richer glow,
    As it mirrored a Form above,
That bent o'er the fire, though unseen by us,
    With a look of ineffable love.

Can we think it pleases His loving heart
    To cause us a moment's pain?
Ah, no, but He saw through the present cross
    The bliss of eternal gain.

So He waited there with a watchful eye,
  With a love that is strong and sure,
And His gold did not suffer a bit more heat
  Than was needed to make it pure.[3]

If God is refining your heart, don't seek to escape the furnace of affliction. Yes, it's hot in the furnace, but you can bear it when the "fourth man" goes there with you.

---

3. "The Refiner's Fire," author unknown, *Out of My Treasure*, edited by Willie W. White (Joplin, MO: College Press, 1964), p. 209.

Chapter Five

THE GOD WHO HEALS - OR DOES HE?

"I am Jehovah that healeth thee" (Exod. 15:26).

There has been a healing question since the inception of sin. The almighty, all-wise, all-loving Father climaxed His creation by forming man out of the dust of the earth and breathing into his nostrils the breath of life. This crown of creation was placed in a beautiful garden, planted eastward in Eden. Here all was perfect. The God Who made it all had looked upon His completed creation and pronounced it "very good."

Eden was no jungle where the stronger lay in wait for the weaker. Here was no dread of tooth or claw or poisoned fang. Here was no grinding toil; no heavy burden for tired shoulders . . . just the happy employment of "dressing" and "keeping" the garden, and of walking in sweet communion with the Creator. In Eden there was no sickness, sorrow, pain, nor death. If man had continued this intimate fellowship with his Maker there would never had been a healing problem.

But the omnipotent God Who made it all did not desire His child to be an animal nor a robot. It pleased Him to equip His creature with a will and with the power of choice.

> And Jehovah commanded the man saying, of every tree of the garden thou mayest freely eat: but of the tree of the knowledge of good and evil, thou shalt not eat of it: for in the day that thou eatest thereof thou shalt surely die (Gen. 2:16-17).

Yet how perverse we are! How we desire that which is forbidden!

> And when the woman saw that the tree was good for food, and that it was a delight to the eyes, and that the tree

was to be desired to make one wise, she took of the fruit thereof, and did eat; and she gave also unto her husband with her, and he did eat (Gen. 3:6).

What is God to do? The creature has rebelled against the Creator. The sweet fellowship has been broken. God has declared, "In the day thou eatest thereof thou shalt surely die." Sin has entered the world, and God's holy justice demands that death must follow. Man must be denied access to the tree of life, lest he eat and live forever. The curse is complete: the serpent is to slither in the dust; the woman is subjected to the man and is to know pain in child-bearing; the earth is cursed with thorns and thistles; the man is to know wearisome toil, and is to return unto the ground from which he was taken. The stream of agony flows outward from Eden.

And thus it is, ever since that dark day in Eden, when man rebelled against his Maker, that sickness and pain and death have been the common lot of the human race. The birth of the babe is wrought through pain. The first sound uttered by the newly born is its cry. Sickness, disease, and injury bring pain. Despite our miracle drugs and medical technology, old age is usually accompanied by pain. How frequently our hearts are touched by the intense pain of the dying. We have inherited the burden of pain and suffering, and under this burden we cry out for relief. The question of divine healing is inextricably woven into the problem of suffering.

Healing Among the "Heathen"

Search the records of ancient civilizations and note the many references to the healing arts. Physical infirmity is looked upon as the work of evil spirits. Primitive men called upon their idols and their deities for deliverance. Sorcery and witchcraft are practiced. Walk through the Egyptian museum in Cairo, or look into the glass cases in the museum at the ruins of old Pompeii, and note the many instruments and devices employed by the physicians of old. Five hundred years before the birth of Christ, there is the traditional story of a blind man who was supposedly healed by Buddha. We have no monopoly upon the healing question. The question of suffering is the question of the ages.

Healing in the Old Testament

God's first great promise of healing was given soon after the deliverance of the children of Israel from the land of bondage and the crossing of the Red Sea. In the wilderness of Shur, Jehovah made this conditional promise to His people:

> If thou wilt diligently hearken to the voice of Jehovah thy God, and wilt do that which is right in his eyes, and wilt give ear to his commandments, and keep all his statutes, I will put none of the diseases upon thee, which I have put upon the Egyptians: for I am Jehovah that healeth thee (Exod. 15:26).

Dr. S. I. McMillen has produced a brilliant treatise, based upon the above text. On the very first pages of the splendid book, *None of These Diseases,* he points out, so vividly, the many diseases which were prevalent among the Egyptians and the preposterous prescriptions which have been deciphered from the old papyrus manuscripts.[1] The application

---

1. S. I. McMillen, M.D., *None of These Diseases* (Westwood, N.J., Fleming H. Revell Company, 1963), pp. 11, 12.

of these prescribed "cures" frequently produced more serious results than the diseases themselves.

The people of God who had been held in Egyptian bondage those many years were well aware of the diseases which God had "put upon the Egyptians," and how amazed and thrilled they must have been at this divine promise: If they would but be obedient to Him, they would avoid all of these diseases which they had witnessed, and to which they had been subject, in the land of their bondage.

Our God is a promise-keeping God. Following forty years of wilderness wandering, Moses recounts to Israel Jehovah's gracious dealings with His wandering children, and reminds them, "Thy raiment waxed not old upon thee, neither did thy foot swell, these forty years (Deut. 8:4). Some two and one-half million wanderers had been immune to physical infirmity as long as they obeyed the voice of their God.

Not only did the caring God hold a divine shield between His people and disease throughout the wilderness wandering, but He gave a divine plan for physical fitness which, if followed carefully, would guard against sickness and disease. The all-wise God, Who formed man out of the dust of the earth and breathed into his nostrils the breath of life, knows what is best for the bodies of His creatures. What wonderful laws for health and well-being are given through His servant Moses.

The books of Leviticus and Numbers provide an outstanding model for effective quarantine and sanitary legislation, pre-dating the findings of modern medical science by some 3,500 years. God gave Moses instructions as to how to wash the hands after handling the dead or the touching of bodies of the infected living. Mid-way through the twentieth century, following epidemics of staph infection, the Department of Health delineated the proper method for washing the hands, which is approximately that which God gave through Moses in the 19th chapter of Numbers. Man finally learned, and that very dearly, what God had revealed to Moses those many centuries ago.

One of the perplexing problems confronting medical researchers for many years was the comparative absence of cervical cancer among Jewish women. They have now agreed that this spectacular freedom results largely from the circumcision of Jewish men—a practice which God instituted through Abraham some four thousand years ago!

Another remarkable fact in connection with the instructions as to the circumcision of the babes is the time specified: the eighth day. Why the eighth day? Modern research has found the answer. Dr. McMillen points out that vitamin K, a vital blood-clotting element, is not produced in the baby's intestinal tract until the fifth to the seventh day, therefore the first safe day to perform circumcision would be on the eighth day, the day selected by Him Who first made the vitamin K.[2]

Another vital component to the clotting of blood is prothombrin. An eight-day-old baby has more available prothombrin than on any other day of its entire life.[3] God's timetable is always best! "O the depth of the wisdom and the knowledge of God! how unsearchable are his judgments, and his ways past tracing out!" (Rom. 11:33).

The pages of the old covenant scriptures are replete with references to physical healings. Critical, complaining Miriam is punished by leprosy and subsequently healed (Num. 12). A fiery serpent is set upon a standard that those suffering from the serpents' bites might look and live (Num. 21).

2. McMillen, op. cit., p. 22.
3. loc. cit.

Naaman, the leper, finds fulness of cleansing as he obeys the voice of the prophet and dips himself seven times in the muddy Jordan (II Kings 5). King Hezekiah, who is "sick unto death," recovers when, at the direction of the prophet, the cake of figs is laid upon the boil (II Kings 20). In the classic illustration of agonizing Job, his captivity is turned when he prays for his friends, and he lives a hundred and forty years following his restoration (Job 42).

How appropriately King David exults of the One "Who forgiveth all thine iniquities; who healeth all thy diseases" (Psalm 103:3).

Healing in the New Testament

> And Jesus went about in all Galilee, teaching in their synagogues, and preaching the gospel of the kingdom, and healing all manner of disease and all manner of sickness among the people (Matt. 4:23).

Jesus of Nazareth is truly the Great Physician. No case is too difficult for Him to cure, nor too obscure to command His attention. He speaks, and the deaf hear. He touches sightless eyes, and they are opened. He reaches out His hand to the leper, and the leper feels, surging through those wasted veins, the cleansing, pulsating power of the divine touch. A woman who has had an issue of blood for twelve years touches the border of his garment, and is made whole. A man with a withered hand stretches it forth, and it is restored. The palsied servant of a Roman centurion is healed from a distance, with but a spoken word. The Gadarene demoniac is freed, clothed, comforted, and seated at the feet of Jesus. In the last recorded healing of His ministry, He touches the severed ear of the servant of the high priest and heals him.

86

It was very early in the ministry of our Lord that He cured Peter's mother-in-law of her fever. Matthew continues the story:

> And when even was come, they brought unto him many possessed with demons: and he cast out the spirits with a word, and healed all that were sick: that it might be fulfilled which was spoken through Isaiah the prophet, saying, Himself took our infirmities, and bare our diseases (Matt. 8:16-17).

He "took our infirmities." They became His. Every pain becomes His pain. Every weakness becomes His weakness. Every care becomes His care. It was Goethe who cried out, "If I were God, this world of sin and suffering would break my heart." O, but it does! How we read how the caring Jesus looked upon suffering humanity and was "moved with compassion." He sees. He understands. He cares.

> O yes, He cares, I know He cares,
> His heart is touched with my grief;
> When the days are weary, the long nights dreary,
> I know my Savior cares.[4]

As the twelve were sent out before Him, they were commissioned and empowered: "Heal the sick, raise the dead, cleanse the lepers, cast out demons . . ." (Matt. 10:8). The Book of Acts recounts healings wrought by disciples. In Acts 3 Peter takes the hand of the one who was lame from his mother's womb and raises him up. Acts 5:16 speaks of the sick and those who were vexed with unclean spirits being brought to the apostles, "and they were healed every one."

Among the miraculous manifestations of the Spirit, imparted to selected leaders in the early church was the gift of

---

4. Frank E. Graeff, "Does Jesus Care?"

healing (I Cor. 12:9). It was the practice of the inspired apostles to lay their hands upon selected leaders in the church, to confer upon them special miracle-working powers (Acts 8:18). Doubtless, many of these who thus became spiritually-gifted brethren became elders in their congregations. Perhaps this helps us to better understand the instruction which James gave to the twelve tribes which were of the Dispersion:

> Is any among you sick: let him call for the elders of the church; and let them pray over him, anointing him with oil in the name of the Lord: and the prayer of faith shall save him that is sick, and the Lord shall raise him up; and if he have committed sins, it shall be forgiven him (James 5:14-15).

Whether this anointing with oil was the formal anointing, such as was used in setting aside prophets, priests, and kings, or whether it was the application of warm olive oil, as used for therapeutic purposes, will probably never be fully resolved. Perhaps this instruction is given because God wants us to do our part in relieving suffering and infirmity. Whatever the meaning may be, it is the "prayer of faith" that shall save the sick, and God's primary desire is the healing of the soul ("and if he have committed sins, it shall be forgiven him"). God is more interested in the salvation of men's souls than in the healing of their bodies.

Does God Heal Today?

Note well that the question is not, "*Can* God heal?" That question would be ridiculous. He Who formed the first Adam from the dust is certainly capable of healing that which He has made.

It was a Master Craftsman Who designed and constructed the body of man. He built the two hundred and six bones and secured them with six hundred muscles. For building materials He used sixty thousand billion cells, each containing about two hundred thousand billion molecules, and each molecule containing up to thirty thousand atoms. The Builder installed thermostatically controlled heat, sealed and lubricated bearings, sound and sight recording, and a pump which circulates life-giving fuel throughout the body for seventy to one hundred years without faltering.

The Divine Craftsman built a tongue which is flexible enough to form words and an ear which can hear and understand. He equipped His masterpiece with an automatic control called a brain. In the cortex of that brain there are ten billion nerve cells, with dendrites, axons, and synapses, enabling thought, memory, and character development, and this three pound brain can store about fifty times more information than is contained in the nine million volumes of the congressional library. Dr. William W. Orr has summarized it well:

> It is God who planned the intricacies of our circulatory systems with its 25 trillion red blood corpuscles. It is God who built into the human ear the little grand piano with its 24,000 strings. It is God who fashioned the human eye with its retina containing 2,000,000 rods and cones. It is God who planned the human hand which is the most utilitarian instrument on earth. Surely such a God who planned all these amazing things would know full well how to restore them to usefulness.[5]

The director of a large hospital in Chicago testified: "As a doctor, I have seen recoveries after prayer and healing services

---

5. William W. Orr, *Does God Heal Today?* (Los Angeles: Bible Institute of Los Angeles), p. 4.

that defy all present scientific knowledge." Dr. Robert Laidlaw, chief of Psychiatry at New York City's Roosevelt Hospital, osberved: "Does a healing power exist? I believe we can answer with an unconditional 'yes'." He who has felt the healing touch of the Great Physician, or he who has carefully considered the testimony of recipients of physical blessing from their Maker, unite in declaring, "Yes, God heals. God heals today. He can heal but, in His wisdom, He does not always choose to do so." His wisdom is higher than ours.

All Healing Is Divine

Those who have visited Harvard Medical School tell us that over one of the doors is inscribed these words: "We dress the wound; God heals it." The world's greatest surgeon does not have the ability to heal the smallest wound. The dedicated surgeon may practice all of the medical skill at his command, but it is God Who must do the healing. What a comfort and source of strength it is, after being wheeled into surgery and receiving the anaesthetic, to hear the petition, as the surgeon, to whom you have entrusted your life, turns to his assistants and quietly says, "Now, let us pray!"

The child of God who has searched the Scriptures, who has walked in sweet communion with the Creator, and has committed body and soul to the One Who gave him being, must reach the conclusion that all healing is of God, whether it be wrought through natural means (rest, sleep, exercise, diet), through medicine or surgery, through manipulation (chiropractic), through mental suggestion or through prayer. God is the ultimate Healer. He is in the healing business.

No case is too difficult for Him, and when God heals it is complete; there are no failures with Him.

Not only does God heal, but He has given our bodies the power to fight disease and the marvelous ability to recuperate from illness, disease, and trauma. He has mustered a battalion of white corpuscles to attack and destroy the enemy of infection. He has formed the prothrombin to coagulate the blood. He washes our eyes with tears to expel any damaging substance. He has given our bodies the ability to build immunity systems which may spare the ravages of disease.

One of the most marvelous of the protective agents with which the Maker has equipped the body is that which is known to medical science as the T_4 bacteriophage virus, which attacks and destroys unwanted bacterium. In less than thirty minutes from the onslaught, the bacterium is dead, and an army of two hundred new T_4 viruses are ready to do battle with subsequent invaders.[6]

The Creator continues to express concern over the bodies He has made. He protects. He provides. He heals.

. . . BUT NOT ALWAYS

Our God is a miracle-working God: nothing is too difficult for Him. Yet a careful reading of the scripture, the observation of the sickness and suffering of the faithful, and a thoughtful analysis of our own experience, must lead us to conclude that He does not always heal.

Doubtless there were many lepers in Syria, but only Naaman was healed. There was a multitude of sick, blind, halt, and withered at the pool of Bethesda, but only one

6. G. Merwyn Maxwell, *Man, What a God!* (Mountain View, CA: Pacific Press Publishing Association, 1970), pp. 9, 10.

was made whole. The apostle Paul had his "thorn in the flesh" to buffet him, concerning which he thrice requested that it might depart. This was not in harmony with the divine will, but God answered, "My grace is sufficient." One of Paul's closest companions, Trophimus, was "left at Miletus sick." Paul's child in the faith was instructed to "use a little wine for thy stomach's sake and thine often infirmities" (I Tim. 5:23). Paul certainly possessed the gift of healing; why then did he not restore these dear friends? Has his faith run low, or could it be that God had a purpose in sickness and suffering?

When God does not see fit to heal is it not that He desires to accomplish a greater good? When suffering ones pray much and find no apparent relief many lose faith. May He grant us the realization that it is far more important to keep our faith than it is to keep our health.

When we are numbered among the suffering; when we have cried out for relief and petitioned earnestly for healing, and the infirmity remains, how shall we respond? There are many who are convinced that when God does not heal there is either something wrong with them or with God, and this failure to be healed may result in loss of faith, in disillusionment, and even in death. When suffering lays its dark hand upon our lives, how prone we are to forget that immunity from sickness and pain and sorrow are never laid down in the scripture as a proof of special divine favor, nor as a reward for our "goodness" or for our faith.

Is it not conceivable that God's plan for our lives may include sickness, and that suffering, in some strange way, may be the gift of a loving God? Peter admonishes us, "Let them also that suffer *according to the will of God* commit their souls in well doing unto a faithful creator" (I Peter 4:19. Italics are the author's.).

SICKNESS MAY BE A TEACHER. The psalmist learned the lesson well. He declared, "It is good for me that I have been afflicted; that I may learn thy statutes" (Ps. 119:71). Kahlil Gibran, the Lebanese poet, expressed it thus: "Your pain is the breaking of the shell that encloses your understanding." Paul explained that his "thorn in the flesh" was a messenger of Satan, sent to buffet him, lest he should be exalted over much. God may use our sickness to prevent pride. Sickness may teach dependence upon God. God may place us on our backs so that it is easier for us to look up. We may never see so clearly as when our eyes are washed with tears.

As a young minister, I had three wonderful friends who lived next door. These boys were vibrant, alert, optimistic— and completely blind. One was a brilliant college student and splendid musician. One was a saxophone player and a technician. He was an outstanding radio repairman. Although totally blind, he constructed his own short-wave transmitter and receiver. The third boy was a wrestler and a singer. There were few dry eyes in the audience on that Lord's Day morning when he stood before our little congregation and sang that stirring solo, "The Blind Plowman."

How he poured out his heart in the petition, "Set my hand upon the plow, my feet upon the sod; turn my face toward the east, and thanks be to God." Many were the souls that were searched and the hearts that were turned heavenward, as he sang of the God Who took away his eyes that his soul might see.

It was John Mark, the evangelist, who related the strange story of the healing of a blind man (cf. Mark 8:22-26). After the Master had spit on his eyes and laid His hands upon Him, his healing was incomplete. He could see men, but they

93

appeared "as trees walking." How strange! Was the Miracle-worker losing his touch? Would His healings no longer be successful? And then the Great Physician laid His hands upon him the second time and he saw all things clearly. When we long for healing, and can not see clearly through the mist of His wise design, it may be that we need but await the second touch.

SICKNESS MAY GLORIFY GOD. Seeing a man blind from birth, the disciples asked, "Rabbi, who sinned, this man or his parents, that he should be born blind?" In our thoughtlessness, we often pose the same question: "Who sinned?" It is true that some sickness results from the individual's sin, but not all of it. The Master set the record straight, as He declared, "Neither did this man sin, nor his parents: but that the works of God should be made manifest in him" (John 9:1-3). How wonderful it is when the works of God are made manifest in those who suffer.

The apostle Paul suffered much, but he wrote that he rejoiced in his sufferings for the sake of the saints at Colossae, and that he could fill up that which was lacking in the afflictions of Christ for His body's sake, which is the church (Col. 1:24). Not all of the suffering for the church was completed at Calvary. Peter's challenge to rejoice when we partake of Christ's suffering is not easily received. He further explains this commandment as he writes that none should suffer as an evil-doer, but if a man suffer as a Christian, let him not be ashamed; but let him glorify God in this name (I Peter 4:13-16).

As Jesus warned His disciples of the suffering which awaited them, He pointed out that "It shall turn out unto you for a testimony" (Luke 21:13). Sickness and suffering afford an opportunity to witness. Some of God's greatest preachers had a sick bed for a pulpit.

94

She sat near the front of the sanctuary, her face aglow with the glory of heaven. She was living out her days in a wheel chair. She had no feet. Her hands were twisted and drawn next to her body, yet she could take a brush in those deformed hands and paint so very beautifully. I cherish a beautiful book mark which portrays a cheery floral bouquet, sketched by those crippled hands. I visited in her home many times to "cheer her up." Guess who it was that did the cheering.

It was the closing Lord's Day morning of the evangelistic crusade, and the little crippled saint was there, drinking deeply from the Water of Life. As I spoke to the church, encouraging them to "press on toward the goal," I chanced to make the statement, "My best for God is wonderfully important." In the offering that night there came an envelope, beautifully inscribed, and I knew that it must have been placed there by those crippled hands . . . and I wondered: what could the contribution of the cripple be? I have treasured for many years that little note, bearing the simple testimony: "Thank you for my new life motto which you gave me this morning—My best for God is wonderfully important." She glorified God through her suffering!

SICKNESS MAY ENHANCE CHRISTIAN CHARACTER. Paul again displays that deep insight into the purpose of tribulation as he declares that "we also rejoice in our tribulations, knowing that tribulation worketh stedfastness; and stedfastness approvedness; and approvedness, hope" (Rom. 5:3-4). God may permit infirmity of body that there may be wholeness of soul. Peter takes up the refrain to remind us that after we suffer a little while, God will perfect, establish, and strengthen (I Peter 5:10). How often the loving God uses affliction to keep us in His divine will. The psalmist grasped this truth and exulted, "Before I was afflicted I went astray: but now I observe thy word" (Ps. 119:67). The good, the true, and the beautiful come out of the crucible of suffering.

The end of life is character. Without the possibility of pain Christian character can not be attained, and the world misses the impact of a character enhanced through suffering. This tremendous truth is captured well in the "Prayer of the Handicapped."

I asked God for strength, that I might achieve,
I was made weak, that I might learn humbly to obey . . .
I asked for health, that I might do greater things,
I was given infirmity, that I might do better things.
I asked for riches that I might be happy,
I was given poverty, that I might be wise . . .
I asked for power, that I might have the praise of men,
I was given weakness, that I might feel the need of God . . .
I asked for all things, that I might enjoy life,
I was given life that I might enjoy all things . . .
I got nothing that I asked for, but everything I had hoped for;
Almost despite myself, my unspoken prayers were answered.
I am among all men most richly blessed.[6]

SICKNESS MAY BRING A CLOSER WALK WITH GOD. Our Master suffered much for us and, in so doing, He left us an example, that we should follow His steps (I Peter 2:21). What a paradox that His disciples should desire to suffer with Him. Paul's greatest desire was to know Him, and the power of His resurrection, and the fellowship of His sufferings (Phil. 3:10). We begin to be like our Lord

---

6. Father Keller, of "The Christophers," "Prayer of the Handicapped," from *Out of My Treasure,* edited by Willie W. White (Joplin, MO: College Press, 1964), p. 207.

when we can welcome any suffering which brings us any nearer the side of the suffering Savior. How much have we grown in Christ-likeness? Do we thank God for the cross for forgiveness but shun the cross to bear? A cross for Jesus— but none for me?

> Must Jesus bear the cross alone,
> And all the world go free?
> No, there's a cross for every one,
> And there's a cross for me.[7]

"To you it hath been granted in the behalf of Christ, not only to believe on him, but also to suffer on his behalf" (Phil. 1:29). The lessons learned in the School of Affliction can bring us nearer our sympathizing Savior, if we will but have it so.

SICKNESS MAY BETTER EQUIP US FOR A HOME IN HEAVEN. Beloved John, on the isle of Patmos, for the word of God and the testimony of Jesus, writes letters of encouragement, rebuke, and instruction to the seven churches of Asia. It is to the church in Smyrna that these words are addressed: "Fear not the things which thou art about to suffer . . . Be thou faithful unto death, and I will give thee the crown of life" (Rev. 2:10). When God has an especially bright crown awaiting one of his saints, He frequently imparts an equally heavy cross. Longing for the crown, we do not weary of the cross.

Philip Yancey, in *Where Is God When It Hurts?*, devotes an entire chapter to the story of Brian Sternberg.[8] Brian was an outstanding athlete. While a freshman in the University of Washington, he set a national collegiate freshman

7. Thos. Shepherd, et. al., "Must Jesus Bear the Cross Alone?"
8. Philip Yancey, *Where Is God When It Hurts?* (Grand Rapids, Michigan: The Zondervan Corporation, 1977), pp. 99-110.

record in the pole vault, and in 1963 he set his first world mark, with a vault of 16'5". This was followed quickly with the taking of titles in both the NCAA and AAU.

Brian was preparing to tour Russia with the U.S. track team when the tragedy occurred. He had gone to the university gym for a warm-up. While working out on the trampoline, he fell on his neck, injuring his spine and paralyzing his body. For forty-eight hours the doctors did not know whether Brian would live. But Brian did live. His mind was alert, but his body useless . . .

And then came the nightmares, the hallucinations, and the emotional depression. The strong, supple body of a world-champion athlete, hopelessly confined to a hospital bed. No one with Brian's injury had ever walked again. Brian didn't walk again, but something better happened: Brian placed his life in the hands of God as he became a Christian.

Brian Sternberg told his story for *Look* magazine. In this beautiful article he concludes his testimony with these words: "Having faith is a necessary step toward one of two things. Being healed is one of them. Peace of mind, if healing doesn't come, is the other. Either one will suffice."[9]

When sickness comes—When we have prayed much and committed all to God—and there is still no relief—what shall we do? May the gracious God enable us to accept it—to bear it with Him—and to *use* it for the glory of God and the good of our fellowman.

---

9. Brian Sternberg with John Poppy, "My Search for Faith," *Look*, March 10, 1964, p. 80.

Chapter Six

I COME TO THE GARDEN

All those who journey, soon or late,
Must pass within the garden's gate;
Must kneel alone in darkness there,
And battle with some fierce despair.
God pity those who cannot say,
"Not mine but thine"; who only pray:
"Let this cup pass," and cannot see
The purpose in Gethsemane.
— *Ella Wheeler Wilcox*[1]

Standing atop the Mount of Olives and looking west-ward, there is spread before us the panorama of the Holy City, Jerusalem. It is a breath-taking and emotion-fraught experience for the Christian. Walking down the rock-walled "Palm Sunday Way," approaching the Brook Kidron, we arrive at the Church of All Nations. Here is the Rock of Agony and, close beside the church, the traditional Garden of Gethsemane. Whether this is the actual site of our Lord's agony we cannot know, and the place is not that which is important.

The Garden of Gethsemane is beautifully kept. The shrubs and the flowers are beautiful to behold, and within the confines of the garden there are eight gnarled old olive trees. Expert horticulturists estimate the age of the trees at 2,000 years, and they are still bearing fruit!

Looking through the branches of the old olive trees, and across the Kidron Valley, there looms before us the eastern wall of Jerusalem and the sealed Golden Gate. It is all beautiful to behold—far more beautiful, I am sure, than on that

---

1. Ella Wheeler Wilcox, "Gethsemane," *Out of My Treasure, Volume Two*, edited by Don Earl Boatman (Joplin, Mo: College Press, 1965), p. 263.

dark night nineteen and one-half centuries ago, when twelve dark figures emerged from the city gate, crossed Kidron, and entered the garden. Their leader, knowing full-well what awaited them, bade the disciples, "Sit ye here, while I go yonder and pray" (Matt. 26:36).

"And he taketh with him Peter and James and John." How the humanity of Jesus longed for the companionship of His closest friends as He approached Gethsemane alone. There are friends who will go part of the way with us, but the wrestling must be ours alone. How often we turn back to our friends and find them sleeping.

"And he went forward a little and fell on his face" (Matt. 26:39). How mistaken the artists have been as they have portrayed the Christ in Gethsemane—patiently kneeling, His features composed, His robes falling serenely to the ground. With the weight of the world on His shoulders, the Savior of mankind went forward and fell on His face. It was a sweaty, grime-covered face, and His dust-covered garments fell in disarray about Him. This was no tourist attraction—no beautiful flowers—no well-kept pathway.

As we lead our annual Holy Land tours, and come reverently to the garden called Gethsemane, we give our little band of pilgrims a few moments to enter the chapel and meditate by the Rock of Agony and take pictures of the garden. Then we lead them out of the crowds and a short distance up the Mount of Olives, to a natural little olive orchard, and here, alone, we read "Not my will but thine," sing "I Come to the Garden," and bow heads and hearts in humble, contrite prayer.

"And he said, Abba Father." Under the burden of His deep suffering, He used both the Aramaic and Greek words for "father." The trials and the victories of Gethsemane are for

Jew and Gentile alike. "Abba, Father" may have been the manner of address in His childhood prayers, and now, approaching the culmination of His ministry, He looks up with simple, trusting faith and says, "Father."

It is doctor Luke who seems to be most impressed with the intricacies of the agony in the garden. He relates it thus: "And being in agony he prayed more earnestly; and his sweat became as it were great drops of blood falling down upon the ground" (Luke 22:44). The word translated "agony" is an ancient word, indicating "conflict" or "contest," and is used only here in our New Testament. It would appear that the agony was so intense that blood issued from His pores and mingled with His perspiration as it fell upon the ground.

What could be the cause of this intense suffering in the garden? For what is He petitioning as He cries out, "My Father, if it be possible, let this cup pass away from me"? Is He praying to escape the physical suffering which lies immediately at hand? True, the Roman crucifixion, preceded by the scourge, was the most painful death ever devised by sinful humanity, yet there have been martyrs who bore such pain with composure, submission, and even joy. It was in the divine plan that our Savior suffer as a man, but surely this is more than the cry of humanity for deliverance. It is not human weakness that causes our Master to shrink from the ordeal He now faces.

Some who have wrestled with the problem of the agony in the garden have surmised that death was imminent in Gethsemane, and that Jesus is praying to be spared to complete the atonement at Calvary. True, He did declare, "My soul is sorrowful, even unto death," and the bloody sweat might well indicate that death was at hand. Commentators have cited instances of bloody sweat under

101

abnormal conditions, and death has invariably followed quickly. However, there is no indication in the language employed that Jesus feared that He might die before completing His sacrifice on Calvary.

May it not be that the Gethsemane agony is caused primarily by the realization that the hour has now arrived—the hour for which He has been prepared since the foundation of the world? He realizes that He is to be betrayed, forsaken, and mocked. He knows, full well, that the Palestinian thorns will pierce deeply into His brow—that His back will be bared to the Roman scourge, under which strong men frequently died—that a rough-hewn cross will be laid upon that bruised and bleeding back—that He will be lifted up to the taunts and jeers of those He came to save—that there will be the excruciating pain, the cramped muscles, the hours of struggling for breath, the crawling insects, but there is more, much more!—a suffering which will be far more difficult to endure than the physical.

The agonizing Savior knows that as He expires on Calvary there will be wrung from His lips the cry, "My God, My God, why hast thou forsaken me?"—and that this will be no idle cry. God did forsake His Son upon the cross; it was imperative that He do so! As Jesus was offered up as a sacrifice, He *became* sin. Paul reminds us, "Him who knew no sin he made *to be sin* on our behalf" (II Cor. 5:21. Italics are the author's). As the Savior offered the perfect sacrifice for sin He became sin, and the pure and holy heavenly Father, Who can not look upon sin, had to hide His face and, in the span of six hours upon the cross, it broke the heart of His Son.

An understanding of the contents of "the cup" makes it easier for us to appreciate the divine dread of draining its contents. B. W. Johnson has spoken eloquently of the cup in these words:

> The cup, which He felt it so dreadful to drink, had in it ingredients which were never mingled by the hand of His Father, such as the treachery of Judas, the desertion of His disciples, denial on the part of Peter, the trial in the San-hedrin, the trial before Pilate, the scourging, the mockery of the soldiers, the crucifixion, etc., etc. All these incidental and unessential ingredients were put into the cup by men, wilfully and wantonly. Hence the petition, *Remove from me this cup,* this cup as it is. Without these superadded ingredients the potion would have been unquestionably bitter enough; and it need not be doubted that, in consideration of the bitterness, the exquisite sensibility of our Lord would be conscious of a feeling of shrinking and instinctive recoil. But still He had come for the very purpose of 'tasting death for every man,' and was no doubt willing and wishful to die.[2]

. . . Is it cause for marvel that He cries out, "If it be possible, let this cup pass?" How strange the phrase, "If it be possible." With God all things are possible, but it was not possible for His Son to fulfill His divine mission of redemption without draining the cup.

But the battle is short-lived. The Savior is the victor and the victory is found in submission: "Nevertheless not my will, but thine be done." He is ready now to drain the cup to its bitterest dregs. The victory brought infinite submission to the will of His Father.

How we empathize with that dark figure in the garden, for we, too, experience the struggle which inevitably comes

---

2. B. W. Johnson and Don DeWelt, *The Gospel of Mark* (Joplin, Mo: College Press, 1965), pp. 419-420.

through the conflict of will. Have you not stood on the hillside, with the wind blowing in your face, and then, looking high above, seen the clouds moving exactly in the opposite direction? Down here is the current of air which brings the wind in your face; up there is the current which carries the clouds apparently into the very teeth of the gale. And when you witnessed that strange phenomenon of nature, did you think of God's declaration through the prophet Isaiah, "For my thoughts are not your thoughts, neither are your ways my ways, saith Jehovah. For as the heavens are higher than the earth, so are my ways higher than your ways, and my thoughts than your thoughts" (Isa. 55:8-9).

And what do you do, dear friend, when your will moves in one direction and God's will moves in another? You say, "I want to do this," and He replies, "No, my child, I want you to do that." What do you do? As His disciple, what can you do? I know of but one place to find the answer: Go at night out the gates of the city; cross the brook; walk alone in the garden until you come upon a lonely figure with His face buried in the dust. Stand there a moment, with your back to a gnarled old olive tree, and listen. What is that He is saying? "Oh God, if it be possible, let this cup pass." For the moment, there is the conflict of will—down here is the human; up there is the divine. You need not tarry long for your answer, for the victory is soon won: "Nevertheless, not my will, but thine be done."

Have you been in the garden with Jesus? Have you learned to follow His example in prayer? When our stubborn, selfish will is in conflict with the divine, God teach us that the secret of victory is found in submission: "Not my will, but thine be done." And this is the victory which alone brings peace.

104

PEACE

With eager heart and will on fire,
I fought to win my great desire.
"Peace shall be mine," I said; but life
Grew bitter in the weary strife.

My soul was tired, and my pride
Was wounded deep: to Heaven I cried,
"God grant me peace or I must die."
The dumb stars glittered no reply.

Broken at last, I bowed my head,
Forgetting all myself, and said,
"Whatever comes, His will be done,"
And in that moment peace was won.

— *Henry Van Dyke*

It would be altogether possible to read, somewhat casually, the Gethsemane narrative and thoughtlessly conclude, "There is a prayer which was never answered." Oh, but it was! What we should have said was that the petition was not granted. If the cup had been removed, think what would have resulted: no atoning Savior, no lifting of sin's burden, no newness of life, no indwelling Spirit, no assurance of a home in heaven. The answer is seen in the angel from heaven who was sent to strengthen Him. If we will but have it so, there need be no Gethsemane without its consoling angel.

There are two ways in which burdens may be removed from tired shoulders. They may be taken from us so that we are no longer required to bear them, or we may be given such strength that the burden is no longer a burden. The latter is very far better.

The apostle Paul suffered greatly. He referred to his physical infirmity as a "thorn in the flesh." Three times he besought the Lord for its removal. The request was not granted, but the prayer was answered, as the Lord replied, "My grace is sufficient for thee: for my power is made perfect in weakness" (II Cor. 12:9). Sufficient grace! How very much better to enjoy the fellowship of grace than the invariable removal of all infirmity.

God answers prayer! God *always* answers prayer! Many years ago, in the city of Portland, Oregon, there lived a sightless saint. Her life was the epitome of Christian faith and reliance upon her Heavenly Father. She was a teacher of preachers. Every week there were scores of Christian workers who came to sit at her feet and to listen to the gracious words which proceeded from her mouth. The visitors never departed without partaking of physical, as well as spiritual, nourishment. No one knew her background, her church affiliation, or the source of her bounty. She knew the Book. If you misquoted a passage in her hearing, she would kindly reply, "Pardon me, dear, but this is what it says . . ."

On the wall of the blind teacher's home there hung a motto, a motto which she could not see, but which bears one of the most precious promises in the precious Book: "Call unto me, and I will answer thee" (Jer. 33:3).

God answers prayer! God *always* answers prayer! Listen to the promise of the divine Christ, as recorded in John 14:13: "And whatsoever ye shall ask in my name, that will I do." And that, my friend, is the word of a Gentleman. It is the promise of the One Who never told a lie. God always answers, but He, in His infinite wisdom, dare not always answer, "Yes." A wise father does not give his child everything he asks, but a loving father always answers. Our all-wise Father may answer, "Yes," or "No," or "Not yet," but He always answers. Trust Him.

THIS I KNOW

I know not by what methods rare,
But this I know, God answers prayer.
I know that He has given His Word,
Which tells me prayer is always heard,
And will be answered, soon or late,
And so I pray and calmly wait.

I know not if the blessing sought
Will come in just the way I thought;
But leave my prayers with Him alone,
Whose will is wiser than my own,
Assured that He will grant my quest,
Or send some answer far more blest.

— *Eliza M. Hickok*

Have you been in the garden with Jesus? Have you walked with Him and talked with Him there? When your will comes into conflict with the Divine, have you learned the secret of victory which comes only through submission? Do you rest in the assurance that He always answers, and that the answer may be far superior to the request?

* * * * *

The key to the mystery of the Gethsemane experience is found in the submission of the human will to the Divine Will. There is one battlefield where victory is attained through surrender. Let us utilize the remaining pages of this chapter to think deeply together about the victory which comes through surrender.

Listen again to the fervent, heart-sprung plea of Apostle Paul, as he writes to the beloved saints in Rome:

I beseech you therefore, brethren, by the mercies of God, to present your bodies a living sacrifice, holy, acceptable to

107

God, which is your spiritual service. And be not fashioned according to this world: but be ye transformed by the renewing of your mind, that ye may prove what is the good and acceptable and perfect will of God (Romans 12:1-2).

Our initial response to this urgent plea might well be: "Why should I? Why should I present my body to God? Why should I surrender my will to the divine will?" If we could but realize that it is not *in order to* belong to Christ, but *because we do* belong to Him. First Corinthians 6:19-20 sets the record straight as it declares, ". . . ye are not your own; for ye were bought with a price: glorify God therefore in your body."

If the foregoing be true, if God robbed heaven of its dearest treasure to purchase you, where is the title to your life? Is it not with Him Who paid the purchase price in full?

Let us suppose that your old "clunker" has seen better days, and that you have determined to purchase some new wheels. You know just the car that you want: the make, the model, the design, the color. You go into the automobile agency with your request and the salesman replies, "We do not have the particular number in stock, but we have a shipment soon to arrive, and the car that you want is in that shipment." Eager for his commission, he continues, "We have sufficient information that we could complete the deal, and we will deliver the car to you just as soon as it is received and serviced."

With assurance, you pay the price and sign the papers. Now, who owns the car? Is it not yours? You have paid the price; you hold the title; the possession is elsewhere. My friend, God paid the price, and God holds the title to your life. The question is not, "Do I belong to God?" but "Have I delivered the goods?"

The surrender of your life to God is in response to the price that He paid for your redemption. James H. McConkey relates a beautiful story of a redeemed slave's response to his purchaser.[3]

In the days of human bondage, a trembling slave stood on the auction block. At his feet were the wife and children whom he dearly loved. He stood there with head bowed, knowing that when the gavel fell, and the auctioneer cried, "Sold to the highest bidder," that he would be parted, perhaps forever, from these who were dearer than life to him.

The bidding soared higher and higher, for the slave was young and strong. He would make someone a good animal. At last the gavel fell. The auctioneer cried, "Sold to the highest bidder," and the buyer stepped forward to claim his property.

The one who had paid the unprecedented sum for the slave looked upon the one he had purchased and declared, "Well, I have bought you." "Yes, Massa." "I have paid a great price for you." "Yes, Massa." "But, more than that, I have paid this price that you might be free. Return to your wife and children!" And the slave, who had been redeemed at such a great price, fell at his purchaser's feet and cried out, "Oh Massa, I am your slave forever!"

Christian, has there fallen upon your heart of hearts, the realization of the tremendous price that has been paid that you might be free, and has there come a willingness to prostrate your life in the dust, throw your arms about blessed, pierced feet, and cry out for all the world to hear, "Oh Master, I am your slave forever!"?

---

3. James H. McConkey, *The Surrendered Life* (Pittsburgh, PA, Silver Publishing Society, 1902), p. 16.

Peter reminds us, so forcefully, "knowing that ye were redeemed, not with corruptible things, with silver or gold, from your vain manner of life handed down from your fathers: but with precious blood, as of a lamb without blemish and without spot, even the blood of Christ" (I Peter 1:18-19).

Surrender is the answer to the suffering Savior. Consecration is the response to Calvary.

How often we hear the apostle cry out, "I am a bond-slave of Jesus Christ." Bondslave! What does he mean? Those who lived in Bible days knew full-well what it meant to become a bondslave. When the servant had completed his term of servitude, and had a right to freedom, but he so loved his master that he had no desire to be freed, he came to his master's door and stood with his back to the door-post, while the master pierced his ear with an awl—the mark of the bondslave.

Christian, with your back to the door-post, let us pledge, "I love you, Lord. Master, I am your slave forever." This is the way to victory.

And the surrender which leads to victory dare not be half-hearted nor partial. Our Master did not equivocate nor hestitate when questioned as to what commandment of the law is the first of all: "thou shalt love the Lord thy God with *all* thy heart, and with *all* thy soul, and with *all* thy strength" (Mark 12:30. Italics are the author's).

There is a story which has come to us from the days of the Roman Legions. It was during the reign of Constantine, when men were becoming Christians (at least in name) in a wholesale fashion. We are told that an entire regiment of soldiers embraced Christianity. When the time arrived for their baptism, they were marched, in rank and file, through a river, where each soldier dipped himself for his

110

baptism. The account, whether it be legendary or factual, continues that as each soldier dipped himself, he held out of the water his right hand. This was his sword hand. This was the hand with which he must draw blood, and he was saying in effect, "Lord Jesus, I give myself to you. I am your man, but please, Lord, here is something which I would like to reserve for myself."

The way of surrender is the way which holds out nothing from Christ. The way to victory, victory through surrender, is not the way of conquest, nor of truce, nor of compromise, but the way of unconditional surrender to the King of Kings and the Lord of Lords.

It was long ago that I came across the words of an unknown author, words which embody so beautifully the decision of unconditional surrender:

> Here, Lord, I give up all my plans and purposes, all my hopes and desires, and accept thy will for my life.
> Whatever thou dost want, take;
> Whatever thou wouldst have come, send;
> Wherever thou wouldst have me go, lead;
> Whatever thou wouldst have me surrender, reveal.

I have long felt that George MacDonald was writing particularly to me. I was raised in the beautiful hills of Oregon. I have always loved the mountains, the lakes, and the streams. I always shall. I never cared for the city. I wanted the natural beauty of God's great out-of-doors. When I first realized that God was asking me to devote my life to His service, I felt that I was making the supreme sacrifice in entering a ministry which would take me frequently to the city. How mistaken I was, but this is the reason that the words of "Obedience" are of special meaning to me.

I said: "Let me walk in the fields."
　　He said: "No, walk in the town."
I said: "There are no flowers there."
　　He said: "No flowers, but a crown."

I said: "But the skies are black;
　　There is nothing but noise and din."
And He wept as He sent me back—
　　"There is more," He said, "there is sin."

I said: "But the air is thick,
　　And fogs are veiling the sun."
He answered: "Yet souls are sick,
　　And souls in the dark undone."

I said: "I shall miss the light,
　　And friends will miss me, they say."
He answered: "Choose tonight
　　If I am to miss you or they."

I pleaded for time to be given,
　　He said: "Is it hard to decide?
It will not seem so hard in heaven
　　To have followed the steps of your Guide."

I cast one look at the fields,
　　Then set my face to the town;
He said, "My child, do you yield?
　　Will you leave the flowers for the crown?"

Then into His hand went mine;
　　And into my heart came He:
And I walk in a light divine,
　　The path I had feared to see.[4]

If you would know the pathway to peace, to effective service, and to victory, go with Him into the inner recesses of the garden, bow your face in the dust, and learn to pray: NOT MY WILL, BUT THINE BE DONE.

---

4. George MacDonald, "Obedience," *212 Victory Poems,* compiled and written by Clifford Lewis (Grand Rapids, MI: Zondervan Publishing House, 1941), pp. 51-52.

Chapter Seven

PENIEL

(The Face of God)

One of the most difficult things for us to comprehend as we read the Divine Word is how God was able to use some of the people whom He employed in the accomplishment of His purpose. One of the unsavory characters of the Old Testament was a man named Jacob. Even at his birth there was portent of conflict and treachery to come. Israel's wife, Rebekah, was pregnant with twins, and the children struggled within her womb. The first to be born was named Esau. As the other was born his hand was holding Esau's heel, and he was named Jacob, meaning "one that takes by the heel" or "supplanter."

Jacob's young life is a story of connivance and treachery. He took advantage of his brother who was faint from hunger by purchasing his birthright for a mess of red pottage. Abetted by a scheming mother, he presented himself to his blind father in the guise of Esau and lied as to his identity, that he might receive the blessing which was reserved for the firstborn.

As Jacob journeyed toward Haran, to take a wife from among his mother's relatives, God appeared to him in a dream: a ladder reaching to heaven, and angels ascending and descending upon it. And here God made the promise of possessions and posterity and the Divine Presence, that in the seed of this deceiver all the nations of the earth would be blessed. Think of it! A conniving schemer is to be ancestor of God's messiah! God uses some very unlikely vessels in the accomplishments of His divine purpose.

Following the account of Jacob's vision we find one of the most beautiful love stories in the Bible: Jacob's love for Laban's daughter, Rachel, and his servitude for seven years that he might have her as his wife. Laban, also a trickster, gave his older daughter, Leah, to Jacob instead of his beloved Rachel, necessitating seven more years of servitude that Rachel might be his. Laban's treachery was repaid by some crafty schemes on the part of Jacob, resulting in wealth and abundant possessions of his own. It was at this point that God called Jacob to return to the land of his fathers, and reiterated the promise of His presence.

At long last, Jacob takes his wives, his children, his cattle, and all of the substance which he has gathered in Haran, to return to his boyhood home. But, as he journeys, there stands before him the specter of Esau, the brother whom he has tricked and defrauded. Will the brother whom he has wronged find it in his heart to forgive him, or will Jacob forfeit all that which he has gained, and perhaps life itself, to the hand of his brother? Ever scheming, and now somewhat desperate, he decides on his strategy: He will send a gift to pacify his brother. And quite a substantial gift it is: 550 head of livestock. The animals are divided into droves, and the servants who accompany them are carefully coached as to their conciliatory speeches, designed to gradually mitigate the wrath of a wronged and envious brother.

It was then that Jacob came to the Brook Jabbok. The Jabbok is a winding little stream which flows westward through a deep valley to the Jordan River. By the ford of the Jabbok Jacob encamped for the night with his family. It was a long night for the Supplanter. Was it his conscience, or the fear of his brother, or the tension of the journey that caused that sleepless night? Unable to sleep, Jacob arose in the night and took his family over the ford of the Jabbok, and Jacob was left alone. We have all experienced those dark nights in life's journey when it seems that we are left

114

alone: experiences in which even those who are dearest to us can not share.

It was during that dark night at the Jabbok that one of the most fascinating and mysteriously sublime incidents in the Old Testament occurred (cf. Gen. 32:22-32). God appeared to Jacob in the form of a man and wrestled with him until the breaking of the day but "prevailed not against him." At the dawning of the new day, the angel touched the hollow of Jacob's thigh and it was strained. Despite the injury, Jacob clung to his adversary, protesting, "I will not let thee go, except thou bless me." Perhaps at last Jacob realizes that he must be reconciled to God for his past misdeeds before he can receive the blessing.

Do you recall that dark night that you wrestled all night with God, seeking the blessing, and receiving no response? One of the most difficult experiences known to the Christian is to encounter the silence of God. King Saul knew the agony of God's silence. His arch-enemy, the Philistines, had come up against Israel. The prophet Samuel was dead and Saul was afraid, "and his heart trembled greatly." At long last, the king called upon the God Whom he had once known and served, but "Jehovah answered him not, neither by dreams, nor by Urim, nor by the prophets" (I Sam. 28:6).

Another to encounter the mysterious silence of God was a Canaanitish woman who was burdened in soul over a demon-possessed daughter. Hearing of a man of Nazareth who could cast out demons, she came with her petition: "Have mercy on me, O Lord, thou son of David; my daughter is grievously vexed with a demon. But he answered her not a word" (Matt. 15:21-23). How strange! How unlike our Master! Could it be that the silence of God is testing of our faith and of our willingness to persevere in prayer?

115

Jacob persevered—and he received the blessing. Wrestling with adversity may not be the most pleasant of exercises, but it can bring a blessing and produce a strong soul.

Here at Jabbok Jacob receives a new name and a new heart. Jacob the Supplanter is now to be called "Israel"—"striving with God" or "Prince of God." From this point on, Jacob is a new man. He is no longer the old Jacob; he is now the new Israel. No longer a fugitive and an exile, but now at home in the land of promise. The one who had been partner to that cruel hoax upon his father and brother, who fought Laban's treachery with crafty schemes of his own, who was guilty of sinful cunning, now becomes beloved Israel, the father of the twelve tribes of Canaan, an ancestor of the coming Messiah.

As the new "Israel" receives the divine blessing and realizes that he has seen God face to face and that his life has been spared, he immediately settles upon a name for the place where he has prevailed with God and men: Peniel—the face of God.

The blessing came, but Jacob had to pay the price. The hollow of his thigh was strained, and he "limped upon his thigh." The effort left its mark, a constant reminder of that long night of wrestling and of that which had brought it about. Jacob had to suffer and persevere and overcome before he could walk stedfastly with God, just as the Christian must take up that yoke of self-crucifixion before he can walk stedfastly with Christ. Passionate, personal, prevailing prayer does not come easy, and he who would know the secret must pay the price.

What is the secret of power in prayer? How can we get on praying ground? Is it the eloquence of our prayer that touches the heart of the Father? The prayer which Jesus

116

taught His disciples to pray is an extremely simple prayer. Is it the length of our prayers that makes them effective? Some of the most powerful prayers in the Bible are very brief: "Lord, help me"; "Lord, save me"; "Lord, be merciful." Is it the bodily posture that counts with God: upraised hands, closed eyes, kneeling reverently before Him? Sam Walter Foss negates this humorously in "The Prayer of Cyrus Brown."

"The proper way for a man to pray,"
Said Deacon Lemuel Keyes,
"And the only proper attitude
Is down upon his knees."

"No, I should say the way to pray,"
Said Reverend Doctor Wise,
"Is standing straight, with outstretched arms,
And rapt and turned up eyes."

"Oh, no; no, no," said Elder Snow,
"Such posture is too proud;
A man should pray with eyes fast closed
And head contritely bowed."

"It seems to me his hands should be
Austerely clasped in front,
With both thumbs pointed toward the ground,"
Said Reverend Doctor Blunt.

"Last year I fell in Hodkin's well
Headfirst," said Cyrus Brown,
"With both my heels a-stickin' up,
My head a-p'intin' down.

An' I made a prayer right then an' there—
Best prayer I ever said,
The prayin'est prayer I ever prayed,
A-standin' on my head."[1]

---

1. Sam Walter Foss, "The Prayer of Cyrus Brown," *Out of My Treasure,* edited by Willie W. White (Joplin, Mo: College Press, 1964), p. 113.

Then what is the secret of effective prayer? How we need to rethink the whole area of "answered" prayer. Day after day we bring our petitions before the throne. In His divine wisdom, there are many of those petitions which He does not grant—and we say, "That prayer was not answered." Oh, but it was! The petition may not have been granted, but the prayer was answered.

Every heart-sprung prayer of the child of God is answered. Of the 650 distinct prayers in the Bible, 450 are followed by distinct answers. The One Who can not lie has promised, "Call unto me, and I will answer thee" (Jer. 33:3). He may answer, "Yes." He may answer, "No." He may answer, "Not yet"—but He will answer. Can you love Him and continue to trust Him even when the answer is "no"?

There are keys which "open heaven's door." He has not told us to pray and then left us to stumble about until we chance upon praying ground. His Word is filled with direction as to *how* to know power in prayer.

1. Pray in Jesus' name.

It was during the last night the Master spent on this earth that He gathered the little band of disciples about Him and made a promise: "And whatsoever ye shall ask in my name, that will I do, that the Father may be glorified in the Son" (John 14:13). Granted petitions are for man's good and God's glory. What does it mean to pray "in Jesus' name"? Is this not infinitely more than an appendage to our prayer ("In Jesus' name, Amen")? To pray in Jesus' name indicates a position: we are coming as His people, *within* His name. The blind teacher, to whom we have made previous reference, captured this truth so beautifully in the following.

118

Within the Name of Jesus
　　Where peace and plenty lie,
I rest securely sheltered—
　　No evil can come nigh.

Within the Name of Jesus
　　From condemnation free,
He canceled each and every sin
　　That I might ransomed be.

Within the Name of Jesus
　　His power and might are mine,
And Satan is a conquered foe
　　By that great Power Divine.

Within the Name of Jesus
　　Sheltered from every storm,
The Hiding Place of all who trust—
　　From every false alarm.

Within the Name of Jesus
　　All upward shall ascend,
To greet Him at His coming
　　With joys that never end.[2]

2. Pray in faith.

Mark relates the rather mysterious incident of Jesus cursing the barren fig tree, which withered immediately. As Jesus and His disciples passed by on the following morning, the disciples marvelled at the withered tree. It was in this setting that Jesus made that remarkable promise, "All things whatsoever ye pray and ask for, believe that ye receive them, and ye shall have them" (Mark 11:24). In the original

---

2. M.E.H., "Within the Name of Jesus," *212 Victory Poems*, compiled and written by Clifford Lewis (Grand Rapids: Zondervan Publishing House, 1941), p. 112.

language the verb "receive" is in the past tense: "Believe that *ye received*." The request is already granted; the deal is consummated; we are just awaiting the delivery. What faith! According to your faith, be it done.

For many years, in the State of Oregon, the "99" men's movement sponsored a series of summer camps for boys. It was my privilege and joy to direct these camps over a period of five years. Some of the experiences of those little fellows might well serve as a lesson for those of us who are more advanced in years. There are times that we stand humbled and rebuked before the faith of a little child.

One of our counsellors was teaching a class on prayer. In the course of his instruction he dramatized the story of the prophet Elijah, praying that it might not rain, and it rained not for three years and six months. And he prayed again, and the deluge came. As the teacher related this miracle he noticed two lads in particular: one was drinking it all in, his eyes big as saucers; the other was listening with the expression of a skeptic.

Following the class, the skeptical lad approached the believing lad and asked, "Do you believe that stuff, about a man praying and making it rain?"

"Sure, I believe it," was the prompt reply.

"Naw, I don't," the doubter replied, "A man can't pray and make it rain."

"Oh, is that so?" our little believer responded, "Well, I tell you what—I'm going to go over there under that tree and pray that God will make it rain just to show you." And, sure enough, the boy walked over to a tree and bowed his head in earnest prayer.

The teacher who witnessed this incident said, "The amazing thing was that, although it was a beautiful mid-summer day, it wasn't long until the clouds came up and the rain literally poured." Although it was "rest hour," as the rain began, the little prayer warrior tumbled off his bunk, ran across the court yard to the skeptic's cabin, stuck out his chin and said, "See?"

We smile at such incidents, but far be it from me to believe that God may not have honored the faith of a little child. Pray in faith!

3. Pray from a righteous heart.

As the Psalmist exults in the mercies of God, he declares, "If I regard iniquity in my heart, the Lord will not hear" (Psalm 66:18). James reminds us that it is the "supplication of a *righteous* man" that avails much. To know power from God we must strive to be right with God. Surely this does not mean that we are to refrain from prayer when we are conscious of our transgressions. How grateful we ought be that we have a Father to Whom we can bring all things: our sorrows as well as our joys, our failures as well as our successes; our sins as well as our righteous acts. We sin and we do not feel like praying. When we find it the hardest to pray is just the time that we need to pray the hardest.

King David, God's man that he was, sinned and sinned grievously. At the time of year when kings went out to battle, David tarried behind in Jerusalem and sent others to do the work which God expected him to do. As he walked at eventide on his rooftop, David looked with lust on the wife of another and, because he had the power to do so, he had Bathsheba brought to him and committed adultery. Then, in a clumsy effort to cover his sin, he caused the murder of the husband, Uriah, the Hittite.

121

God is not pleased with disobedience, lust, adultery, hypocrisy, or murder, so He sent Prophet Nathan to the sinful king with his story of the poor man whose one little pet lamb was taken by the rich man to feed his guest. The king was wroth and declared that such a despicable character was worthy of death. Good old Nathan shook a bony finger under the king's nose and declared, "Thou art the man!" (II Sam. 11, 12).

The 51st Psalm is entitled "A contrite sinner's prayer for pardon," and the heading informs us that this is "A Psalm of David; when Nathan the prophet came unto him, after he had gone in to Bath-sheba."

In this penitential psalm the sinful king is pouring out his soul to God. He does not spare himself, nor give soft names to his sin. He cries out for pardon, for a pure heart, for a right spirit, for fellowship with his Maker, for restored joy, and for a willing spirit, then discerningly concludes, "Then will I teach transgressors thy ways; and sinners will be converted unto thee."

Powerful, prevailing prayer springs from a righteous heart.

4. Pray humbly.

Among the potent parables of the Master Teacher is that of the Pharisee and the publican who went to the temple to pray. The Pharisee prayed *with himself,* thanking God that he was not as other men. The despised tax collector would not so much as lift his eyes to heaven, but smote his breast, saying, "God be merciful to me a sinner." And the One Who knows the hearts of men declared that this was the one who went to his house justified (Luke 18:9-14). "Humble yourselves in the sight of the Lord, and he shall exalt you" (James 4:10).

122

One of the beautifully familiar passages of the Old Testament is found in II Chronicles 7:14: "If my people, who are called by my name, shall humble themselves, and pray, and seek my face, and turn from their wicked ways; then will I hear from heaven, and will forgive their sin, and will heal their land." If *my people* . . . will *humble themselves* and pray . . . I will hear. Look at the church in the New Testament and the church today—and be humbled. Look at our plenty and a starving world—and be humbled. Look at lives unlived, services unrendered, victories unwon—and be humbled. When life knocks you to your knees you are then in a position to pray!

5. Pray unselfishly.

James lists two reasons as to why we don't always have that which we feel we ought: "Ye have not because ye ask not. Ye ask and receive not because ye ask amiss that ye may spend it in your pleasures" (James 4:2-3). Jesus taught His disciples to pray "Our Father." The first word in this model prayer casts aside all selfishness. Note the prayer carefully. It is "our" and "thy" and "thine." It is never "I." The selfish prayer is a powerless prayer.

The prophet Samuel felt it a sin if he neglected to pray for others. As he addressed Israel, he cried out in I Samuel 12:23, "Moreover as for me, far be it from me that I should sin against Jehovah in ceasing to pray for you." When those times come, as they surely will, when you feel helpless to minister and witness for Christ as you know you ought, you can always pray. J. Sidlow Baxter said it well: "Men may spurn our appeals, reject our message, oppose our arguments, despise our persons, but they are helpless against our prayer."

6. Pray with a forgiving spirit.

As the disciples were being taught how to pray, the Master instructed them to ask, "Forgive us . . . as we have forgiven," and "If ye forgive not men their trespasses, neither will your Father forgive your trespasses" (Matt. 6:12, 15). How much are we asking when we pray, "Forgive us *as we have forgiven?*" Could it be that some of our petitions ascend no higher than the ceiling because we are possessed of an unforgiving spirit? The Father's forgiveness does not come as a reward for our forgiving others, but a forgiving spirit does place us in a position where we are capable of receiving forgiveness.

How frequently we hear some wronged soul cry out, "I can forgive, but I can't forget." What they mean is that they are unwilling to forgive. Someone has observed that the way some folks forgive they would bury a dead dog with his tail sticking out. When some bury the hatchet they want to mark its resting place well, that they may disinter it at the slightest provocation.

The individual who is unable (or unwilling) to forgive those who sin against him ought climb a lonely hill outside a city wall, see a sinless man spiked to a Roman cross, listen to the cursing, jeering mob that spiked Him there—and then be attentive to His petition, "Father, forgive them; for they know not what they do" . . . or stand among the mob outside the city gate, as the stones fall upon the defenseless body of the first Christian martyr, and listen to him pray: "Lord, lay not this sin to their charge." What is one more stone when you are at peace with God and with your fellowman?

The hand of the Father is unshackled when His children learn to pray with a forgiving spirit.

124

7. Pray in harmony with others.

Matthew 18:19 gives us another key to effective prayer, as Jesus declares to His disciples, "If two of you shall agree on earth as touching anything that they shall ask, it shall be done for them." When we approach the throne with hands and hearts joined with those of other members of the family of God, how much more apt we are to present those petitions that are in harmony with the Father's will. Could it be coincidental that this promise is given immediately following the instruction on how to be reconciled to our brother? What power is released when His people join hands about the throne!

In a little lumber town in Oregon there stands a beautiful church building, and it is filled with beautiful saints of God. The reason that there is a church in that community is that nine concerned Christians agreed to ask God for it. A dear member of that church family relates the thrilling story in the following bit of verse.

> While sitting on my porch one eve, watching the sun go
>   down,
>   I heard an old man talking to a stranger in the town;
> "Yes, that's our new church, stranger," I heard the old man
>   say;
>   "How come, you say? I'll tell you. Nine people knelt to
>   pray.
>
> "How many years, you ask me, in a village that's so small,
>   To raise the money that it takes, to build a church so tall?
> One year ago today, sir, that place was only sod;
>   Today you see the Church. And how? Nine people trusted
>   God.

"How did we know He'd help us? We read His message
true—
'Where two or three are gathered, there will I be too;
The harvest fields are ready. Come Christians, one and all';
And just one year ago, sir, nine people heard that call.

"How many members have we? I can't exactly say;
But ninety-seven gathered for Sunday School today.
How did we get them out, you say? True Christians never
shirk;
And praying, hoping, trusting, nine people went to work.

"You asked me where they came from. They came from far
and near.
Don't you know the world is hungry, the Word of God to
hear?
And near one hundred people are praising God today;
The reason why—One year ago nine people knelt to pray."

The stranger walked on down the street, the old man went
his way,
But Faith and Hope were born anew within my heart
that day.
For only God, the Father, Who knoweth all, can say
How great will be the answer, when people kneel to pray.

8. Pray specifically.

How prone we are to take the easy way and pray in gen-
eralities: "Bless all the sick—Minister to all the needy—
Strengthen all who are facing temptation—Restore all the
sinful—Bless all the missionaries." Blind Bartimaeus approached Jesus with his cry for mercy, and Jesus answered
(just as He answers every sincere cry), "What wilt thou that
I do unto thee?" and, without a moment's hesitation, the blind
man cried out, "Rabboni, that I may receive my sight." He
had a specific need; he made a specific request. The "rifle"

126

prayers which go straight to the target are far more effective than the "shotgun" type which scatter our petitions all over the landscape.

Jane Merchant displayed a deep insight into the power of specific, heart-sprung prayer as she penned "The Little Prayers."

> The little prayers that people whisper low
> And deep within their spirit, as they go
> About their work, are seldom finely phrased:
> "Lord, help poor Sarah. She's so sick and dazed
> With grief. Lord, teach her what is best to do."
> "O Father, be with Tom and see him through."
> "God, don't let the children laugh at Jimmy's crutch."
> "Give me the patience that I need so much."
> "Guide me, O Father, help me do Thy will."
> Such short and simple prayers they are, but still,
> Of all the little prayers that people pray,
> I doubt that any ever went astray.[3]

9. Pray gratefully.

As Preacher Paul writes to his beloved church in Philippi, exhorting them to be stedfast in the Lord, he gives the secret of the carefree life: "In nothing be anxious; but in everything by prayer and supplication *with thanksgiving* let your requests be made known unto God" (Phil. 4:6. Italics are the author's). How prone we are to approach the throne only when we desire something for ourselves. Evangelist Sam Jones used to say, "We can't get within a mile of God without holding out our hands and saying, 'Give me.'" May God help us to turn back and say, "Thank you," as did the Samaritan leper

---

3. Jane Merchant, "The Little Prayers," *Out of My Treasure*, edited by Willie W. White (Joplin, MO: College Press, 1964), p. 121.

who was one of the ten that Jesus healed, rather than to go thoughtlessly on with the nine.

10. Pray earnestly.

Doctor Luke informs us that as the Son of Man wrestled for the victory of submission in Gethsemane "He prayed more earnestly, and his sweat became as it were great drops of blood falling down upon the ground" (Luke 22:44). With a deep sense of our need and that of our fellowman, how we need to learn to go into the inner recesses of the garden and pray "the third time more earnestly."

One of the greatest missionary gatherings in America is held every summer at beautiful Camp Wi-Ne-Ma, on the northern Oregon coast. Here missionaries from all about the world come to inform and inspire and rebuke the eager listeners. In 1976, one of the missionary speakers was Jim Moon Kim, of Korea. He spoke eloquently on the Christian's privilege of prayer, and told how the Korean Christians meet for prayer every morning at 4:30. When asked his impression of our American churches, he thought for but a moment and then replied, "You have nice buildings. They are warm. They are air-conditioned. You have elders and deacons and Sunday School teachers . . . but in America I have never seen tears in prayers." What an indictment!

He was just a little four-year-old boy, but he was an integral part of a Christian home, and he had learned to pray. One of the problems which confronted the family was that they lived near the railroad tracks, and little Marvin, despite frequent warnings from his loving parents, persisted in wandering onto the tracks. He was apprehended once more on forbidden ground and father really "got to the seat" of the problem. That night, as little Marvin said his prayers, he petitioned earnestly, "O Lord, keep old Marvin off the railroad tracks, and what I mean is keep him off the railroad tracks!" That, my friend, is fervency in prayer!

11. Pray persistently.

Our Lord was a masterful story teller. His matchless teachings are saturated with stories: parables to help us remember the basic truths of His message. He once gave a parable to teach us that we should be persistent in prayer. It is the story of an unjust judge who was disturbed by a poor widow who came to him repeatedly, asking to be avenged of her adversary. For a time she received no response but, in response to her persistence, the judge said, "Lest she wear me out by her continual coming, I will avenge her" (Luke 18:1-13).

What a strange story this was which came from the lips of the Master. Certainly, we are not to think of our God as One Who becomes weary by our oft-coming, nor One Who becomes "worn-out," but Jesus spoke the parable "to the end that they ought always to pray, and not to faint." To learn the secret of power in prayer we must learn to "pray without ceasing" (I Thess. 5:17).

12. Pray in the will of God.

This final key to effective prayer is one of the most difficult to discover, but without it we can not unlock the door of heaven. Beloved John, who was just a little nearer the Lord than the other disciples, is the one who gives us this key: "If we ask anything according to his will, he heareth us" (I John 5:14). Our minds go back at once to that dark night in the garden, as the human will struggles with the Divine. As we listen to the conflict, we hear the exultant cry of victory, "Not my will, but thine be done," and the Son of Man and Son of God goes onward to complete our redemption.

Since to be effective in prayer we must request that which is within the will of God, it behooves us to consider well the question, "How is it possible for me to know the Divine will?" God's will is revealed in God's Word. The greater our understanding of the Bible, the more complete will be our understanding of His will. The closer we walk to Him, and the better we know Him, the more we will comprehend what His will is, and will request that which we are confident is within the Divine desire.

How frequently, in our infirmity and our fleshly limitation, we cry out with the apostle, "We know not how to pray as we ought." And, in times like these, what assurance there is to discover, as did Paul, that "The Spirit himself maketh intercession for us with groanings which cannot be uttered" (Rom. 8:26).

> More things are wrought by prayer
> Than this world dreams of. Wherefore, let thy voice
> Rise like a fountain for me night and day.
> For what are men better than sheep or goats
> That nourish a blind life within the brain
> If, knowing God, they lift not hands of prayer
> Both for themselves and those who call them friend?
> For so the whole round earth is every way
> Bound by gold chains about the feet of God.[4]

Since there are "more things wrought by prayer than this world dreams of," and since all that we could ever need or hope for are in the hand of the Almighty, may we, like Jacob

---

4. Alfred Lord Tennyson, "Prayer."

of old, wrestle with God—all night, if necessary—and the blessing will come—and the place will be called Peniel—the face of God.

* * * * *

Joseph Scriven was a graduate of Trinity College in Dublin, Ireland. At the age of 25 he migrated to Canada where he met a delightful and dedicated young Christian lady. At the time they were engaged to be married they knelt together in prayer. As their love continued to deepen, and their wedding day drew near, they resolved that throughout their married life they would take every problem to God in prayer.

On the day before the happy young couple were to be wed, Joseph was handed a letter, bearing the tragic news that his beloved fiance had drowned. The groom-to-be was stunned, then turned bitterly on God. It was not right! It was not fair! How cruel of God to "take her!" . . . and then Joseph remembered the resolution which they had made: take every problem to God in prayer.

The bereaved young man fell to his knees and for three hours he begged God for light and guidance and strength. And God answered, as He always does. Joseph Scriven was granted the grace of Christ, and he arose from his knees and penned the words which have brought solace and strength to myriads of aching hearts:

> What a Friend we have in Jesus,
> All our sins and griefs to bear!
> What a privilege to carry
> Everything to God in prayer!
> O what peace we often forfeit,
> O what needless pain we bear,
> All because we do not carry,
> Everything to God in prayer.

131

Have we trials and temptations?
Is there trouble anywhere?
We should never be discouraged,
Take it to the Lord in prayer.
Can we find a friend so faithful
Who will all our sorrows share?
Jesus knows our ev'ry weakness,
Take it to the Lord in prayer.

Are we weak and heavy laden,
Cumbered with a load of care?—
Precious Savior, still our refuge,—
Take it to the Lord in prayer.
Do thy friends despise, forsake thee?
Take it to the Lord in prayer;
In His arms He'll take and shield thee,
Thou wilt find a solace there.[5]

---

5. Joseph Scriven, "What a Friend We Have in Jesus."

Chapter Eight

THOUGH HE SLAY ME

One of the grandest portions of all inspired scripture appears midway through the Old Testament: the Book of Job. It stands unique and independent among the books of the Bible. It is grand in its subject matter, in its composition, and in its conclusions. A careful reading of the book will result in a profoundly moving religious experience and a more complete understanding of many of the deeper issues of life, death, and eternity.

The Book of Job is a masterful work of literature. Thomas Carlyle's evaluation of the book was as follows: "I call this book, apart from all theories about it, one of the Grandest things ever written. Our first, oldest statement of the never-ending problem: Man's Destiny, and God's Ways with him in the earth. There is nothing written, I think, of equal literary merit."[1]

This book is a historical poem: an ancient record of an actual experience which befell a godly man. The prologue and the epilogue are presented in prose. The remainder of the story is presented in masterful Hebrew poetry. It is studded with passages of beauty and grandeur. It runs the gamut from faith to doubt, from confidence to despair, and from daylight to darkness.

It is extremely difficult for our western minds to understand and appreciate oriental poetry. We ask of our poetry that it rhyme, that it be properly measured out by feet and meters, and that the syntax be well pleasing to our ear. The outstanding characteristic of Hebrew poetry is that of parallelism: the rhythm of thought and the sentiment of

---

1. Henry H. Halley, *Halley's Bible Handbook* (Grand Rapids: Zondervan Publishing House, 1965), p. 240.

one line repeated in different terminology in the line following. The Psalms are replete with such examples. Halley explains this well in the following paragraph.

> Hebrew poetry did not have metre or rhyme, like the poetry of our language. It consisted rather of parallelisms, or thought rhythm, in synonymous or antithetical couplets. "The sentiment of one line echoed in the next." "Sometimes the couplets being doubled, or trebled, or quadrupled, making 2-liners, 4-liners, 6-liners, or 8-liners."[2]

We can not say for a certainty as to the time of the writing, nor as to its author. In all probability, the Book of Job was written during the patriarchal period. Job was priest for his family and, as such, offered burnt offerings for them (Chapter 1, verse 5). There are literary features in the book which belong to the time of the patriarchs, and it contains no reference to Israel nor to the law of Moses, although there would have been ample opportunity to quote from this source were it then known. There is the strong possibility that the Book of Job was the first of the 66 books in our Bible to be written.

Jewish tradition ascribes the book to Moses. No author is given. Perhaps the writer may have been Job himself or someone who listened to or participated in the debate. It is certain that God had to reveal certain of preliminary facts to whoever did the writing. The time and place and author are not of utmost importance. Most important is the subject matter and the lessons that the Master Teacher would have His pupils to learn. How fitting that the first book of the Bible to be written should address itself to the questions of the ages: "If there be an all-powerful, all-wise, and all-loving God, why does He permit the innocent to suffer?"

---

2. Halley, loc. cit.

The central issue of the Book is the problem of divine justice. It is not "why does God permit suffering?" but "why do the righteous suffer, while the unrighteous are frequently spared? Why do bad things happen to good people?" This is one of the most serious obstacles to faith in God—and we find God's answer in this masterful didactic poem.

There are three major themes which run like an unbroken thread throughout these 42 chapters:

1. Regardless of external circumstances, Jehovah God is worthy of our complete love, trust, adoration, and praise.

2. God does not cause suffering and misfortune, but He uses it to strengthen the faith and purify the lives of His children.

3. The wisdom of the infinite God far surpasses the wisdom of finite man.

We view the issues of life from our limited, earth-bound perspective. The Book of Job enables us to view them from the perspective of heaven. Let us turn now to the Book and listen carefully as the God Who gave us being answers those questions which are as universal as the sufferings and the misfortunes of His creatures.

THE PROLOGUE: "Hast thou considered my servant Job?" (Chapters 1 & 2).

The hero is introduced in the very first verse of our text: "There was a man in the land of Uz, whose name was Job; and that man was perfect and upright, and one that feared God, and turned away from evil." God's evaluation of him was that he was perfect, upright, God-fearing, and righteous (verse 8). If there was ever a "good man," it was truly Job. Surely no one deserved suffering less than he.

Job was a family man. There were born unto him seven sons and three daughters. The perpetuation of his name and his reputation seemed assured. Job loved his family and was concerned for their well being and their relationship to God. In his concern he arose early in the morning to offer burnt offerings on their behalf, in case they had sinned and renounced God in their hearts (verse 5).

Job was a wealthy man. His capital consisted of 7,000 sheep, 3,000 camels, 500 yoke of oxen, 500 she-asses, and a very great household. He was the greatest of all the children of the east. Job must have been chairman of the Board of Directors of the First National Bank of Uz. Surely misfortune could not touch such a man as this.

The scene now shifts abruptly to heaven. From His celestial throne God is reviewing His angelic troops. Satan is among them, and God challenges him: "Hast thou considered my servant Job? for there is none like him . . ." and Satan replies, "He is just a phony. He serves you for what he can get out of it. Every man has his price! Just take away the things upon which he relies and he will renounce you to your face."

Jehovah accepts the challenge. The stage is set. The conflict begins. God says unto Satan, "Behold, all that he hath is in thy power; only upon himself put not forth thy hand."

Satan wastes no time. It must have been with great glee that the Adversary set about to carry out the permitted testing. His first attack is upon possessions. If Job served God for what he could get out of it, surely the loss of his possessions would be accompanied by the loss of his faith. In quick succession, Job loses his oxen, asses, and herdsmen to the marauding Sabeans, his sheep to the "fire of God" (probably a severe electrical storm), and his camels and their attendants to the Chaldeans. How cruel was Satan's timing! The loss of all of Job's possessions came on the day of a birthday party for one of his dear children.

The most cruel and the most trying blow of all was reserved for the last. If the loss of possessions would not break the spirit of Job and cause him to renounce God, surely the loss of his loved ones would. The announcement of Job's loss of substance had not died out when a fourth messenger informed him of the hurricane which destroyed the mansion where his children were celebrating, killing them all.

Countless parents have grieved over the loss of a child. What a heart-break it is to be deprived of that young life which you have provided for, directed, cherished, and loved—but Job lost them all: ten dear children, and that in one cruel blow.

Immediately there comes the question: "How could a God Who is loving, merciful, and just permit the death of this entire, innocent family in order that Job might be tested?" To answer such a question would require the mind of the Infinite. God knows best, as eternity alone will reveal. His object lessons are at times fraught with grief and pain.

And how did Job respond to this tragic loss? He expressed his grief according to the prescribed custom of his day by tearing his clothes and shaving his head. But Job did something more: he fell upon the ground *and worshiped:* "Jehovah gave, and Jehovah hath taken away; blessed be the name of Jehovah." And in all of this Job "sinned not."

Gleason Archer summarizes Job's response to his tremendous loss in well chosen terms:

> Job, in his prayer to God, resigned himself humbly and submissively to His will, even though he could not understand it. Even in this emotional extremity Job remembered that he and all of his loved ones and possessions really belonged to the Lord who had given them to him. And so he

137

openly acknowledged before the Almighty that He had a perfect right to do with His own whatever He chose to.[3]

"In all of this Job sinned not." The first test is completed— and Job has passed with flying colors!

Chapter Two again ushers us into the Divine Presence, as the stage is set for the second severe testing of God's man. The sons of God are again presenting themselves before Jehovah, and Satan is there. The old boy sure gets around! It is God Who again challenges Satan: "Hast thou considered my servant Job? for there is none like him in the earth, a perfect and an upright man, one that feareth God, and turneth away from evil: and he still holdeth fast his integrity, although thou movedst me against him, to destroy him without cause" (Job 2:3).

Satan is about to lose face before the cohorts of heaven so, in desperation, he resorts to another diabolical maneuver: "Skin for skin, yea, all that a man hath will he give for his life." Satan's argument is that Job is holding fast his faith in order to protect his health. The devil's strategy seems to be that if Job is subjected to intense physical pain and that if he loses his noble appearance so that he will appear repulsive to his friends and neighbors he will surely renounce God.

Jehovah accepts the challenge and permits the painful testing: "He is in thy hand; only spare his life. So Satan went forth from the presence of Jehovah, and smote Job with sore boils from the sole of his foot unto his crown." As a young man, this writer was afflicted with boils, and can testify that when you are suffering from a single boil

---

3. Gleason L. Archer, Jr., *The Book of Job* (Grand Rapids: Baker Book House, 1982), p. 36.

you hurt all over! But Job's body became a raw mass of throbbing, ulcerated abscesses.

In his misery, Job picked up a piece of broken pottery to scrape the encrusted puss which oozed from the boils and headed for the city dump, or the dunghill outside of town, which was frequented by the dogs and the outcasts. He was following the prescribed custom. When tragedy came, men sat in ashes or threw ashes on their heads in mourning (Jonah 3:6; Ezek. 27:30).

In his time of testing Job has now lost his possessions, his children, and his health. All that he has left is his wife, and she is scant comfort! A person can endure a great deal when he has a loving and caring companion to stand by him, but apparently Job's wife has been seething with rebellion against God, and she turns upon her husband with the tirade, "Dost thou still hold fast thine integrity? renounce God, and die." It appears that Job's wife held the shallow, distorted philosophy which is so prevalent in our day: that life should always be pleasant and prosperous, and that if it is not it isn't worth living.

But faithful Job rebukes her blasphemous suggestion, tells her that she is speaking as one of the "foolish women," and astutely observes that the Giver of all has a right to withhold as well as to bestow His gifts upon His creatures, and in all of this Job did not "sin with his lips." Job has passed his second test with a perfect score.

Destitute—bereaved—afflicted—misunderstood! If ever a person needed an understanding friend it was Job. Job was widely known throughout the ancient world, and three friends came from afar to "bemoan" and "comfort" him— three would-be comforters who were ill-equipped to counsel. In the latter part of Chapter Two we are introduced to these callous comforters.

139

The first is Eliphaz the Temanite, a pious sage who tried to be compassionate as he rebuked Job for his "sin." Eliphaz was probably the oldest of the three, since he exercised the prerogative of making the first speech.

Bildad the Shuhite was well-versed in the philosophies and traditions of his day. He seems to be more interested in justifying his own philosophy, and that of sages past, than in comforting the sufferer.

Zophar the Naamathite is the stern dogmatist of the group. His "comfort" consists of condemning Job and telling him that he had better "get right with God."

James Strauss has given appropriate nicknames to Job's friends: "Bilious Bildad," "Zealous Zophar," and "Enterprising Elihu."[4] After listening to the three exhausting speeches of Eliphaz, we might well dub him "Exasperating Eliphaz!"

As the friends approached Job, they were at first unable to recognize him because of his disfigured appearance. When they drew near and witnessed the anguish of their friend, they wept, tore their clothing, sprinkled dust on their heads, and did the kindest thing of all that they did in their ministry to Job: they kept silent for seven days. There are times when words are such inadequate vessels to carry comfort.

When the week of silence was past, the dialogue and the debate and the "comfort" began. Job spoke nine times; Eliphaz, three times: Bildad, three times; Zophar, twice; Elihu, once; and God, once. In some of the speeches of these "friends" we wonder if they knew just what they wanted to say or if they only desired to display their wisdom and exercise their rhetoric. God calls all of their rhetoric "windy words."

---

4. James D. Strauss, *Job* (Joplin: College Press, 1976), p. xxviii.

The speeches of Job's friends sound very much like those of many in our day, as they preach the "gospel of health and prosperity": if you but have sufficient faith, and turn from sin to God, you will always be in good health, be immune to suffering, and be prosperous. The problem with this "gospel" is that it is not Jesus' gospel. The call of the Master was, "If any man would come after me, let him deny himself, and take up his cross, and follow me" (Matt. 16:24). It is not possible to take a rough cross on a lacerated back and fail to experience suffering.

Job's comforters are agreed upon one thing: all suffering comes as a result of sin, and if our sins have been secret, our suffering reveals our hypocrisy. They elaborate their premise: health and prosperity are inseparably linked with sinfulness.

His possessions are gone. His children are gone. His health is gone. His wife has turned against him. His friends berate him. His God is silent. And you think you've got trouble! How dark and hopeless the situation would be if our story ended with the close of Chapter Two.

1. Jobs speaks: "Let the day perish wherein I was born" (Chapter 3).

Throughout the prologue Job has remained silent and submissive. The inner turmoil is now too much to contain, and Job speaks. There is a therapy in sharing our burdens with understanding friends, and Job feels free to express to his friends the bitterness and rebellion which has been welling up within him. In this first speech Job does not ask for understanding nor relief, but proclaims his misery.

In his anguish, the suffering one does not curse God. He curses the day of his birth and he cries out, as have countless other suffering ones, "Why me, Lord?" He is saying,

"If this is all that is left to life, it would have been far better if I had never been born, for then I would have been at rest."

In this first speech Job expresses the philosophy of the world, that life without comfort and happiness is not worth the living. How we need to be reminded that there is a happiness which is totally unrelated to "things" and to the exterior circumstances of life. Our Lord declared to the little band of followers, just before He went out to face His own suffering and death, "Peace I leave with you; my peace I give unto you: not as the world giveth, give I unto you. Let not your heart be troubled, neither let it be fearful" (John 14:27).

2. Eliphaz's first speech: "Who ever perished, being innocent?" (Chapters 4 & 5).

Eliphaz, who is probably the oldest of Job's friends, seems to esteem him highly and to be genuinely sorry for his misfortune. His theology seems to interfere with his compassion. Although bringing little comfort to the sufferer, his speech is one of the most masterful in the book. The burden of his discourse seems to be "Why don't you practice what you preach? You have taught others to bear misfortune, but when it lays its hand upon you, you can't take it. You are being justly punished, for who ever perished, being innocent? They that plow iniquity, and sow trouble, reap the same." Some comfort this!

Strauss says of verse 9: "The wicked perish. This doctrine says that misfortune is divine retribution. This teaching is at the heart of America's 'Success Syndrome,' i.e., if you are prospering, you are being blessed; if you are in destitute circumstances, it is God's way of expressing retributive justice."[5]

---

5. Strauss, op. cit., p. 38.

Perhaps the most profound observation in this eloquent discourse by Eliphaz is the question, "Shall mortal man be more just than God? Shall a man be more pure than his Maker?" He goes on to point out that "man is born unto trouble, as the sparks fly upward," that man is altogether insignificant in comparison to the almighty God, and that there are benefits to be found in chastisement ("Happy is the man whom God correcteth.")

Eliphaz suggests that if Job will but turn to God that all of his troubles will disappear.

3. Job answers Eliphaz: "Is my strength the strength of stones?" (Chapters 6 & 7).

In Job's reply to Eliphaz he acknowledges that his words have been rash, but that it is because of the extreme calamities which have befallen him. In all of his anguish he has not denied the words of the Holy One, but he questions whether or not he has the strength to see it through. Strong as he is, he does not have the "strength of stones."

Job then turns upon his friends, accuses them of deceitfulness, expresses his disappointment at their counsel, and appeals to them for a little kindness.

Not finding encouragement or surcease from his friends, Job appeals to God for relief. One of the most distressing features of his suffering is that he can find no reason for God to afflict him. He closes his pathetic speech by imploring God to forgive his sin, whatever it might be, before he dies.

4. Bildad's first speech: "Does God pervert justice?" (Chapter 8).

It is time now for a younger one to speak, and Bildad

picks up the now familiar refrain: "God can do no wrong. Suffering is a result of transgression. Job, if you were pure and upright you would be spared these calamities and would be prosperous. Furthermore, your children were killed because of their sin. They got what they deserved." How cruel! Bildad is certainly not known for his tact nor for his compassion.

Callous Bildad has a simple solution for all of Job's problems: "Just confess your sins to God and He will deliver you out of all of your trouble. Surely this must be true, for this is what was taught by the 'forefathers'! The righteous are always blessed; the sinners are always destroyed."

5. Job's third speech: "There is no umpire betwixt us." (Chapters 9 & 10).

As Job responds to Bildad, he cries out for justice from the hand of God and man. He acknowledges the power of the omnipotent God, but complains that He destroys the perfect with the wicked. Job wrestles with the problem of how to present his case to God, since God is not a man as he is, and since there is no umpire between man and God to settle the case justly.

In his agony and confusion, Job accuses God of injustice, in that it appears that He makes no distinction between the righteous and the wicked. He is later rebuked for this outburst, both by Elihu and by Jehovah.

Chapter 10 contains a magnificent description of how God frames the body of man, from conception to birth. Job seems to be saying, "God, if you formed me so carefully, why have you now forsaken me?"

Job closes his third speech by crying out for comfort before he goes to "the land of darkness and of the shadow of death."

6. Zophar's first speech: "If iniquity be in thy hand, put it far away" (Chapter 11).

How strange that Zophar should be styled a "comforter." He is blunt, severe, and brutal. In effect, he says, "Job, you are a fine orator. You are full of talk, but eloquence is not enough to solve your problem. If God would reveal what He knows about you, you would see that your punishment is far less than you deserve. Your finite mind cannot possibly fathom the infinite. If you will put away your sin, your sufferings will pass and you will again know peace, prosperity, and happiness."

Zophar was a "pressure evangelist." He attempted to force Job to confess his secret sins on the basis of the benefits which would accrue through his repentance.

The three friends have now spoken, and they are in agreement that Job's basic problem is secret sin, that he needs to get right with God and that peace and prosperity will again be his.

7. Job's fourth speech: "Ye are all physicians of no value." (Chapters 12 - 14).

Job begins this lengthy speech by turning on his friends with biting sarcasm: "No doubt but ye are the people, and wisdom shall die with you." He declares that he is in no way inferior to them. He affirms God's power, as perceived in His creation and in His divine providence. He charges his friends with falsehood and declares that their sayings are "proverbs of ashes."

145

As the suffering one continues his discourse, he speaks eloquently of the fraility of man and the finality of death, then propounds the question of the ages: "If a man die, shall he live again?" Two millenniums later, at an empty tomb in the garden of Joseph of Arimathea, the question is answered, once and for all, and it is answered in the affirmative. The risen Christ declared, "Because I live, ye shall live also."

The character and the determination of Job are beautifully declared in Chapter 13, verse 15. I like the rendering of the King James translation here (supported by the New American Standard and the New International translations): "Though he slay me, yet will I trust Him." Job has found that which every individual, consciously or unconsciously, longs for: the Life of Trust.

The Life of Trust

The Old and New Testament Scriptures, alike, are shot through with the tender appeal of the Almighty: "Trust me." He gave us being. He provides all things that are needful. He confirmed His love towards us in that, while we were yet sinners, Christ died for us. This God of limitless love is worthy of limitless trust. You can trust one who would die for you. You can trust Him with all that you are and all that you have.

How many perplexed and troubled souls have found peace and purpose and direction by accepting His gracious invitation: "Trust in Jehovah with all thy heart, and lean not upon thine own understanding: In all thy ways acknowledge him, and he will direct thy paths" (Prov. 3:5-6).

Another blessed formula is found in Psalm 37:5, "Commit thy way unto Jehovah; trust also in him, and he will bring it to pass." Are you troubled, friend, over the way that you should take? Commit—trust—and He will . . .!

Men of God, throughout the ages, have found the answer to life's problems in the Life of Trust. Listen again as the great sufferer Paul exults, "For I know him whom I have believed, and I am persuaded that he is able to guard that which I have committed unto him against that day" (II Tim. 1:12).

He wants us to trust Him even when we can't understand Him. He desires that we cling to Him, even as Job did, although we may think that we have every reason to deny Him. "Blessed is the man that maketh Jehovah his trust" (Psalm 40:4).

8. Eliphaz's second speech: "The wicked man travaileth with pain all his days." (Chapter 15).

It is time now for the second cycle of speeches to begin, and it is Eliphaz's turn. He does not sound much like the Eliphaz of Chapters four and five. Job has not submitted to the advice of his friends, so Eliphaz turns from compassion to abuse in this blistering denunciation of Job.

Exasperating Eliphaz begins by implying that Job is full of hot air: "filling himself with the east wind." As we listen to these lofty speeches, we wonder just who it is that is full of hot air. "Job," says Eliphaz, "don't you know that the ancients all knew that suffering is caused by sin? How dare you defy our traditions?"

This frustrated and frustrating speech closes with the description of the fate of the wicked. According to the philosophy of Eliphaz, man pays in full for his sins during this life.

147

9. Job's fifth speech: "Miserable comforters are ye all."
   (Chapters 16 & 17).

Job is becoming weary of the verbosity of his friends and turns on them with the charge, "Don't judge me until you have walked in my moccasins. If my soul were in your soul's stead, I could speak as you do, but I believe that I would speak a bit more kindly than you."

Job continues his complaint of the treatment he is receiving from the hands of God and man, although there is no violence in his hands, and his prayer is pure. He challenges his friends to continue their attack and declares that even if they repeat the same words it will in no wise make them valid.

In his agony, Job fails to trust in the love of God. He concludes sadly that his only hope may be in Sheol, where he will find rest in the dust.

10. Bildad's second speech: "The light of the wicked shall be put out." (Chapter 18).

It appears that Bildad has concluded that because Job refuses to repent he must have a burden of unconfessed sin, so Bildad launches into a legalistic tirade as to the fate of sinners: "terror—calamity—disease—homeless—no progeny—wanderer—forgotten." Bildad thought to force Job to repentance by depicting the terrible fate of the wicked.

There is not a word of compassion, comfort, or consolation in Bildad's second speech.

11. Job's sixth speech: "I know that my Redeemer liveth." (Chapter 19).

The plethora of words is beginning to break Job's composure, and he protests against the reproaches of his friends.

How pathetic the picture which Job draws of his own wretchedness: broken on every side; his hope gone; forsaken by kinsfolk, friends, and servants; utter loneliness. In his agony, Job reaches out for someone who might understand and care: "have pity upon me, O ye my friends."

Then, suddenly, out of the depths of darkness and despair, Job bursts forth into one of the most sublime expressions of faith ever uttered:

> But as for me I know that my Redeemer liveth, and at last He will stand up upon the earth: and after my skin, even this body, is destroyed, then without my flesh shall I see God; whom I, even I, shall see, on my side, and mine eyes shall behold, and not as a stranger (Job 19:25-27).

Here are the central and the most eloquent verses of the entire book: Old Testament verses which affirm a firm belief in the resurrection. Job may not have understood the *why,* but he knew the *Who.* We can face most anything in life when we have the assurance that our Redeemer lives and that it will be worth it all when we see Him, face to face.

> Oftimes the day seems long, our trials hard to bear,
> We're tempted to complain, To murmur and despair;
> But Christ will soon appear To catch His Bride away,
> All tears forever over in God's eternal day.
>
> Sometimes the sky looks dark with not a ray of light,
> We're tossed and driven on, No human help in sight;
> But there is one in heav'n Who knows our deepest care,
> Let Jesus solve your problem, Just go to Him in pray'r.
>
> Life's day will soon be o'er, all storms forever past,
> We'll cross the great divide To glory—safe at last;
> We'll share the joys of heav'n—a harp, a home, a crown;
> The tempter will be banished, We'll lay our burden down.

149

It will be worth it all when we see Jesus,
Life's trials will seem so small when we see Christ;
One glimpse of His dear face All sorrow will erase,
So bravely run the race Till we see Christ.[6]

12. Zophar's second speech: "The triumphing of the wicked is short." (Chapter 20).

Assuming Job's wickedness, as have the others, Zophar launches into a coarse and irrelevant discourse on the fate of sinners. His speech produces more heat than light. He declares that sinners will know swift vengeance in the here and now, that they will experience poverty, that their children will resort to begging, and that God's wrath will be upon sinners to destroy them.

Archer summarizes this speech well, as he states, "Here again we see how unrelenting was the fanatical hostility aroused by Job's refusal to confess to sins he never committed"[7]

13. Job's seventh speech: "Why should I not be impatient?" (Chapter 21).

"Regardless of what you say, Zophar, the wicked are not always punished in this life"; thus Job begins his seventh speech. He contradicts Zophar's premise that the wicked always receive their just due in this life by pointing out the very obvious fact that unrighteous men are frequently prosperous men. Job has seen, as have his friends, that sinners are often successful in business; their children are happy; they spend their days in prosperity, yet they do not desire to know God.

---

6. Esther K. Rusthoi, "When We See Christ."
7. Archer, op. cit., p. 77.

Job points out vividly that the righteous and the wicked "lie down alike in the dust, and the worm covereth them." He concludes, "How then comfort ye me in vain, seeing in your answers there remaineth only falsehood?"

14. Eliphaz's third speech: "Is not thy wickedness great?" (Chapter 22).

The third cycle of the debate now begins and Eliphaz is the first speaker. Since he can find no fault in Job, and since he stubbornly holds to his preconceived premise that all suffering results from sin, he conjures up a long list of sins which Job must surely have committed to cause God to punish him so severely. He must have cheated his brethren, withheld help from the needy, and oppressed the widows and the orphans. According to Eliphaz's concept of retribution, only such cruelties could possibly account for Job's extreme misfortune.

Eliphaz concludes by urging Job to return to God, so that He would hear and bless. Amidst all of the faulty reasoning of Job's friends, Eliphaz makes an appeal which all people of all time would do well to heed: "Acquaint now thyself with him, and be at peace" (verse 21).

15. Job's eighth speech: "I shall come forth as gold." (Chapters 23 & 24).

In former speeches Job has replied to the accusations of his friends. Now he looks within in an effort to analyze his own feelings and expresses his yearning for access to God, that he might present his case before Him. God would understand! God would care! God would extend justice and mercy!

Despite his intense suffering in body and mind, Job is able to take the long look and to realize "When he hath tried

151

me, I shall come forth as gold." True, he is now in the furnace, but the Refiner will discover no dross—only pure gold!

Job again protests his integrity, questions God's apparent indifference to the course of the wicked, and closes with the challenge: "And if it be not so now, who will prove me a liar, and make my speech nothing worth?"

16. Bildad's third speech: "How can a man be just with God?" (Chapter 25).

Believe it or not, Job's friends are about to run out of words. Bildad's final speech is the shortest of them all. He contrasts God's majesty and man's frailty and asks, "How then can man be just with God?" He seems to scoff at Job's appeal to the Almighty. Bildad is through. He has failed miserably in bringing comfort and light.

17. Job's final speech: "I will not put away my integrity from me." (Chapters 26 - 31).

In his final speech, Job turns upon his friends with a burst of sarcasm for their lack of feeling and insight. His tenacious faith in the Almighty is again seen as he glories in the transcendence of divine wisdom and power, as contrasted to the frailty and ignorance of man.

Overcome by nostalgia, Job cries out for his prosperity, happiness, honor, and respect which he had known in days gone by. What a contrast to his present wretched state!

With amazing insight, Job speaks of facts which were unknown prior to the discoveries of modern astronomy: the empty space at the north, the earth poised in space, the curvature of the earth's surface, etc. Who taught astronomy to Job, unless these insights came by divine revelation?

In Chapter 31 Job catalogues the sins of which he is not guilty. The substance of Job's final speech is "Till I die, I will not put away my integrity." Job had a faith and a determination that just wouldn't quit! He is a shining example of one who was determined to remain faithful, even when his world caved in.

"The words of Job are ended." What more could he say? There is no record of his speaking again to his friends in the final eleven chapters of the book.

18. Junior speaks up: "God is greater than man." (Chapters 32 - 37).

This is the first we hear of Elihu. He is the youngest of the group and has modestly waited until the last to speak, although he has almost choked on the silence. Elihu may have tagged along, hoping to learn something from the sages, or to have opportunity to display his own wisdom and rhetoric.

Elihu is angry: angry at Job because he has justified himself rather than God, and angry at his friends because they haven't been smart enough to answer Job's arguments. Most of Elihu's speech seems to consist of telling him what great things he is about to say. When he has finished we aren't quite sure what he has said, and neither is Elihu.

Elihu speaks of the awesome nature of God and seems to indicate that suffering may be preventive and corrective rather than punitive. In a sense, Elihu is a better theologian than his friends in that he points out that suffering may be permitted by God toward the accomplishment of His wise design.

The conversation between Job and his friends is a profound example of man's attempts to solve the perplexing

153

problems of life through purely rationalistic or theological processes. When neither Job nor his friends can find a satisfactory answer to suffering and loss, *then God speaks.*

19. God speaks—and men listen in awe. (Chapters 38 - 41).

Throughout the thirty-five chapters of dialogue, as Job and his friends have wrestled with the suffering problem, and have berated one another, the God Who had permitted it all has remained strangely silent. Perhaps the most difficult experience to face in all of life's journey is to encounter the silence of God. But now, at last, the silence is broken, in what Strauss repeatedly styles "The Shattering of Silence." And God answers from a most unlikely and most unexpected source: out of the whirlwind. There are times when the answer is found in the very heart of the turmoil and strife. The important thing is to know that eventually *God will speak.*

Perhaps the most striking thing in all of Jehovah's speech is that Job's problems are completely ignored. Job has repeatedly expressed a longing for a personal audience with God. The audience is now granted, but Job is given no opportunity to present his case, nor does God reveal to him the reason for his misfortune. God simply asks a series of questions which bring Job to his knees.

In these grand and majestic chapters, God propounds questions which display Job's ignorance of creation, nature, earth, sea, heavens, beasts, and birds. He reminds Job of His power as revealed in the celestial and the terrestrial. Tremendous wisdom and power were required to design and construct the hippopotamus and the crocodile. God seems to be saying, "Job, if you are incapable of the simplest answers, how can you be expected to understand the depth of God's dealings with man?"

Men, with their finite minds, ought not expect to fully understand the mind of the Infinite. The majestic power of God as seen in the natural realm extends also to the moral realm. Therefore, man must bow before the wisdom and the power of the Creator, recognizing that His way is best and that He does all things well.

As Job begins to view the human scene through the eyes of God, he is brought to repentance.

20. At long last, Job submits: "I abhor myself, and repent in dust and ashes." (Chapter 42:1-6).

It is enough. God has spoken. Job has heard and seen Him, and he cries out, "I abhor myself, and repent in dust and ashes."

"Repent?" Of what does Job have to repent? Was Job not "perfect and upright, and one that feared God, and turned away from evil?" Did not Job retain his integrity? In all of his pain and grief Job had never renounced God, as the devil had predicted that he would. Job has questioned God's justice and bitterly complained over the "injustices" of life. He has lashed out at his friends. His faith has run low. Before the Divine Presence, he now acknowledges that he has uttered that which he had not understood and, before the Almighty One, he abhors himself and repents.

In repentance Job wins the victory. In conquering himself he has conquered Satan, and he has entered the peace which comes only through complete surrender to the will of the Redeemer. There is no more dissension, no more bitterness, no more doubt. God has spoken. Job has acquainted himself with his Maker and he is now at peace.

THE EPILOGUE: "Jehovah blessed the latter end of Job more than his beginning" (Chapter 42:7-17).

155

Having drawn aside the curtain, that Job might see the majesty of God, examine his own frailty and unworthiness, and be brought to repentance, God turned upon Job's three friends with a scathing denunciation. They were instructed to bring a burnt offering, for they had not spoken that which was right as Job had. Man must always approach God through an acceptable mediator. In this instance, Job was the man—the one whom they had so vehemently accused of unconfessed sin. How humiliating to be required to come crawling to the man whom they had so criticized and condemned! Job offered the sacrifices for his friends. He did so willingly—and he prayed for them!

"And Jehovah turned the captivity of Job when he prayed for his friends." Intercessory prayer is held forth as a mighty force throughout the scriptures. Are you ever held in bondage by an unforgiving spirit, brought about by the unjust criticism of your friends? Have you ever prayed for them? Perhaps that is just what is needed to break the shackles and set you free. Try it. It works!

"And Jehovah gave Job twice as much as he had before": possessions, the fellowship and comfort of friends and loved ones, posterity, health, and long life. Job's prosperity is restored, but not as a reward. The grand lesson of the book is not that God grants success to the faithful, but that when man sees God and submits to His will he has won the victory, and that others, witnessing the triumph, will come to glorify God.

Pain and suffering are an integral part of life, and believers are not exempt. It is the testimony of God throughout His Word that we are not to be shocked or surprised when misfortune strikes us or our loved ones. Probably we don't understand the problem any better than men did in Job's day, but we should be better able to understand and to cope than did they for, in the meantime, God wrapped Himself in human flesh and visited this earth in the person of His Son. This Son became partaker of our suffering and, as we come to know and love Him, He helps us to understand.

It is after we have met Christ, and only then, that we realize the answer to the problem before us, and the only answer, is that which is revealed in Romans 8:28: "And we know that to them that love God all things work together for good, even to them that are called according to his purpose." Note well that He does not say that all things that happen to us are good, but that the Master Craftsman is able to work all things together for good, in the fulfillment of His wise and perfect design.

Many years ago, Brant Lee Doty wrote with deep insight on the problem of suffering, as seen in the Book of Job. He concluded his discourse beautifully: "So may we learn to be patient and establish our hearts, to suffer affliction without complaint, and learn that the Lord is filled with pity and tender mercy, and that our own High Priest is, indeed, touched with the feeling of our infirmities."[8]

---

8. Brant Lee Doty, "Job—The Problem of Suffering" (*Christian Standard*, December 14, 1967), p. 4.

157

Chapter Nine

MAKE ME A BLESSING

Out in the highways and by-ways of life,
Many are weary and sad;
Carry the sunshine where darkness is rife,
Making the sorrowing glad.

Tell the sweet story of Christ and His love,
Tell of His pow'r to forgive;
Others will trust Him if only you prove
True, ev'ry moment you live.

Give as 'twas given to you in your need,
Love as the Master loved you;
Be to the helpless a helper indeed,
Unto your mission be true.

Make me a blessing, Make me a blessing,
Out of my life may Jesus shine;
Make me a blessing, O Savior, I pray.
Make me a blessing to someone today.

— Ira B. Wilson

The church at Corinth was hurting. They were hurt by discord and division: some said, "I am of Paul"; some said, "I am of Apollos"; some said, "I am of Cephas"; some said, "I am of Christ." They were hurt by sin among their members: one was living in open adultery with his father's wife. They were hurt by lawsuits among brethren. They were hurt by misunderstanding as to the proper relationship between the sexes, the eating of meat sacrificed to idols, sharing with the poor saints, the abuse of the Lord's Supper, the use and abuse of spiritual gifts, and doubts about the resurrection body. It was to this suffering church that preacher Paul wrote that beautiful, but pungent letter of Second Corinthians.

Blessed be the God and Father of our Lord Jesus Christ,
the Father of mercies and God of all comfort; who comforteth us in all our affliction, that we may be able to comfort

them that are in any affliction, through the comfort wherewith we ourselves are comforted of God. For as the sufferings of Christ abound unto us, even so our comfort also
aboundeth through Christ. But whether we are afflicted, it is
for your comfort and salvation; or whether we are comforted,
it is for your comfort, which worketh in the patient enduring
of the same sufferings which we also suffer; and our hope
for you is stedfast; knowing that, as ye are partakers of the
sufferings, so also are ye of the comfort (II Cor. 1:3-7).

"Blessed!" How like Paul to sing praises in the midst of
affliction! Immediately our minds go back to that dark midnight in the Roman prison in Philippi, as Paul was seated
on the cold floor of the inner prison, his back streaming
blood, yet he was praying and singing hymns unto God.
Faith sings in the prison at midnight! T. R. Applebury comments with deep insight into this characteristic of the apostle:

> This attitude came, in part at least, from the fact that he
> had once been the chief persecutor—and the chief sinner
> because of it—of the church. He now rejoiced that he had
> become identified with Christ. In no way was this more
> evident than in his suffering the same kind of affliction that
> Christ had suffered during his ministry.
> Persecution and affliction do not always produce faith-
> fulness and rejoicing. But those who have strong convictions
> about Christ and are fully assured about His resurrection
> and coming again rejoice in spite of hardships.[1]

This second epistle to the church in Corinth is a comforting epistle. Paul not only instructs these beloved disciples
as to how to deal with problems and with pain, but he points
them to the sources of comfort which are available. Notice

1. T. R. Applebury, *Studies in Second Corinthians* (Joplin, MO: College Press, 1966), p. 18.

that he points out in Chapter One that our God is a comforting God, our Christ a comforting Christ, and God's people are to be a comforting people.

Our God Is a Comforting God

Paul exults in "the Father of mercies and God of all comfort." Some eight hundred years earlier Isaiah had rejoiced in the comforting God: "for Jehovah hath comforted his people, and will have compassion upon his afflicted" (Isa. 49:13). To prostrate Zion God held out arms of love and cried out, 'I, even I am he that comforteth you" (Isa. 51:12). And, as he is about to close this beautifully prophetic book, God again promises, "As one whom his mother comforteth, so will I comfort you; and ye shall be comforted in Jerusalem" (Isa. 66:13).

"As one whom his mother comforteth": the mothering God! All of us encounter sorrows and misfortunes in this life which can only be healed by the mothering instinct of God. And whose comfort can compare to that of a mother? The mother who nurtured us in her own body, near her heart; the mother who travailed in pain to give us birth; the mother who held us securely to her breast; the mother who picked our splinters, bandaged our wounds, and wiped away our tears—and God has promised comfort like that of a mother for her child. When the child cries out for help, the loving mother does not wait for the child to come to her, but hastens to the side of the child for her ministry of love. God is like that: ready to hasten to those who call upon Him.

As the Son of the Comforting God preached that matchless sermon which we have styled "the sermon on the mount,"

He spoke eloquently of the happy mourners: "Blessed are they that mourn: for they shall be comforted" (Matt. 5:4). Certainly not all of those who mourn are comforted, but those who have come to place their trust in the Comforting God have found surcease from sorrow.

Our Christ Is a Comforting Christ

The Galilean had emerged the Victor in the wilderness temptation and had returned to His home town of Nazareth. It was the sabbath day, and He entered, as His custom was, into the synagogue, and stood up to read. The scroll of Isaiah was delivered to Him and He opened it to the prophecy which we find recorded in our sixty-first chapter:

> The Spirit of the Lord Jehovah is upon me; because Jehovah hath anointed me to preach good tidings unto the meek; he hath sent me to bind up the broken-hearted, to proclaim liberty to the captives, and the opening of the prison to them that are bound; to proclaim the year of Jehovah's favor, and the day of vengeance of our God; to comfort all that mourn; to appoint unto them that mourn in Zion, to give unto them a garland for ashes, the oil of joy for mourning, the garment of praise for the spirit of heaviness . . ." (Isa. 61:1-3).

. . . and He said, "Today hath this scripture been fulfilled in your ears" (Luke 4:21).

When comfort was needed Jesus was there. Mary and Martha were weeping over the death of brother Lazarus— Jesus was there. The little daughter of a ruler of the synagogue was dead. Relatives and friends were bewailing her— Jesus was there. A funeral procession was proceeding from the gates of Nain: the only son of a widowed mother— Jesus was there. An outcast woman came at noon to draw

161

water from a well in Samaria—Jesus was there. There were deaf and dumb and blind and lame and leprous—Jesus was there. The Savior is always there when needed. He is the Comforting Christ.

This morning, as I was enjoying my daily visit with God, I read a story which I have read countless times, but found something in it which I had never before discovered. Matthew Fourteen relates the tragic story of the death of John the Baptist. Courageous John had confronted the wicked king Herod and denounced him for taking his brother Philip's wife. At a birthday party for the king, his wife's daughter had performed a voluptuous, seductive dance before the king and his guests, and Herod, perhaps inflamed by too much wine and by lust, had promised to give her whatever she might ask.

Herodias seized upon this opportunity to be rid of her accuser, once and for all, and instructed her daughter to request the head of John the Baptist. The king was grieved at the request but, rather than lose face before his guests, sent and had John beheaded in the prison, and his disciples came and told Jesus.

John the Baptist—the cousin of Jesus . . . the one who had leaped with joy in his mother's womb upon hearing the voice of the Lord's mother . . . the one who was clad in camel's hair, subsisting on locusts and wild honey . . . the one who came preaching, "repent, for the kingdom of heaven is at hand . . . the one who had baptized the Man of Nazareth . . . the one of whom Jesus declared, "Among them that are born of women there hath not arisen a greater than John the Baptist" . . . faithful, courageous John the Baptist was dead.

Jesus was grieved. He had lost a close relative and a dear friend. He entered into a boat to go to a quiet place where, for a brief moment, He might be alone with His sorrow. The Miracle Worker could not avoid the crowds. When the boat landed the multitude was there, "and he had compassion on them and healed their sick." The sorrowing Jesus was comforted by His Father, but He shared that divine comfort with needy humanity.

Jesus must have been extremely weary that evening. He was burdened with grief. He had worked hard all day. But before Him were needy people, and He satisfied the hunger of five thousand men, besides women and children. Many of our churches have the beautiful and helpful custom of serving dinner for bereaved families, following the funeral or memorial service for a departed loved one. Here Jesus reversed the procedure: the sorrowing one provided the meal. What a beautiful picture of the comforting Christ: He comforted those in affliction through the comfort wherewith He was comforted of God.

His Spirit Is a Comforting Spirit

As Paul points his readers to the "God of all comfort," he uses an old Greek word, *parakléseōs,* which literally means "to call to one's side." This is the same beautiful word that Jesus used when, on His last night upon the earth, He promised the little band of disciples, "and I will pray the Father, and he shall give you another Comforter, that he may be with you for ever, even the Spirit of truth" (John 14:16). Jesus had been a great Comforter to them and, now that He must leave them, He promises another Comforter: the paraclete, the Holy Spirit—One Who will stand alongside them forever.

A prominent professor of Greek once stated that there is only one word in our English language that approaches the

163

meaning of the Greek word "paraclete," and that is our semi-slang word "Buddy." Wonderful! We can relate to that. A buddy is one who understands us, is genuinely concerned over us, and will stand by us, come what may. The Holy Spirit is like that, and He would like to be a "Buddy" to all.

The Holy Spirit becomes the Abiding Guest of all who will obey God (Acts 5:32). On the first Pentecost following the crucifixion and resurrection of our Lord, inspired Peter instructed the inquirers to "Repent ye, and be baptized every one of you in the name of Jesus Christ unto the remission of your sins; and *ye shall* receive the gift of the Holy Spirit" (Acts 2:38. Italics are the author's). Note that he does not say, "you may," nor, "it is possible," but, "ye shall." If you are His obedient child, don't hesitate to claim your promised Guest.

The *paraclete,* the Comforter, the Holy Spirit, by which the Christian walks (Gal. 5:16), bears good fruit (Gal. 5:22-23), puts to death the deeds of the body (Rom. 8:13), and knows power in prayer (Rom. 8:26), is a comforting Spirit.

God's People Are to Be a Comforting People

Why is it that God desires to comfort the sorrowing? Perhaps our first response to this question might well be, "Because He is God. It is His nature. He is the kind of God Who is touched with the feeling of our infirmities. It is natural that Father God should comfort His sorrowing children." All of which is certainly true, but our text reveals another precious reason why God comforts: "that we may be able to comfort . . . through the comfort wherewith we ourselves are comforted of God." God does not comfort us to make us comfortable, but to make us comforters.

164

Some seven hundred years before the birth of Christ, God gave a commission through Prophet Isaiah: "Comfort ye, comfort ye my people, saith your God" (Isa. 40:1). The purpose of God's comfort to us is that we might comfort others. The Comforting God is saying, "Pass it on."

C. S. Lewis has learned the lesson well, and he eloquently points out a twofold purpose of suffering: "What is good in any painful experience is, for the sufferer, his submission to the will of God, and, for the spectators, the compassion aroused and the acts of mercy to which it leads."[2]

What a thrilling, but humbling, discovery to realize that the Comforting God is dependent upon us to continue His work. This thought is beautifully amplified by Leslie Weatherhead in the following paragraph:

> One of the most glorious thoughts in the world, is, surely, that God depends on us to get his will done—that there are some things he literally cannot do apart from ourselves. When he wants something done in the world, he does not mobilize his angels; he will bring two people together, not by force, but the winsomeness of love, and they will have a baby who will become a Moses or an Isaiah, a Luther or a Wesley, an Augustine or a Livingstone. If he wants to comfort some broken heart, he will put into your heart to go and say kindly words for him. . . . It is amazing how the eternal, omnipotent God has so condescended to co-operate with man that apart from man he is helpless fully to reveal his nature or to accomplish his purpose.[3]

We learn compassion for others who suffer by our own endurance of suffering. When in trouble, we instinctively

---

2. C. S. Lewis, *The Problem of Pain* (New York: MacMillan Publishing Co., Inc., 1962), p. 110.

3. Leslie D. Weatherhead, *Why Do Men Suffer?* (New York-Nashville: Abingdon Press, 1936), p. 29.

turn to one who has experienced the same trouble. This is, partially at least, the key to the success of Alcoholics Anonymous. The drinker who has become alcoholic is free to unburden his soul and to lean on one who has walked down the same road and has emerged victorious. Compulsive eaters find help through Overeaters Anonymous. Those with abnormal sexual desires are assisted by the counsel of those who have conquered the same problem.

In no area of life is this desire for comfort from those who have experienced God's comfort more pronounced than in the loss of a loved one. I have just returned from conducting a funeral service for a dear saint of God. She had lived long, and she had lived well. She was well prepared for her meeting with the King, but, even so, there were children, grandchildren, relatives and friends who stood in need of comfort. This was my first funeral since the loss of my own dear wife, and I found anew the meaning of comforting with the comfort wherewith I was comforted of God. It was a joy to find that because my Heavenly Father had comforted me, I was better able to permit His comfort to flow through me to the aching hearts of others.

There is a little booklet which I have given to many in times of bereavement. It is entitled, "Be Assured." The author is unknown. The flyleaf bears the words of Psalm 147:3: "He healeth the broken in heart and bindeth up their wounds." From the page, "The Fellowship of Suffering," come these two significant paragraphs:

> Your bereavement admits you to one of the great fellowships in the world, that fellowship of those who have suffered. Nothing which one can say or do can help in the hour of grief as much to bring comfort as the companionship and sympathy of one who, also, has passed through the valley of the shadow of death.

166

God has a way of opening the eyes of those who suffer. To them are revealed the great secrets of his kingdom. Perhaps one of the great missions of your life, from this hour, will be to help others to understand these secrets. You can be the means of bringing "light in the hour of darkness."[4]

One of the divine purposes of affliction in the Christian life is to qualify the sufferer to minister to others. As Carl Ketcherside has expressed it, in his inimitable way, "By suffering we are qualified to fill the role to which God has called us."[5] The personal experience of God's comfort is necessary before we can pass it on to others. There is a definite correlation between suffering and comfort. In our text in Second Corinthians, Paul declares, "For as the sufferings of Christ abound unto us, even so our comfort also aboundeth through Christ." The word "abound" means to "overflow." Just as the sufferings which Christ experienced came like a flood upon Paul, and the comfort of Christ overflowed him, so our comfort should over flow toward others.

How indebted we are to our comforters! David was an honor student in the School of Affliction. He was the object of the wrath of a jealous king and was forced to become a fugitive and wanderer. His beloved friend Jonathan was slain by the Philistines. His young son died. Another dear son led a rebellion against him and was slain in battle. David knew what it was to suffer, but while enduring persecution, he wrote the Psalms, which have brought solace and strength to myriads of aching hearts.

Paul was another who was a "straight A" student in the School of Affliction. The course was exacting and the

___
4. The Fellowship of Suffering, *Be Assurred* (Cleveland: Church World Press, Inc.)

5. Carl Ketcherside, *Talks to Jews and Non-Jews* (Cincinnati: The Standard Publishing Co.), p. 155.

examination was rigorous. He was imprisoned, beaten, stoned, shipwrecked, mocked and misunderstood but, through it all, he was comforted and was thereby able to comfort others through the comfort wherewith he was comforted of God.

When we have been there—so desperately in need of comfort—and have been ministered to by the Comforting God, we are better qualified and more willing to reach out to others. Reuben R. Youngdahl, in "The Secret of Greatness," pictures a little lad, outside the walls of Versailles, tenderly holding in his hands a sparrow with a broken wing. A kind lady, passing by, asked, "Wouldn't you like me to take the sparrow home? I could care for it until it is well, then bring it back to the gardens and let it fly again." The little lad responded, "No, lady, if you don't mind, I'll care for this bird myself because, you see, I understand this bird." When the little fellow stood up, with the crippled bird in his hands, the would-be benefactoress saw that his leg was in a cast. He understood the bird!

We live in a hurting world—sickness and disease, marital and family problems, broken homes, misunderstanding, bereavement and frustration—and the church is not immune. Remember that time when you hit the wrong nail with your hammer? How it hurt! and all of the members of the body hurt right along with that throbbing thumb. When the members of the body of Christ hurt, we must be there, hurting right along with them.

A famous surgeon who was once asked if he ever worried about the day when his fingers would eventually lose their skill, replied, "No, my greatest worry is that one day I will no longer feel the pain of my patients." How we ought feel the pain of others for, as S. R. Smalley expressed it, "We cannot heal the wounds we do not feel."

June Beeman recently wrote a beautiful, sensitive article entitled "Where Are You When It Hurts?" In this heart-searching column she offers some very practical suggestions as to how we may minister to our hurting world. She speaks of the very obvious hurts which we observe and experience within our church families, and then continues:

> The truly sensitive Christian sees even less obvious hurts among the members. These are those who take a lonely young wife to lunch the day her husband catches the early bus for his new military post. They visit a middle-aged mother the day her last child leaves home. They share the work of an elderly person who makes a daily trek to the nursing home to visit a spouse. They care for the small children of a potential child abuser for a few hours so the parent can have a bit of free time to help preserve her sanity. They sit with a loner during the church service. They minister to the family of a surgical patient during the long hours in the waiting room.[6]

How desperately we need the compassion of our Master as we view our hurting world. The story is told of a small girl who was given some money by her mother and sent on an errand to the neighborhood grocery store. The little one was gone for a long while and the mother became worried. When the girl finally returned, the mother asked, rather sharply, "Where in the world have you been?"

"Well, mother," replied the daughter, "On the way to the store I lost my money. While I was looking for it, I heard a little girl crying. She had lost her money, too, and she was sitting there on the sidewalk crying."

---

6. June Beeman, "Where Are You When It Hurts?" *Christian Standard* (Cincinnati: The Standard Publishing Co.), October 2, 1983.

"Oh," responded the mother, "I suppose you helped her look for her money."

"No, mother," the little one responded, "I sat down with her on the sidewalk and helped her cry."

That's it! That's what the world needs! Someone to sit down with us and help us cry.

Alfred Lord Tennyson once wrote, "I am a part of all that I have met." Every life that we touch leaves something of our life there. To have suffered much is like knowing many languages, in that it gives the sufferer access to so many more people. Are we leaving something of the comfort of God on those lives which we touch daily?

We live in a world which is torn by conflicting philosophies as to what constitutes success. There is the ever-popular philosophy of the world, which declares that success is determined by the amount of "things" which you take out of the world for yourself: the size of your pile in the bank, the number of acres you own, the kind of house in which you live, the style of clothing you wear, the number of cars in your garage, and where you go for your vacation. There is a diverse philosophy which is not so widely held: the philosophy which dares to suggest that success may be measured by the amount of your life which you invest in a needy world. I take comfort in realizing that this is the philosophy which was embraced by a Man Who came out of the hilltown of Nazareth some 2,000 years ago. This is the way of life which would revolutionize this old world if we but had the courage to put it into practice!

I have always thought of myself as "fundamental," believing firmly in the Scriptures, and Biblically sound in the "plan of salvation," but as I look upon the judgment scene which the Master portrayed in Matthew 25, where all the nations are gathered before the throne, I hear but one question asked: *"What did you do for others?"* Did you feed the hungry? Did you clothe the naked? Did you visit the sick and the imprisoned? Did you demonstrate by your ministry to others that you knew the serving and comforting Christ?

And the service and the comfort, to be effective, must be personal, rather than professional. There is an oft-told illustration of a group of American businessmen who were touring the orient. As they passed through a mission station, they came upon a missionary nurse, bent low as she tenderly bathed the gangrenous foot of a leper. One of the men drew back in revulsion, and exclaimed, "I wouldn't do that for a million dollars! The nurse looked up briefly from her labor of love as she softly murmured the reply, "Neither would I!" It is love that sanctifies the ministry and bestows the comfort.

There are some things for which there is no "next time." We have no yesterdays; time took them away. There may be no tomorrow. *Now* is really the only time that we have. May God grant us the grace to realize that we shall not pass again this way—and minister accordingly.

> The bread that giveth strength I want to give;
> The water pure that bids the thirsty live;
> I want to help the fainting day by day:
> I'm sure I shall not pass again this way.
>
> I want to give the oil of joy for tears,
> The faith to conquer cruel doubts and fears.
> Beauty for ashes may I give alway:
> I'm sure I shall not pass again this way.

I want to give good measure running o'er,
And into angry hearts I want to pour
The answer soft that turneth wrath away:
I'm sure I shall not pass again this way.

I want to give to others hope and faith;
I want to do all that the Master saith;
I want to live aright from day to day;
I'm sure I shall not pass again this way.[7]

It was many years ago that I was privileged to hear a newspaper editor present an outstanding address to a civic group, in which he related the gripping story of a vivid dream. A man dreamed, so goes the story, that he died and was escorted by an angel to view the awful agonies of hell. Here before him was a huge banquet room, tables bountifully spread with all kinds of food that one might desire, but those who were seated at the tables were lean, emaciated, and bewailing their wretched state. Then the visitor saw the reason for their sad situation: each person had iron bands about his elbows, making in impossible for him to feed himself—starving to death in the midst of plenty.

Then, in his dream, the man was escorted to the pearly gates of heaven. Looking within, he beheld a huge banquet room, tables bountifully spread with all kinds of food that one might desire, but those who were seated at these tables were well-fed, cheerful, and rejoicing in their happy situation. Upon closer examination, these, too, were seen to have iron bands about their elbows, so that they could not feed themselves, but there was this difference: each person, with his arms straight ahead of him, was feeding the one whom he faced across the table!

---

7. Ellen H. Underwood, "I Shall Not Pass Again This Way."

It was a "certain lawyer" who once asked Jesus, "Who is my neighbor?" The Master responded with the parable of the man who, on the Jericho road, was robbed, beaten, and left half dead. A certain priest saw him and passed by on the other side. A member of the priestly tribe also passed by on the other side. It was a mongrel Samaritan, despised by these religionists, who was moved with compassion, bound up the wounds of the unfortunate, and provided for his care. "Go," said Jesus, "and do thou likewise" (Luke 10:30-37). On which side of the Jericho road are you?

How sad that in this hurting world there are so many who are "passing by on the other side." A young woman is held for hours on a pool table while she is gang-raped by a group of men, and no one comes to her aid. Another young woman's car is stalled in a tough area of the city as a gang approaches, and only one little black boy goes for help. The others were afraid to get involved. This hurting world is crying out for involvement, and if you, Christian, won't become involved, who will?

How sad it is when one loses physical eyesight, and can no longer thrill to the exquisite beauty of the handiwork of God. Many are blinded by glaucoma: the disease in which the tear ducts close so tightly that there is no lubrication for the eye. This causes the surface of the eye to harden and may, eventually, cause the loss of sight. May God save us from glaucoma of the soul! Without tears of compassion the soul hardens and the victim becomes spiritually blind.

The sermon was eloquent and moving. There were many who were shedding tears. Through it all there was one listener who appeared to remain unmoved. When, following the service, he was asked why he was unaffected by the message, replied, "I don't belong to this parish." Those who don't want to get involved in comforting and ministering to a hurting world must belong to a different parish. Certainly it is a "parish" which is unknown to the compassionate Christ.

How we who have been comforted by God ought to feel for those who are hurting, and share our comfort with them. In "Uncle Tom's Cabin," Little Eva's father does not want her to hear the terrible stories of the plight of the slaves and their families. He explained that she was "too tender" to be exposed to such things. Little Eva replied with deep insight: "You want me to live so happy, and never to have any pain—never suffer anything—not even to hear a sad story, when other poor creatures have nothing but pain and sorrow all their lives; it seems selfish. I ought to know such things, I ought to feel about them."

In recent years, the marathon races have become a very popular athletic event. Those who follow track events are familiar with the Boston Marathon. Great throngs of athletes participate in this grueling race, and many who start never finish. The marathon course covers 26 miles and 385 yards. One of the most difficult points in the race is at a hill which is situated at approximately the 20-mile marker. Runners and fans have named this obstacle "Heartbreak Hill," because of the large numbers of runners who are too exhausted to continue on from this point; it is a point of heartbreak for them. Aware of this extremely difficult portion of the race, many loyal fans now station themselves at the hill to shout encouragement to the runners. Several successful runners have testified that they would never have made it were it not for the faithful fans at Heartbreak Hill. How we ought to realize that there are many in the race of life who have arrived at the place of heartbreak. They have reached the end of their endurance. They are ready to give up the race and concede defeat. Let's station ourselves at Heartbreak Hill and cheer them on to victory.

To be effective in our comfort, and to be made "a blessing to someone today," it is imperative that we identify with the suffering, the sorrowing, and the needy. The story of Father Damien is a familiar story. He was the leper priest on the isle of Molokai. He was a part of an unscriptural hierarchy. He wore a title which Jesus said men ought not wear. His ignorance of scriptural doctrine was appalling, but Father Damien offered himself on the altar of sacrificial service to the lepers of Molokai.

For eight long years Father Damien labored among his leper parish with scant success. How that would break the heart of the average minister: eight years without a response! Then, one sad day, Father Damien looked upon his own flesh and saw the telltale marks: he, too, was a leper.

The next Lord's Day the priest stood before his beloved leper congregation to preach the sermon which he had prepared. As he began to speak, he held out his hands and began, "We lepers." That was as far as he got. There was no sermon preached that morning; there was none needed! With a hoarse, inarticulate, animal-like cry, they arose as one man and surged upon him. Father Damien had become one of them.

When we identify with suffering humanity, hungry are fed, naked are clothed, sorrowing are comforted, and souls are saved.

One of our most effective missionaries in the orient is Yoon Kwon Chae. He ministers tirelessly: exhausted, ill, and inadequate, he presses on. Day after day, he teaches and preaches. He leads an effective institute to train native teachers and preachers. He oversees a large children's home. He and his wife have adopted several Korean children. His writings reflect an overflowing heart of love and compassion. Many of us have heard Chae relate the story of his conversion to Christ.

It was during the Communist invasion of Korea, and Chae had gone to look for his preacher-father whom the Communists had slain. There were many others on the same sorrowful mission that day. There were so many blackened corpses that Chae could not find his father. The bereaved ones about him were crying in hopelessness and despair. It was a scene of heartbreak.

But then, as the futile search continued, a grieving Christian looked up and lifted his voice in song: "There's a land that is fairer than day, and by faith we can see it afar; for the Father waits over the way, to prepare us a dwelling place there." Another voice joined in, others picked up the refrain, and soon a great chorus was swelling the song of assurance: "In the sweet by and by, we shall meet on that beautiful shore; in the sweet by and by, we shall meet on that beautiful shore." Over and over again, they sang their song of hope and trust.

When the singing was ended, every eye was dry, and they were looking up with a new-found hope and faith. It was then and there that Yoon Kwon Chae gave himself to Christ, and launched a life of dedicated Christian service. He has comforted others with the comfort wherewith he was comforted of God.

Since penning the foregoing gripping story, I have received a newsletter from Chae. In this communication he reports that there are now 92 children in the Geon Christian

176

Children's Home. He closes his account with a vivid illustration of the compassion which consecrates his ministry:

> I remember one cold night two days before Christmas that I spent in a cold storage room. I made some regulations and if any child violate them, I made a rule that he will have to spend one night in a cold storage room. One boy violated and I had to send him to the storage room (wrapped with blankets). But I could not sleep myself and in the middle of the night, I sneaked into the storage room and spent a night there. I could not sleep well there either; but it was an inspiring night as I felt a little bit of God's pain, Who couldn't sleep with us suffering on this world, Who sent His only begotten Son to be born in a cold manger for us all. And that's why we wish you again MERRY CHRISTMAS AND HAPPY NEW YEAR!
>
> Yours as ever,
> YOON KWON CHAE

May we who have been comforted of God pray the prayer of Helen Hunt Jackson—and then practice what we pray:

> If I can live
> To make some pale face brighter and to give
> A second luster to some tear-dimmed eye,
> Or e'en impart
> One throb of comfort to an aching heart,
> Or cheer some way-worn soul in passing by;
> If I can lend
> A strong hand to the fallen, or defend
> The right against a single envious strain,
> My life, though bare
> Of much that seemeth dear and fair
> To us on earth,
> Will not have been in vain.[9]

---

9. Helen Hunt Jackson, "If I Can Live."

Chapter Ten

THE DEVIL DIDN'T MAKE ME DO IT

Blessed is the man that endureth temptation; for when he hath been approved, he shall receive the crown of life, which the Lord promised to them that love him. Let no man say when he is tempted, I am tempted of God; for God cannot be tempted with evil, and he himself tempteth no man: but each man is tempted, when he is drawn away by his own lust, and enticed. Then the lust, when it hath conceived, beareth sin: and the sin, when it is fullgrown, bringeth forth death. Be not deceived, my beloved brethren. Every good gift and every perfect gift is from above, coming down from the Father of lights, with whom can be no variation, neither shadow that is cast by turning. Of his own will he brought us forth by the word of truth, that we should be a kind of firstfruits of his creatures (James 1:12-18).

The word "temptation" does not lend itself readily to definition. The dictionary indicates the meaning to be a trying or testing in a venturesome way, an enticement or allurement. Both the Hebrew and the Greek words translated "tempt" or "temptation" carry the thought of proving, trying, or testing. I recall that a Bible College professor defined temptation as "an undesirable, inside response to an outside appeal." I am not at all sure that this is accurate, for many do not regard the temptation experience as something undesirable. When we are beset by temptation we do not desire to define and analyze; we want to know what to do about it and how to overcome it.

Of all of the trials and struggles of life, there are none more agonizing and discouraging and debilitating than the constant battle we wage with temptation. Temptations are the common lot of man, and, weary of the struggle, we confuse the temptation with the yielding and fail to realize that the sin is not in the temptation but in the surrender. How often we cry out with philosopher Seneca, "Oh that a hand would come down from heaven and deliver me from my besetting sin!"

One of the reasons that temptation may be so devastating to the Christian life is our tendency to feel that if we are truly Christian we will not experience the allure of temptation and the desire to yield. Erwin Lutzer speaks to this tendency with keen insight: "Many Christians think that victory over sin means that they will no longer be tempted. Or they think that God will change their nature so that they will no longer desire to do evil. Either way, they are wrong. Temptation is not a sin: it is a call to battle."[1] Where there is no battle, there can be no victory.

We are amazed when we hear James admonish, "Count it all joy, my brethren, when ye fall into manifold temptations" (James 1:2). We do not consider it a very joyful experience to be beset with temptations.

Let us consider what James has to say about the "joy of temptation." He implies that instead of lamenting or becoming discouraged over temptation, we should rejoice, "knowing that the proving of your faith worketh patience." Temptation comes as a testing of our faith. After all, is not life a situation which God has devised as a training school for possible citizens of His Kingdom? We are strengthened by temptations that are faced squarely and overcome. As the hymn-writer expressed it, "Each victory will help you some other to win."

James continues his lesson: "Let patience have its perfect work." The successful endurance of temptation must not be

---

1. Erwin H. Lutzer, *How to Say No to a Stubborn Habit*, (Wheaton, Ill.: Victor Books, 1979), p. 50.

a passive experience. We must work out its complete results. Don't try to ignore it. Don't throw it away. Build it into life. Use it for the good of man and the glory of God!

In the text with which we introduced this chapter, the author exults, "Blessed (happy) is the man that endureth temptation." He does not say that all who are tempted are happy, but he that *endures* temptation is blessed, for he shall receive the crown of life. The writer then warns his readers against blaming God for their temptation: "Let no man say, I am tempted of God." When some fall under temptation they are prone to place the blame on God. There can be no temptation unless there is something within which responds to the outside appeal. "Each man is tempted when he is drawn away by his own lust, and enticed."

The unhappy course of sin is depicted as a birth process— "the lust, when it hath conceived, beareth sin—and the sin, when it is fullgrown, bringeth forth death." Lustful desire, declares James is the conception. When the desire sees its fruition in the deed, the sinful deed is the birth. The final result of the lustful desire and the sinful deed is death. Man must now be either forgiven or punished.

When temptation comes to me, as it comes to all, what comfort and encouragement is mine to listen to that great Christian conqueror, as he confesses to the saints at Rome, "That which I do I know not: for not what I would, that do I practice; but what I hate that I do . . . Wretched man that I am! who shall deliver me out of the body of this death?" (Rom. 7:15-25). Some scholars see here an allusion to the ancient barbaric practice of binding the body of the murder victim to the body of the murderer—dragging about that putrefying carcass until the contagion exacted its terrible toll. How we need deliverance from the body of sin!

180

How pathetic would be the state of us all if there were no twenty-fifth verse in the seventh chapter of Romans! We do what we would not. We do not that which we would. In our agony, we acknowledge our wretchedness. We cry out for deliverance. The triumph lies just one verse beyond: "I thank God through Jesus Christ our Lord."

The story of temptation is almost as old as the story of man. It reaches back through the ages to that beautiful garden planted eastward in Eden. Here the loving Father has placed His perfect children, and has given them freely all that they could possibly desire. The fruit of every tree in the garden was theirs—all but one: the fruit of the tree which was in the midst of the garden. Every need was supplied. The man and his wife knew a sweet fellowship one with the other and with their Creator. They were made in His likeness, and the all-wise Father had instilled within them the power of choice. Would you have it otherwise? Without the power to choose we would be puppets, not people, mannequins, not men. Thank God for the power of choice!

One day Eve had a call from an exceptionally good salesman—the subtle serpent. He came, as the tempter so often comes, with a question: "Has God said 'Ye shall not eat of any tree of the garden?'" And the woman, in her innocence replied, "We may eat of all the trees in the garden but one. If we eat of it, or touch it, we will die." "Not so," replied the tempter, "You will not die, but you will be as God, knowing good and evil." And, for the first time, the woman realized she had a choice. Attention was now focused on the forbidden fruit; it was beautiful, and who would not desire to be wise? So she ate of the fruit and gave also to her husband, and he did eat.

181

Temptation—yielding—penalty. "And the eyes of them both were opened," but how they wished that they were still blind! "They knew that they were naked"—innocence is now left behind. "And the man and his wife hid themselves from the presence of Jehovah"—how natural for sinful man to attempt to hide from a holy God, but how futile! When confronted with their sin, the man blamed the woman and the woman blamed the serpent. The devil was the tempter, but man was the chooser. The devil didn't make them do it!

Every man reads his own biography in the account of the first temptation. The tempter comes, as he came to Eve, questioning the word of God, then denying the word of God. Sin becomes alluring. We rationalize. We yield. Our hands are stained with forbidden fruit. We refuse to admit blame. We stand naked before God. We go into hiding—and then comes the terrible realization that we cannot hide from God: "Be sure your sins will find you out."

We have all gone through the garden with Adam and Eve. "All have sinned, and fall short of the glory of God" (Rom. 3:23). And "the wages of sin is death" (Rom. 6:23). How dark and how hopeless the picture would be if God forsook us just outside the garden!

When Temptation Comes

1. Be ready to recognize.

When temptation comes be ready to recognize it for what it is: a strong desire to do that which is not in keeping with the loving Father's will, nor for our ultimate good. Recognize that temptation is of the devil, and that he will do all within his power to thwart God's will for our lives. Recognize that sin is not in the temptation, but in the yielding. Recognize that yielding brings sin, and that sin brings death. Recognize that if we do not master temptation, temptation will master us. Recognize that God has a reason for permitting the temptation experience.

If you are prone to rebel against temptation, and to cry out, "Why doesn't God take it away?" remember that temptation, with all of its frightful possibilities for failure, is God's method for testing our loyalties. Temptation is the divine curriculum to teach us how to climb the ladder of spiritual maturity, and through the triumph over temptation God demonstrates His grace and His power.

2. Be motivated.

Knowing that temptation will attack you, be ready, and be motivated by a strong desire to be an overcomer. Our problem is that the temptation is so strong and appealing that our fleshly desire is to yield. The story is told of a small boy who was forbidden by his mother to go swimming. The day was hot; the cool water was appealing; the voice of his friends was enticing, and it was not long until Johnnie returned home with the tell-tale marks of disobedience adorning his wet head. "Johnnie," cried the distraught mother, "why did you go swimming, after I told you that you could not?" "Because I was tempted so badly," the urchin replied. "And how did you happen to have your swimming suit with you?" "Because I thought I might be tempted," was the ready response. Johnnie wasn't prepared to resist temptation; he was prepared to yield.

3. Cut off sin at its source.

James reminds us that we are tempted when we are drawn away by our own lust, the lust bears sin, and the sin

183

brings death. The devil gets into the garden where the fence is the weakest. We need keep a constant watch on those weak places in our fences. The problem comes when, desiring the thrill of the temptation experience, we deliberately place ourselves in a position where we are vulnerable to temptation. "If you don't want the fruit of sin, stay out of the orchard!"

Temptation is not addressed to the outward, but to the inward man. The response to temptation comes from what the Scriptures style as man's "heart." The wise man who wrote the book of Proverbs appealed to his "son" to "Keep thy heart with all diligence; for out of it are the issues of life" (Prov. 4:23). He reminds us again that "as a man thinketh in his heart so is he" (Prov. 23:7). The Master knew the danger inherent in evil thoughts, and in His matchless Sermon on the Mount He warned against the anger which leads to killing and the lust which leads to adultery. He is saying, "Cut off sin at its source."

But how do I escape those tempting thoughts? This is the $64.00 question. It requires more than an act of the will. We will not avoid the wrong thought pattern unless we crowd it out with the right thought pattern. There is an old game which asks you to not think of the figure "8" for one minute. You can't do it, of course, unless your mind is so filled with other thoughts that you have no time for the figure "8".

We crowd out tempting thoughts by opening the door to the King. After Jesus had cast a demon from one who was blind and dumb, He told the intriguing story of the Devil's Hotel. The demon, when cast out, said Jesus, searches for a place of rest, and when he finds none, he returns to the house from whence he was cast out, and finds it empty, swept, and garnished. Then he takes seven other spirits, more evil than himself; they move into the empty building, and the last state of the man is worse than it was before (Matt. 12:43-45).

When you have resolved to not dwell on those vile and sinful thoughts, and are in the process of house-cleaning your mind, don't leave those rooms vacant! Crowd out the evil with the good. Beautiful guests for the rooms of your mind are listed in Philippians 4:8: "Finally, brethren, whatsoever things are true, whatsoever things are honorable, whatsoever things are just, whatsoever things are pure, whatsoever things are lovely, whatsoever things are of good report; if there be any virtue, and if there be any praise, think on these things."

There is a cartoon which depicts a frustrated man, standing beneath a tree in the fall of the year, rake in hand, looking up angrily at one leaf which refuses to fall. Don't worry about it! When the sap arises, and the new buds begin to appear, this new life will push off the old leaves. It is the new life that crowds out the old.

None of us can prevent temptation from coming, but we can keep from welcoming it, reveling in it, and envisioning its fruition. You can't keep temptation from coming, but you don't have to give it a chair to sit on, or, as the old sage observed, "You can't prevent the birds from flying over your head, but you can stop them from building a nest in your hair!"

4. Don't open the flap of your tent.

There is a certain "thrill" in seeing how far we can walk down the road with temptation without yielding to its enticements. But once we have said "yes" to the smallest temptation, there is the very real danger of saying "yes" to them all.

185

It is so like the alcoholic who decides to take that "one little drink," but that is all that is required, regardless of high resolve, to cause him to empty the bottle.

There is an ancient oriental legend of the Arab and his camel, spending the night on the desert sand. As the chill of the night drew on, the camel spoke, "Oh Master, it is cold out here; please permit me to come into your tent."

"No," replied the master, "the tent is not large enough to accommodate both of us."

"But, master," responded the beast, "my nose is so cold; permit me to put but my nose within the tent."

"Very well," replied the owner, "but, mind you, only your nose."

The finale and the application are obvious: when morning dawned, the Arab found himself outside on the sand, and the camel ensconced within the tent.

Recognizing the progressive nature of temptation and sin, don't permit so much as a camel's nose within your tent!

5. Look to the Victor.

How beautiful and how vital is the reminder in Hebrews 4:15: "For we have not a high priest that cannot be touched with the feeling of our infirmities; but one that hath been in all points tempted like as we are, yet without sin." Did I hear you say, "No one has ever been tempted as I am tempted?" Don't you believe it! The God-Man of Galilee was tempted in all points as you are tempted.

Is your temptation a lust of the flesh? Jesus was led of the Spirit into the wilderness to be tempted of the devil (cf. Matt. 4:1-11). There, confronted by the devil and by wild beasts, He fasted for forty days. Commentators have suggested that this is approaching the limit that the fleshly

186

body can endure without sustenance, and that just prior to death there is again an intense hunger for food. Perhaps Jesus was experiencing the pangs of death. The devil always attacks at the weakest point, so he came to the emaciated Jesus with the taunt, "If thou art the Son of God, command that these stones become bread—satisfy the desires of the flesh." But the One Who had tasted no bread for forty days responded, "It is written, Man shall not live by bread alone."

Is your temptation to receive the plaudits of men rather than the commendation of God? The devil took Jesus into the holy city, where he set Him on the pinnacle of the temple (possibly the high porch which overhung the Kidron valley, some 300 feet below), saying, "If thou art the Son of God, cast thyself down—and let the angels bear thee up." He seems to imply that Jesus is a fame-seeker, and that if He is truly God's Son, the angels will rescue Him, and He will have glory from all who witness this miraculous sight. Jesus replied, "It is written, Thou shalt not make trial of the Lord thy God."

Is your temptation to obtain things in the wrong manner, or to arrive at a place of prominence through the wrong route? The devil took Jesus into a high mountain and showed Him all the kingdoms of the world, saying, "All these things will I give thee, if thou wilt fall down and worship me." Jesus claimed to be a King. The devil claimed to be the Prince of this world. All subterfuge is now laid aside. Jesus has selected the way to the throne that is covered with thorns and blood. His way is weary and painful and it is lined with the thoughtless, the scoffers, and the persecutors. The devil is saying, "I'll show you an easier way: Just fall down and worship me, and I will give you a short-cut to the Kingdom—a way in which there will be no self-denial, no cross, and no tomb." But Jesus replied, "It is written, Thou shalt worship the Lord thy God, and him only shalt thou serve."

Satan unloaded his whole arsenal when he tempted Jesus, or, as Carl Ketcherside expressed it, "He scraped the bottom of the temptation barrel." "In all points tempted like as we are, yet without sin," and the very same Power which enabled my Lord to overcome is available to me! Of course, Jesus could have yielded. It would have been no temptation if He could not. It was the *humanity* of Jesus that was tempted. The man of Galilee was the Victor.

Temptations follow high resolutions. It was immediately following the baptism of Jesus, when the heavens were opened, the Spirit descended, and the Father claimed Him as Son, that Jesus entered into the wilderness temptation. There are some vital lessons to be learned in this account of the temptation of our Lord. First, note that Jesus was led of the Spirit, to be tempted of the devil; the Spirit did the leading; the devil did the tempting. Lutzer again reminds us: "God does not shield us from circumstances that provoke us to sin. Remember it was the Holy Spirit who led Christ into the wilderness to be tempted of the devil."[2]

To overcome every temptation our Example quoted from the Book which was given by the inspiration of the Holy Spirit. And when the victory was won, He returned "in the power of the Spirit." Beautiful! Led of the Spirit—overcoming by the Spirit—returning in the power of the Spirit. Would that we could always walk in His steps through our encounters with temptation. Could this be what Paul has in mind when he admonishes, "Walk by the Spirit, and ye shall not fulfill the lusts of the flesh" (Gal. 5:16), and when

---

2. Lutzer, *op. cit.*, p. 14.

he reminds the saints at Rome, "If by the Spirit ye put to death the deeds of the body, ye shall live" (Rom. 8:13).

6. Find victory in Jesus.

How vital it is that we believe that we can be overcomers: that "sin shall not have dominion over you" (Rom. 6:14). What assurance is to be found in I Corinthians 10:13: "There hath no temptation taken you but such as man can bear: but God is faithful, who will not suffer you to be tempted above that ye are able; but will with the temptation make also the way of escape, that ye may be able to endure it." Rest assured that God will always provide a light through every one of your tunnels, and whenever He sees best to send you on a rough path He will provide sturdy shoes!

Meet temptation with prayer. On that dark night in the garden, the suffering Savior admonished sleeping disciples, "Watch and pray, that ye enter not into temptation." It is not easy to pray when temptation beckons, but when it is hardest to pray we need pray the hardest. You have not utilized all of the artillery which God has given you until you have persevered in prayer.

Rely upon that divine power which He Who is Truth Incarnate promised, "I will in no wise fail thee, neither will I in any wise forsake thee" (Heb. 13:5). Utilize that divine and changeless power which is available to aid you in overcoming. He is faithful. In the immortal words of Ashley S. Johnson, "You may tremble on the rock, but you can't get the rock to tremble under you." What assurance and strength and confidence comes when we at last realize that "greater is he that is in you than he that is in the world" (I John 4:4). John is saying, "When the devil rings the doorbell, let Christ answer the door."

189

Is the temptation so strong that you have convinced yourself that you cannot be victor? Consider well the sixth chapter of I Corinthians, where Paul inscribes that sordid list of those who shall not inherit the kingdom of God: fornicators, idolaters, adulterers, effeminate, abusers of themselves with men, thieves, covetous, drunkards, revilers, extortioners. The apostle then reminds them, "And such were some of you: but ye were washed, but ye were sanctified, but ye were justified in the name of our Lord Jesus Christ, and in the Spirit of our God" (I Cor. 6:9-11). If these tempted ones in the surroundings of corrupt Corinth could win the victory, so can you. Trust Him! You can't say "no" to temptation unless you say "yes" to God.

"But thanks be unto God, who always leadeth us in triumph in Christ" (II Cor. 2:14). Our victory is found in the conquering Christ. Never forget that "the Lord knoweth how to deliver the godly out of temptation" (II Peter 2:9).

The king of Syria was in a tizzy. He was warring against Israel, and wherever his soldiers pitched camp the Israelites were warned and avoided the Syrians. Talk about a frustrated king! Surely there had to be a spy in the camp. But one of the servants solved the mystery: the problem wasn't a spy, but that God had a prophet in Israel who sent the warning to save the people of God.

The Syrian king wasn't accustomed to being check-mated by anyone, so he sent to Dothan a great host, with their horses and chariots, to capture one solitary man.

The following morning, when Elisha's servant looked out from the city wall, he saw the host, with horses and chariots, round about the city. Overwhelmed with fear and anxiety, he ran to his master, crying out, "Alas, my master! how shall we do?"

190

God's man calmly replied to the terrified servant, "Fear not; for they that are with us are more than they that are with them. And Elisha prayed, and said, Jehovah, I pray thee, open his eyes that he may see. And Jehovah opened the eyes of the young man; and he saw; and behold, the mountain was full of horses and chariots of fire round about Elisha" (II Kings 6:8-17).

When the devil assembles his troops for the attack, may your eyes be opened to see the protecting forces at your disposal, and may He help you to hear that voice which rings like a clarion call to the besieged of all ages: "They that are with us are more than they that are with them!"

The story is told of a pilgrim who found, one dark night, that he must cross a rugged mountain. The way was dark; the mountain was steep; the trail was dim; he had no light, but go he must, so, with some foreboding, he set out on his journey. He was congratulating himself on his progress when suddenly he stumbled in a patch of shale rock and began to slide rapidly down the mountainside. Suddenly he felt his body slipping over a precipice. In desperation he clutched a clump of brush and endeavored to pull himself back to safety. It was to no avail. He struggled and called out in vain and, finally, unable to hold on longer, he loosed his hold and dropped—six inches to the ground below! What a parable of life. We struggle; we cry aloud; we strive through our own power—but, just beneath, are the everlasting arms.

"We are more than conquerors through him that loved us" (Rom. 8:37). The victory is in Him. Learn to say "no" through Him. Spurgeon, the prince of pulpiteers, admonished, "Learn to say 'no'; it will be of more use to you than to be able to read Latin."

Among the ancient myths is that of the islands of the sirens. According to this myth, Ulysses requests his seamen to bind him to the mast so that he can resist the songs of the sirens as his ship passes their island. It is said that the Argonauts, when nearing the island, asked Orpheus to play on his harp to counteract the sirens' song. If we are but bound to the mast of God, and enthralled by the music of the heavenly choir, we can safely pass the island of temptation.

7. Thank God for temptation.

What a difficult assignment! How can we thank God for that which is so undesirable, so depressing, and so enervating? Remembering that Christianity is the one way of life which throws nothing away, we should strive to welcome temptations and use them as stepping stones rather than stumblingblocks. An opportunist has been defined as a person who, when he finds himself in hot water, decides to take a bath. Temptations, when overcome, can be used to build a character which stands firm in the time of storm and stress. It is altogether possible to find ourselves during temptation, as well as finding the power to overcome.

The story is told of a small boy who was leading his little sister up a mountain pathway. The little one complained, "This isn't a good path. It is too rocky and bumpy." The older and wiser brother replied, "Sure it's rocky and bumpy, but those bumps are the steps that you climb on." Thank God for the temptation—and for the opportunities it presents to your life.

Then, if all of this be true, should we pray that temptation be removed from us? Character is not developed in a vacuum.

192

It is through meeting and overcoming that Christian character is built. Is not the better prayer to ask for grace and power to be an overcomer?

And What Then?

The strong man of Israel was young Samson. He was a physical giant when "the Spirit of Jehovah came mightily upon him." Samson was going courting when he was attacked by a hungry young lion, and he slew the beast with his bare hands. As he was again going to Timnah, to take his new bride, he turned aside to see the carcass of the lion; and, behold, there was a swarm of bees in the body of the lion, and honey—and how Samson liked honey! He gathered some of the honey in his hands and went happily on his way, eating as he went. It is only when the lion is slain that we discover the honey! (Judg. 14:1-9).

What was it that followed Jesus' wilderness victory over temptation? "The devil leaveth him; and behold angels came and ministered unto him" (Matt. 4:11). What a thrill to experience the flush of victory: the joy, the strength, and the assurance when the temptation is overcome. God, grant us the victory which brings the ministration of your angels!

But, best of all, is the eternal reward that awaits the victor: "Blessed is the man that endureth temptation; for when he hath been approved, he shall receive the crown of life" (James 1:12).

. . . But When You Fail

No, you will not always be the victor. You will never reach that hallowed ground in your Christian experience where you are totally immune to temptation. When you slip back from the proud progress which you thought you were attaining, and you again succumb to the wiles of the tempter, don't be a quitter. Don't permit the devil to mock you to discouragement, for sins multiply in the soil of discouragement.

When temptations come, and when you fail, stand back and take the long look. Remember that you can't determine what direction a river is flowing by watching the eddies. Perhaps your failure was just a small eddy in that broad river of life, and you may rejoin the main current which flows irresistibly along to the sea. Maybe the devil won a battle, but you haven't necessarily lost the war.

Temptations come; temptations go, and we face them one at a time. An elderly minister declared that his favorite Bible verse was "and it came to pass." Temptations, too, will pass, and when you have met them squarely, and have overcome with God, you are a stronger saint.

. . .And Again . . . And Again . . . And Again . . .

Are you discouraged, fellow pilgrim, over having fallen so often to temptation? We have all experienced victory, only to, in spite of our high and holy resolutions, again yield to that overwhelming temptation. And, with the yielding, there has come discouragement and despair, and we cry out, "Will God continue to forgive, again and again, or has He given up on me?" No more agonizing cry than this can fall from the lips of a defeated child of God.

Peter was bothered about forgiving the brother who sinned against him. Doubtless he thought he was being overly generous when he inquired of Jesus if he should forgive the

194

erring one as many as seven times. The Master must have looked deeply into Peter's eyes as he replied, "Not until seven times, but until seventy times seven." Surely our compassionate God would do no less. Tempted friend, don't loosen your grasp on I John 1:9: "If we confess our sins, he is faithful and righteous to forgive us our sin, and to cleanse us from all unrighteousness."

True, there is a sense in which we are denied a new beginning. Lost virginity can never be reclaimed. There are broken homes which have reached the place where they can not be put back together. Health which has been ruined by gluttony, sloth, and/or drugs may not be fully recovered. But, wherever you are, make a new start with God. He is able. Learn to pray, "Lead us not into temptation, but *deliver us from evil*," and you will some day lift your voice in the victor's doxology, "For thine is the kingdom, and the power, and the glory, for ever. Amen."

Chapter Eleven

A WALK THROUGH THE VALLEY

1. God is my shephearde therefore I can lack nothyng: he wyll cause me to repose myselfe in pasture full of grasse and he wyll leade me vnto calme waters.

2. He wyll conuert my soule; he wyll bring me foorth into the pathes of righteousnesse for his names sake.

3. Yea though I walke through the valley of the shadowe of death I wyll fear no euvll: for thou art with me, thy rodde and thy staffe be the thynges that do comfort me.

4. Thou wylt prepare a table before me in the presence of myne aduersaries; thou has anoynted my head with oyle and my cup shal be brymme ful.

5. Truly felicitie and mercy shal folowe me all the dayes of my lyfe: and I wyll dwell in the house of God for a long tyme.

— Bishops' Bible, 1568.

Every individual who has so much as a "speaking acquaintance" with the Bible has a favorite passage of Scripture. You who read these words will think immediately of that portion of Scripture which is peculiarly "yours." Perhaps it is a verse which you learned to lisp at mother's knee. Perhaps it is a passage which you memorized as a child in a Bible School class. Perhaps it is a portion which you found later in life—words to which you were led in a time of abounding joy, overwhelming grief, or difficult decision. Irregardless of the circumstances of discovery, you have a Scripture which speaks to you as does none other.

There are two passages from the Bible which are world favorites: one from the Old Testament, and one from the New. The best known and most beloved New Testament verse is John 3:16, the "Golden Text" of the Bible. The favored portion of the Old Testament is the twenty-third

Psalm. More people can quote this from memory than any other Bible chapter. It is more frequently requested for funeral services than any other passage. More tears have been dried, more aching hearts relieved, and more fears dissipated by this song than by any other.

The Psalms were written to be sung. They comprise the hymn book of the Old Testament. Here can be found songs which are appropriate for all times and all occasions. Many of the Psalms are from the pen of David, the "sweet singer of Israel," the shepherd boy who came to be king.

It is possible that David composed the twenty-third Psalm while he was just a lad, leading his sheep over the hills and through the valleys to the green pastures. I rather think not. The words of this Psalm seem to come from the heart of one who has lived long, thought much, and suffered deeply. They have the ring of one whose heart has been mellowed by passing years; one whose faith has been strengthened by prolonged testing; one who has greatly sinned and has been greatly forgiven. Maclaren amplifies this premise beautifully:

> A young man would not write so calmly, and a life which was just opening would not afford material for such a record of God's guardianship in all changing circumstances. If we think of this psalm as the work of David's later years, is it not very beautiful to see the old king looking back with such vivid and loving remembrances to his childhood's occupation, and bringing up again to memory in his palace the green valleys, the gentle streams, the dark glens where he had led his flocks in the old days; very beautiful to see him traveling all the stormy years of warfare and rebellion, of crime and sorrow, which lay between, and finding in all God's guardian presence and gracious guidance![1]

1. A. Maclaren, *A Homiletic Commentary on the Book of Psalms*, by W. L. Watkingson (New York and London: Funk & Wagnalls Company), p. 111.

The aging king is in his palace, his once strong body now bowed, his once beautiful face now lined and scarred, his once raven locks now white as snow; and he is engaged in visiting his yesterdays. Looking back down that long, rough road which he has traveled, he sees again the hills and valleys and streams of his youth. He thinks of those carefree days in which he had proudly and faithfully led his sheep to pasture and had been their protector. He even remembers some of their names and their peculiarities. There were some which were his particular pets. There were some which were stubborn and unruly. There were some which were always getting into trouble and were in need of constant attention. And as the king mused, and walked in memory among his sheep, he thought, "How like sheep is mankind."

One of the most helpless of animals is the sheep. The Creator never equipped him with claws, of fangs, or swift legs to carry him from danger. The sheep is unpredictable; he is prone to stray purposelessly away. The sheep is easily led, and not always into the best paths. The sheep is frequently entangled in the briars and needs to be rescued.

David thinks of the sheep—and then comes the realization: "I am so much like that. I, too, am a sheep—but all along the pathway of life, I have had a Shepherd."

Jehovah Is My Shepherd

What a wonderful discovery—the Shepherding God! A shepherd is literally "one who feeds." The shepherd is the provider, protector, companion, and guide. And the aging king declares, "Jehovah *is* my shepherd." On what a beautiful note of confidence he introduces his song.

198

But how wonderful the word which follows. One of the most meaningful words in all the song is the monosyllable, *my*: "my shepherd." How right Luther was when he observed that experiential religion is in the personal pronouns. It would have been a wonderful discovery had the psalmist found that the Lord was *a* shepherd, but how far more wonderful to discover that He is *my* shepherd. The new mother looks upon the child of another and remarks, "You have a beautiful baby." How different the tone when she cradles her own little one in her arms and lovingly murmurs, "This is *my* baby." The significance of the Christian faith is to be found in the personal pronouns.

With Jehovah as my shepherd, I shall not want, or, as the New International Version translates it, "The Lord is my shepherd, I shall lack nothing." The remainder of the song exults in all of those things which the Shepherd provides. The sheep want for nothing.

He Maketh Me to Lie Down

I am not a "sheep man"; rather, the Lord called me to be a shepherd of souls, but I have observed that sheep will lie down only when their hunger and thirst is satisfied and when they feel secure. It is after the good shepherd has led his flock to adequate pasture and to the place of watering and has made provision for the protection of his charges that the sheep lie down in contentment. It was some one thousand years later that the Good Shepherd declared, "He that cometh to me shall not hunger, and he that believeth in me shall never thirst" (John 6:36).

Note well that there are times when the all-wise Shepherd *makes* us to lie down. The last sermon that James Earl Ladd

199

ever preached was on the topic, "Green Pastures and Still Waters." In this moving message he tells of an experience of William Evans in Palestine. Mr. Evans had gone with a shepherd to feed a lone sheep. As the sheep was being hand-fed, he noticed that there was a splint on the sheep's leg.

Mr. Evans said, "What happened? Did he fall off a cliff, or a rock roll against him, or an animal bite him?"

The shepherd said, "No, I broke his leg."

He said, "You what?"

The shepherd replied, "I broke his leg. That sheep was wayward. That sheep didn't come when I called. That sheep was always leading others astray so I took him and I broke his leg. Now he eats from my hand. When he gets well he will be a better sheep." Oh, do you see it? "He *maketh* me to lie down."[2]

There are times along the pathway of life that we need to lie down. We are walking too fast. We are missing many things in life which we should be enjoying. We are missing opportunities to serve and to enjoy. We hurry heedlessly on our way, not caring for ourselves, for others, or for our Maker, and He puts us on our backs so that we will be caused to look up. There are times that we just need to be still and know that He is God. Vacation time is not necessarily wasted time. Busy as Jesus and His disciples were, He called to them: "Come ye apart, and rest awhile." He *makes* us to lie down.

He selects the most pleasant spot in which to make us lie down—green pastures. Green pastures are not plentiful

---

2. James Earl Ladd, *As Much As In Me Is* (Portland, OR: Beattie and Company, 1951), p. 222ff.

in the wilderness of Judea. A journey across that arid desert gives us a greater appreciation of green pastures and still waters. The wise and loving shepherd leads his sheep out at a very early morning hour. They may graze first on the rougher herbage, then moving to the better grass, and coming finally to the rich grass of the green pasture, where they can graze and rest in security and contentment.

Green pastures—but not always—

> In "pastures green"? Not always; sometimes He
> Who knoweth best, in kindness leadeth me
> In weary ways, where heavy shadows be.
>
> And by "still waters"? No, not always so;
> Oftimes the heavy tempests round me blow,
> And o'er my soul the waves and billows go.
>
> But when the storm beats loudest, and I cry
> Aloud for help, the Master standeth by,
> And whispers to my soul, "Lo, it is I."
>
> So, where He leads me, I can safely go,
> And in the blest hereafter I shall know
> Why, in His wisdom, He hath led me so.

No, not always in pastures green, but the important thing is not the location of the pasture. The important thing is to follow the Shepherd; He knows the way.

He Leadeth Me

The good shepherd leads his sheep; he does not drive them. One of the unforgettable scenes as you drive through the Holy Land is to observe one of the many flocks of sheep on a desolate hillside, apparently alone and unattended. But not so: there on a rock stands the shepherd, often just

201

a little boy or girl, keeping a close watch over the sheep. When the shepherd determines that it is time to move to other pastures, or to start homeward, he starts out, calling the sheep, and the sheep follow, for they know the voice of their shepherd.

> Like a shepherd, tender, true,
> Jesus leads, Jesus leads,
> Daily finds us pastures new,
> Jesus leads, Jesus leads;
> If thick mists are o'er the way,
> Or the flock 'mid danger feeds,
> He will watch them lest they stray,
> Jesus leads, Jesus leads.
>
> All along life's rugged road,
> Jesus leads, Jesus leads,
> Till we reach yon blest abode,
> Jesus leads, Jesus leads;
> All the way, before, He's trod,
> And He now the flock precedes,
> Safe into the folds of God
> Jesus leads, Jesus leads.[3]

Let Jesus lead; He knows the way.

"He leadeth me beside still waters." Why *still* waters? Only here will the sheep drink. There are many springs on the hillsides of the Holy Land. The water from these springs may rush a short distance down the hillsides and then disappear into the thirsty soil. No matter how thirsty the sheep, they will not drink from these gurgling streams. Their thirst is slaked only when they find a quiet pool; perhaps it is a small basin which has been hollowed out by the hand of the wise and loving shepherd. The actual meaning of "still

---

3. John R. Clements, "Jesus Leads."

waters" in the Hebrew language is "waters of rest." The Good Shepherd knows how to lead us to the quiet waters of peace and contentment. It is for the good of the sheep to follow His leading.

He Restoreth My Soul

How frequently the sheep are in need of restoration: when wandering, when sick, or when in trouble. As David speaks of the restoring God, he is speaking out of his own experience. Perhaps he is looking back to the blackest hour of his life: that dark hour when he forgot the merciful God Who had brought him to the throne, and became guilty of the base sins of lust and adultery and hypocrisy and cold-blooded murder. Yet God never gave up on David. He kept seeking him until He found him and brought him back in line to become ancestor to His Messiah. What wonderful assurance to know that when we stray, and need the healing touch of the Good Shepherd, that we have a seeking and a finding God.

> But none of the ransomed ever knew
> How deep were the waters crossed;
> Nor how dark was the night that the Lord passed thro'
> Ere He found His sheep that was lost.
> Out in the desert He heard its cry—
> Sick and helpless, and ready to die;
> Sick and helpless, and ready to die.
>
> But all thro' the mountains, thunder riv'n,
> And up from the rocky steep,
> There arose a glad cry to the gate of heav'n,
> "Rejoice! I have found my sheep!"
> And the angels echoed around the throne,
> "Rejoice, for the Lord brings back His own!
> Rejoice, for the Lord brings back His own."[4]

---

4. Elizabeth C. Celphane, "The Ninety and Nine."

C. H. Spurgeon, the "Prince of Preachers," wrote extensively, and in depth, on the meaning of the Psalms. In his comments on this Shepherd Psalm, he remarks as follows concerning the Restoring God:

> When the soul grows sorrowful, He revives it; when it is sinful, He sanctifies it; when it is weak, He strengthens it. *He* does it. His ministers could not do it if He did not. His Word would not avail by itself. "He restoreth my soul." Are any of us low in grace? Do we feel that our spirituality is at its lowest ebb? He Who turns the ebb into the flood can restore our soul. Pray to Him, then, for the blessing— "Restore Thou me, Thou Shepherd of my soul!"[5]

He Guideth Me

Rest and refreshment are not an end in themselves, but a means to a greater end. The Way of the Shepherd is not only a fold to lie down in, but a Way to walk in. The trail goes on, and how difficult for the sheep to know the way to take if there is no guide. How often we stand bewildered at the forks of the road, not knowing which way to take, longing to hear that Voice which calls out, "This is the way, walk ye in it."

Countless souls have found satisfying direction by following the instructions which are so clearly given in Proverbs 3:5-6: "Trust in Jehovah with all thy heart, and lean not upon thine own understanding: In all thy ways acknowledge him, and he will direct thy paths."

His paths are the right paths: "He guideth me in paths of righteousness," but it is not for our sake alone, but "for

---

5. C. H. Spurgeon, *Treasury of David*, condensed by David Otis Fuller (Grand Rapids, Michigan: Zondervan Publishing House, 1940), p. 109.

his name's sake." When we follow in the right paths the Shepherd's name is glorified. When you stand bewildered at the crossroads, follow the guidance of the Good Shepherd; He knows the way which you should take.

James Earl Ladd relates a meaningful story of the reason for the Shepherd's guidance. A man had lost a child and, in bitterness of soul, was traveling around the world in a futile effort to forget. In Palestine he found the answer to his quest. A shepherd was endeavoring to lead his sheep across the Jordan, but they refused to enter the water. Suddenly, he splashed through the water, picked up a lamb, and carried it across the river. At the bleating of the frightened lamb, the old ewe, the mother of the lamb, forgot her fear of water as she dashed through the river to be with her baby, and all of the other sheep followed. As the one who had lost his child witnessed the scene, he dropped to his knees by the Jordan river and cried out, "Father, I thank you that I see it now. You took the lamb that I might follow through the waters of the Jordan and be in Thy presence."[6]

Walking Through the Valley

We have come now to the keystone of this beautiful Psalm. "Yea, though I walk through the valley of the shadow of death, I will fear no evil." Here every word is fraught with meaning.

"Walk": The sheep do not run, as if alarmed, nor draw back, as if in fear: they just go calmly on, following the leading of the shepherd.

---

6. James Earl Ladd, *op. cit.*, p. 223.

And it is *through* the valley, not *in* the valley. The trail comes out on the other side.

No, it is not even the valley of death, but the valley of the *shadow* of death. Who is afraid of shadows? What could be more pleasant than to lie in the shadows, beside still waters, on a hot summer day? How we need to remember that wherever there are shadows, somewhere there must be sunshine. Look for it.

There is a sense in which death has been removed. It is only the shadow which remains. The One Who blazed the trail "abolished death, and brought life and immortality to light through the gospel" (II Tim. 1:10).

> Death be not proud
> though some have called thee
> mighty and dreadful
> for thou art not so.
> For those whom thou thinkest
> thou dost overthrow
> die not, poor death,
> nor yet canst thou kill me . . .
> One short sleep past
> we wake eternally
> and death shall be no more.
> Death, thou shalt die.
>
> *— John Donne.*

Shadows may be a place of refreshment, of contemplation, and of beauty. Some of God's most beautiful plants and flowers grow in the shade. Perhaps it will be in the shadows that you will find *Him.*

> Standing somewhere in the shadows, you'll find Jesus;
> He's the One Who always cares and understands.
> Standing somewhere in the shadows, you will find Him,
> And you'll know Him by the nail-prints in His hands.

206

"Death": He who has never contemplated the problem of death has never contemplated life very deeply. And why should we shrink back from speaking of death, when it is an integral part of life? It is said that Louis XV, of France, forbade anyone to mention death in his presence. Pascal, the French monk, once remarked that we spend our lives trying to take our minds off death. Yet death will lay its unrelenting hand upon us all. We are all "terminal"; it is just a matter of when. "It is appointed unto men once to die" (Heb. 9:27). There is nothing more certain about life than death. Kierkegaard said it dramatically: "There comes a midnight hour when all men must unmask."

There is an ancient legend of a merchant in Bagdad who sent his servant to the marketplace. The servant soon returned, pale and trembling. He told his master that in the marketplace he had been jostled by a woman whose name was Death. She had looked at him and had made a threatening gesture. The servant begged his master to loan him his horse, that he might ride to Samarra and hide where Death could not find him. After the servant had fled, the merchant saw Death in the crowd and inquired as to why she had made a threatening gesture toward his servant. "It was not a threatening gesture," Death explained. "It was a gesture of surprise. I had not expected to see him in Bagdad, for tonight I have an appointment with him in Samarra."

It is appointed unto all to pass through this sacred valley. There are some who pass through in tears and gloom. There are others who, passing through the valley, transform it into a place of light and joy. The Psalmist speaks again of those who "Passing through the valley of weeping they make it a place of springs" (Psalm 84:6). Blessed are those who leave springs in the valley.

As we travel through life's shadowed valley,
Fresh springs of His love ever rise;
And we learn that our sorrows and losses
Are blessings just sent in disguise.

(From *Streams in the Desert*)

I am thinking this morning of Anna Rose Morgan. Anna Rose and I were college schoolmates many years ago. She was a brilliant girl, a free spirit innovative in thought, speech, and action. With her keen mind, leadership ability, and dedication to the Lord, it was most natural that she should become a minister's wife, teacher, and author. She has served faithfully for many years with her husband, Newell. They have traveled extensively, and have ministered with distinction.

It was the day before Thanksgiving, 1978, that Anna Rose underwent double surgery. The report included the dread word, "malignant." The surgeon was confident that all of the cancer had been removed, but recommended radiation. In the following month, a series of twenty-seven radiation treatments was begun. Approximately one year from the first surgery, it was necessary to have another operation, due to over-radiation. At this time, twenty-five inches of intestine were removed.

Prior to her radiation treatments, Anna Rose was told by her oncologist that she would be subject to diarrhea for about one year. That was more than five years ago, and the prognosis is that the present extreme situation will continue indefinitely.

Following the first surgery, radiation, and side effects, Anna Rose thought deeply on the issues of life and death, and summarized her thoughts in a book entitled, *The*

208

A,B,Cs of My Dying. This beautiful little book contains twenty-six chapters, each chapter headed by a meaningful word, these words beginning with each letter of the alphabet.

Chapter one of *The A,B,Cs of My Dying* is entitled "Attitude." In her meditation she gives this beautiful testimony:

> As I contemplate death, I must have the right attitude toward it. The attitude I have toward death will color all my thinking. More than that, I must have the right attitude toward my own death. It would not do for me to have one attitude toward death in general, and another attitude toward my own death in particular. I must accept the fact of death as a part of my life. The right attitude will cause me to say to myself, "Some day I am going to die, but that is all right; because my death will only come when God is ready for me to experience it." God has a plan for my life: "A time to be born, and a time to die" (Eccl. 3:2). That attitude will help me to accept the fact that some day my physical life shall cease here, and my soul will live on with God. I must unfailingly maintain this positive feeling toward myself and toward my death. If I would keep from being moody about death, I must have the proper mood about death—and that is accepting it as a fact of life in my life. That comes from the right attitude.[7]

After her condition became somewhat stabilized, and Anna Rose realized that the Lord was loaning her added days of life, she wrote a second volume entitled *Until That Day.* This, too, contains twenty-six chapters, and it is addressed to the "A,B,Cs of her living." To me, the highlight of Volume Two is in the chapter, "Knit Together." Here she reminisces of the three times that she underwent spinal fusion, and relates this to her present condition.

---

7. Anna Rose Morgan, *The A,B,Cs of My Dying* (Bend, OR: Maverick Publications, 1980), p. 1.

The memory of this experience has helped me out in my effort to adjust to the after effects of the cancer radiation treatments. I know that I resented the GAB ("green apple bellyache." Translation by author) that was (and still is) a daily occurrence. I know that I resented the very rigid diet forced upon me. I also knew that I had to get rid of all that resentment before I could be spiritually or physically whole again. What I needed was a spiritual fusion. Instead of asking God for the diarrhea and GAB to stop, the restrictions on the diet to be lifted, I began to pray that God would help me to grow back together again, spiritually. Truly, in Him, everything can be held together! When I coupled that prayer with "Help me to live above the problem," I had an inner acceptance and peace that I really needed. My spirit began to mend. I was, and still am, being knit together by His love. Because in Him is life. A true fusion with Him is a live fusion that holds![8]

When we can pray from our heart of hearts, "Lord, help me to live above the problem," we are on our way to Victory!

If it ever seems dark in the valley, just remember that the sunrise always follows even the darkest night.

> . . . another day
> Shall chase the bitter dark away;
> That though our eyes with tears be wet;
> The sunrise never failed us yet.
>
> The blush of dawn may yet restore
> Our light and hope and joy once more.
> Sad soul, take comfort, nor forget
> That sunrise never failed us yet.
>
> — *Celia Thaxter.*

---

8. Anna Rose Morgan, *Until That Day* (Bend, OR: Maverick Publications, 1982), p. 32.

"I will fear no evil." Notice that he does not say that we will encounter no evil as we walk the valley, but that we need *fear* no evil. To avoid all evil it would be necessary to avoid life. With the Lord as our Shepherd, what is there to fear?

Companionship in the Valley

Why is it that the sheep fear no evil while they walk that lonesome valley? "For thou art with me." Perhaps there are times as we walk that valley that we feel much alone and we cry out, "Is anyone there?" Those are the times we need to listen carefully for the voice of the Good Shepherd: "I am with thee."

Perhaps our most beautiful folk music is the negro spiritual. Born out of hardship, loneliness and suffering, those wistful, haunting melodies have come to be our American heritage. Many of the spirituals speak beautifully of heaven. Out of deep affliction, these black brothers and sisters looked beyond this life to a place of rest and peace. One of the most beautiful is "The Lonesome Valley." The song declares that "You must walk that lonesome valley - You've got to walk it by yourself." It is a beautiful song, but only partially true, for there is One Who walks the valley with us: "Thou art with me."

If the valley ever seems dark, wouldn't you rather walk in the dark with God than to walk alone in the light?

There is a bond, a closeness, between the oriental shepherd and his sheep which is unknown elsewhere. The National Wool Grower Magazine for December, 1949, carried the beautiful and informative story of the Basque Sheepherder and the Shepherd Psalm. James Wallace tells of spending

211

a night under the Nevada stars with an old Basque sheep-herder named Ferando D'Alfonso. As they were preparing to curl up in their blankets for the night, the old man began to speak in a jargon of Greek and Basque. When Williams inquired as to what he had said, the shepherd quoted the 23rd Psalm in English, and pointed out how its daily repetition fills the sheepherders with reverence for his calling.

As the two men sat there that night beside a sparkling pool of water, the sheep securely bedded down, the old shepherd spoke of the relationship of shepherd and sheep in the Holy Land. He told how each sheep takes his place in the grazing line and keeps that place throughout the day, with one exception. Once during the day, each sheep leaves its place in the line and goes to the shepherd. The shepherd gently rubs the sheep's nose and ears, scratches its chin, and talks quietly to it. After a few minutes of this intimate communion, the sheep returns contentedly to its place in the grazing line. How meaningful the phrase, "For thou art with me"—That is companionship in the valley.

Comfort in the Valley

There are those times, even when walking by waters of peace, that the sheep need comfort. Dangers are ever present. There is always the danger of being swept away by flash floods, carried away by thieves, or being torn by the wolves or the wild dogs which lurk in the shadows of the valley. Although there is that which may frighten or injure, the sheep are comforted by the knowledge of the shepherd's ability with his tools—the rod and the staff. Through years of experience, the shepherd has become skilled in throwing his staff, and he uses it to defend his sheep against attack by animals.

212

As D'Alfonso continued his story, he pointed out to Wallace that there is an actual Valley of the Shadow of Death in Palestine. It lies south of the Jericho road, which leads from Jerusalem to the Dead Sea. The valley is four and one-half miles long and, in places, its walls are 1,500 feet high, but the bottom of the valley may be only 10 or 12 feet wide. It is a dangerous valley to travel, for the floor is uneven, cut by gullies which are seven or eight feet deep.

About halfway through the valley the path crosses from one side to the other at a place where the path is cut by an eight-foot gully. The sheep must leap the gully or be assisted by the shepherd. If a sheep falls into the ditch, the shepherd uses the rod, which is an old-style crook, to reach down and lift the sheep to solid ground. Thus the sheep have learned to fear no evil, even in the Valley of the Shadow of Death, for the shepherd is there to help and protect, and the sheep have learned to trust him.

But how about those of us who remain in the green pastures when loved ones have already walked through the valley and have entered the fold? We grieve. We would not be normal if we did not. We sorrow not for the departed, but for ourselves and the great empty space in our own lives. How truly it has been said that "grief is the other side of the coin of love," and the more deeply we have loved, the deeper will be the grief. In our sorrow, where shall we look for comfort?

Comfort is found in the loving Father: "As one whom his mother comforteth, so will I comfort you" (Isa. 66:13).

Comfort is found in memory: "Death cannot destroy a mother's prayer, a father's counsel, a sister's entreaty, a brother's sympathy, a child's love."

Comfort is found in the healing balm of time: "As thy days, so shall thy strength be" (Deut. 33:25).

213

> Time, like an ever-rolling stream,
> Bears all our grief away.

Comfort is found in friends: "Whether one member suffereth, all the members suffer with it (I Cor. 12:26).

Comfort is found in Jesus: "I will not leave you desolate: I come unto you" (John 14:18).

> What a friend we have in Jesus,
> All our sins *and griefs* to bear!

Comfort is found in the Holy Spirit: "I will pray the Father, and he shall give you another Comforter" (John 14:16).

Comfort is found in the Bible: "through comfort of the scriptures we might have hope" (Rom. 15:4).

Comfort is found in the assurance that love can never lose its own.

> Yet love will dream, and faith will trust
>   (Since He who knows our need is just),
> That somehow, somewhere, meet we must.
>   Alas for him who never sees
> The stars shine through his cyprus-trees!
>   Who, hopeless, lays his dead away,
> Nor looks to see the breaking day
>   Across the mournful marbles play!
> Who hath not learned, in hours of faith,
>   The truth to flesh and sense unknown,
> That life is ever lord of death,
>   And love can never lose its own![9]

Refreshment in the Valley

There are many commentators who are of the opinion that at this point in the Shepherd Psalm the figure changes

---

9. John G. Whittier, "Love Can Never Lose Its Own."

from shepherd and sheep to host and guest: "Thou pre-arest a table before me in the presence of mine enemies." But is this necessarily so? Is it not reasonable that the Psalmist should carry the beautiful figure of shepherd and sheep throughout his song? This was the opinion of the old Basque shepherd. He pointed out that in the Holy Land there are many poisonous plants which may be fatal to the sheep, and that every spring the shepherd takes his mattock and grubs out every such plant that he can find, thus preparing the table for his sheep.

The table is not prepared in some secure fold, but it is "in the presence of mine enemies." He does not say that we will have no enemies; we would not be like our Lord if we had none. It is in the presence of our enemies that the table is spread.

The banquet fare may not be elaborate, but it is ample, and the Shepherd is there. "What, all this, and Jesus too!" cried out a poor cottager as she broke a piece of bread and filled a glass with cold water.

Healing in the Valley

"Thou anointest my head with oil." As D'Alfonso sat by his sheep that night, beneath the sparkling Nevada stars, and shared his understanding of the Shepherd Psalm, he declared that by the entry to every sheepfold there is an earthen bowl of olive oil and a large jar of cold water. The shepherd lays his rod above the gateway. As each sheep enters the fold, the shepherd quickly examines it for any injuries. If problems are found, the shepherd drops his rod upon the sheep's back, and it steps out of line.

The sheep's wound is cleansed carefully, then the shep-herd dips his hand into the bowl and anoints the wound with the olive oil. A large cup is then dipped into the jar of water

215

and is brought out overflowing. The sheep can then sink its nose into the refreshing water and drink until contented.

Our Good Shepherd has a water supply sufficient to fill every cup to overflowing: "My cup runneth over," or, as the Bishop's Bible of 1568 translates it, "My cup shal be brymme ful." There is a popular song which petitions, "Fill my cup, Lord; I lift it up Lord . . ." His supply is ample, but we must be careful that the cup which we bring for Him to fill is not dirty or broken. The run-off from our cup may be a blessing to some other thirsty soul.

Attendants in the Valley

"Surely goodness and lovingkindness shall follow me all the days of my life." We have already noted that we have companionship as we walk through the valley: the Shepherd is ever with us. Now the Psalmist thinks of two other friends who will never forsake him: Goodness and Lovingkindness, and how we need these attendants. We need goodness to supply our needs and lovingkindness to forgive our sins.

David never permitted himself to lose sight of the goodness of God. It was a good God Who had led him, protected him, and supplied his every need. The sweet singer of Israel was constantly lifting his praise to his God: "Oh how great is *thy goodness*, which thou hast laid up for them that fear thee" (Psalm 31:19. Italics are the author's).

None knew better than the king the enormity of the sins which he had committed against his Maker, and his consequent need of cleansing. How beautiful and heartsprung his prayer for forgiveness: "Remember not the sins of my youth, nor my transgressions: *according to thy lovingkindness* remember thou me" (Psalm 25:7. Italics are the author's).

216

At the End of the Valley

The sheep are led over varied ways: sometimes through green pastures and by still waters, sometimes over the burning sands of the desert, sometimes along dusty highways, sometimes over rugged mountain passes, sometimes through deep gorges, but they are ever being led to the shepherd's fold.

When the sun is set and day is done, the shepherd does not forsake his sheep, for it is then that the danger is the greatest and they need him the most.

The shepherd carefully admits every sheep to the fold and then, placing his staff well within reach of his hand, he wraps himself in his woolen robe and lies down across the gateway, facing the sheep. No harm can enter, nor can any sheep escape, unless it be over the body of the shepherd.

"And I shall dwell in the house of Jehovah forever.

. . . The years slipped by. The song of the shepherd was never forgotten, but perhaps it had lost some of its significance until that glorious day that a Galilean picked up the refrain: "I am the good shepherd . . . I am the door of the sheep . . . I know mine own and mine own know me . . . I lay down my life for the sheep . . . I go to prepare a place . . ."

* * * * *

Leslie Weatherhead concludes his book on the problem of suffering with this beautiful paragraph of assurance:

So, my friend, be of good cheer! When the long day is over, you will walk in the scented dusk down the last valley; and not alone, for he, the Companion of all men, has

217

pledged his word to be with you. And at the end of that valley, all hushed and quiet, "By velvet darkness folded in," you will see, shining through the trees, the lights of home. One evening the lamps will be lighted for you in the House of New Beginnings. And when you draw near to the house, you will hear music and dancing.[10]

All of us shall take the walk through the valley. May we so know and love and trust the Good Shepherd that we will walk with Him in the pathway that leads us Home.

Let me walk lightly across this last valley,
As one who would hasten to love's rendezvous,
All of life's burdens and shadows behind me,
Ahead of me, everything lovely and new!

Let me walk swiftly across this last valley,
Should footsteps be laggard and fearful and slow
Which carry me finally into His presence
Who loves me, and knows all the way that I go?

Let me walk joyfully through this last valley,
Knowing there waits at the end of the road,
That blest One who sought me, lifted me, bought me,
My precious Redeemer, the dear Son of God!

Let me walk softly across this last valley,
Silently, wonder is wakening here,
Hushing my heart in the presence of glory,
Preparing my soul as the moment draws near.[11]

---

10. Leslie D. Weatherhad, *op. cit.*, p. 224.
11. Martha Snell Nicholson, "The Last Valley."

Chapter Twelve

THE TRANSFORMED CROSS

In the cross of Christ I glory,
Tow'ring o'er the wrecks of time;
All the light of sacred story
Gathers round its head sublime.

When the woes of life o'ertake me,
Hopes deceive, and fears annoy,
Never shall the cross forsake me:
Lo! it glows with peace and joy.

When the sun of bliss is beaming
Light and love upon my way,
From the cross the radiance streaming
Adds more luster to the day.

Bane and blessing, pain and pleasure,
By the cross are sanctified;
Peace is there that knows no measure,
Joys that thro' all time abide.[1]

If you were to launch a new religion what would you select as your distinctive emblem? Would you choose the gallows, or the noose, or the gas chamber, or the electric chair? Jesus did. This unpredictable Galilaean deliberately chose that which was then universally held as an emblem of suffering and shame and transformed it into the symbol of the religion which He had come to establish.

The horrible penalty of crucifixion was reserved for the vilest of criminals. Runaway slaves were frequently spiked to crosses as a warning to others who might be contemplating escape from their masters. The proud and haughty Romans were known to crucify innocent victims to demonstrate their power over subject peoples and thus terrorize them into continued subjection.

---

1. John Bowring, "In the Cross of Christ."

Our most beloved of hymns speaks eloquently of what the cross meant prior to the crucifixion of our Lord: "On a hill far away stood an old rugged cross, the emblem of suff'ring and shame."[2] The writer of the epistle to the Hebrews points out vividly that Jesus "*endured* the cross, despising *shame*" (Heb. 12:2. Italics are the author's). The most painful and the most shameful death ever devised by sinful humanity was cruel crucifixion. The pain of crucifixion beggars description. The shame of crucifixion was emphasized by the victim being stripped of his clothing and bearing his cross-bar to the place of execution.

How unthinkable that the followers of this lone Galilaean should adopt this emblem of suffering and shame as the logo for their religion. To the best of our knowledge, the first symbol of Christianity was the sign of the fish, but this was soon replaced by the cross.

There is a saying that is common among the Egyptians: "You haven't seen Egypt until you have seen Luxor." How fascinating it is to visit this showcase of ancient Egypt and to cross the Nile to marvel at the Valley of the Kings, but one of the most intriguing experiences to be found in all of this area is to travel a short distance to the north of Luxor and walk through the ruins of ancient Karnak.

Karnak was one of the seven wonders of the ancient world. Here are the ruins of three idol temples which once covered an area of 100 acres. The oldest of these buildings dates from 2300 to 2000 B.C. It is awe-inspiring to walk through the "Forest of Columns," containing 134 lavishly carved columns, 75 feet high and 12 feet in diameter. It is said that 100 men could stand on top of each of these pillars. In all of these thrilling and breath-taking experiences, there

---

2. George Bennard, "The Old Rugged Cross."

is none more fascinating than to visit a room in one of these idol temples which was once used as a place of worship by early Coptic Christians. Here in this room there once stood three idols, side by side, but they are no longer idols. They now stand there in the form of an old rugged cross.

What happened to the idols of ancient Karnak? These early Christians remembered that their Maker had once commanded His people, "Thou shalt have no other gods before me," and "Thou shalt not make unto thee a graven image." In their zeal for their Lord, they laboriously chipped away the idols on either side to make the form of a cross, and it stands there yet today—an eloquent testimony to their faith and dedication. They were willing and anxious to transform idols into a cross!

Crosses adorn our church buildings and the walls of our homes. Crosses are proudly worn by men and women and young people as a testimony to their faith. Crosses are frequently seen on automobile bumpers and recreational vehicles. "Cross services" mark the highlight of Christian youth camps. The cross is no longer an "emblem of suffering and shame"; it has become a symbol of allegiance and service and willing sacrifice and glory. New Testament writers had learned to glory in the cross. Paul wrote to the churches of Galatia, "But far be it from me to glory, save in the cross of our Lord Jesus Christ" (Gal. 6:14). The blind hymn writer exulted, "In the cross, in the cross, Be my glory ever; Till my raptured soul shall find Rest beyond the river."[3]

What happened to the cross? The Son of God transformed it!

---

3. Fanny J. Crosby, "Near the Cross."

Jesus Transformed the Cross

How could this be: that the significance of the cross should be reversed so dramatically? How was this beautiful transformation wrought?

1. By dying on it.

What is possibly the most beautiful and the most informative Scripture as to the condescension of the Son of God is recorded in the second chapter of the Book of Philippians. Here Paul points us to the One Who, existing in the form of God and being on an equality with God, willingly lay aside His glory to come into the darkness of a sin-cursed world, and there become obedient unto the death of the cross (Phil. 2:5-8). The cross was transformed because the Son of God died on it.

2. By dying willingly.

Crucifixion was something to be avoided at any cost but, as Jesus approached the culmination of His life of sacrificial service, "he stedfastly set his face to go to Jerusalem," knowing full well that the trail would lead to the cross. His life was not taken; it was given. Although "He could have called ten thousand angels," He yielded to the mob in Gethsemane, to the scourge in Pilate's Hall, to the thorn-crown in the Praetorium, and to the cross on Calvary. There was transforming power in His willing sacrifice.

3. By dying vicariously.

Jesus was crucified for no crime or sin of His own. The Roman governor before whom He was tried pronounced

222

the verdict, "I find no fault in him." The governor's wife styled Him a "righteous man." The one who had betrayed Him cried out in remorse, "I have sinned in that I have betrayed innocent blood." The accusation which was nailed to the cross above His head read, "Jesus of Nazareth, the king of the Jews."

One who had been a blasphemer and an enemy of the cross was so impressed with the substitutionary death of the Savior that he exclaimed, "Him who knew no sin he made to be sin on our behalf." The vicarious death of Jesus of Nazareth transformed the cross.

4. By dying triumphantly.

After six agonizing hours on the cross, Jesus yielded up His spirit, but the cross did not bring defeat. The great veil of the temple was rent in two; the earth shook; rocks were rent; tombs were opened, and the Roman centurion who was set to watch Him die cried out, "Truly this was the Son of God."

The darkest day in history was surely that passover sabbath. The body of the Galilaean lay in the confines of a cold stone tomb; disciples were cowering behind locked doors; sorrowing women had prepared spices to anoint a dead body. At Calvary sinful men had done their worst, but just three days later God did His best. Earth's saddest day and earth's gladdest day were just three days apart. The dawning of the third day revealed the Victor, and He was declared to be the Son of God by the resurrection from the dead (Rom. 1:4).

What assurance and what delight to know Him "who abolished death, and brought life and immortality to light through the gospel" (II Tim. 1:10). The victorious death of the God-man transformed the cross.

If Any Man Would Be My Disciple

The first half of the ministry of the Nazarene was at an end. He was just entering that dark second half when He withdrew with His disciples into the parts of Caesarea Philippi. It was there that He asked, "Who do men say that the Son of man is?" After listening to their varied answers, He put the question which, for many months, He had been preparing them to answer: "But who say ye that I am?" After all, this is the most important question of all, is it not? It is not what others say about Jesus that really matters, but what do *you* say about Him?

Jesus must have listened breathlessly for their response. Had He gotten through to them? Had He failed them? How would they respond? It was Peter who was entrusted with the heaven-borne answer, "Thou art the Christ, the son of the living God." Jesus pronounced a blessing upon the confessor, declared that on this rock He would build His church, and then began immediately to warn the disciples of His rapidly approaching passion and triumph.

It is at this high point in the ministry of our Lord that He throws down the gauntlet: "If any man would come after me . . . ." The service of Christ must be accepted willingly and gladly. No man becomes a faithful disciple unless he desires this above all else. He does not command your following; He lovingly invites it.

LET HIM DENY HIMSELF. How confused we are as to this call to self-denial. Notice that Jesus does not ask us to deny ourselves certain of life's luxuries in order to follow

224

Him (although, at times, this may ensue). Jesus asks us to deny *ourselves*: self-will, self-love, self-interest, self-sufficiency. Oh, how often the old man Self stands in the way of surrender to the Master's call! Self-denial must be the crucifixion of self. Self-denial means the surrendering of our right to choose anything but the will of Christ. Self-denial implies the renunciation of sin. Self-denial dethrones Satan and enthrones the Savior. How well it has been said that in every man's heart there is a throne and a cross: when self is on the throne, Christ is on the cross, but when self is on the cross, Christ is on the throne. Is this not what Paul meant when he declared, "I have been crucified with Christ; and it is no longer I that live, but Christ liveth in me" (Gal. 2:20)? In your heart, is He crowned—or is He crucified?

Harold Fowler displayed a deep insight as to the meaning of self-denial as he penned this paragraph:

> Self-denial is self stepping down from life's throne, laying crown and scepter at the Master's feet and thenceforth submitting the whole of life to His control. It is living out our life, not to please ourselves, but to please our Lord, not to advance our own personal interests, but to do His work. It is the glad making of any sacrifice that loyalty to Him requires. Self gives way altogether as the motive of life.[4]

One of the finest illustrations of self-denial may be seen in the life of the apostle Paul. Saul of Tarsus was a man of position and authority—possibly a member of the Sanhedrin, the royal court of the Jews. He was a highly educated man, having sat at the feet of Gamaliel, the greatest teacher of his day. Doubtless, he was a man of wealth. Saul of Tarsus knew the meaning of self-sufficiency, self-interest, and self-love, but one noontide, on the Damascus road, he

---

4. Harold Fowler, *The Gospel of Matthew*, Volume Three (Joplin, MO: College Press), p. 566.

heard the call to self-denial, and he surrendered self to the Savior. He recounted it like it was as he wrote to the church at Philippi:

> Howbeit what things were gain to me, these have I counted loss for Christ. Yea verily, and I count all things to be loss for the excellency of the knowledge of Christ Jesus my Lord: for whom I suffered the loss of all things, and do count them but refuse, that I may gain Christ, and be found in him, not having a righteousness of mine own, even that which is of the law, but that which is through faith in Christ, the righteousness which is from God, by faith: that I may know him, and the power of his resurrection, and the fellowship of his sufferings, becoming conformed unto his death, if by any means I may attain unto the resurrection of the dead (Phil. 3:7-11).

AND TAKE UP HIS CROSS. These Galilaeans who heard this ringing call to discipleship recognized immediately the import of Jesus' appeal. They knew altogether too well what it meant to take up a cross. The Jews had been familiar with death by crucifixion since the days of Antiochus Epiphanes. Alexander Jannaeus had crucified 800 Pharisees. Josephus, the Jewish historian, reports the crucifixion of 2,000 Jews who had rebelled against their Roman overlords shortly after the birth of Christ. As they heard that call, "take up the cross," they visualized the customary procedure of the criminal carrying his cross-bar to the place of execution. They recognized His challenge as a call to something which was extremely painful and humiliating.

How lightly, and how mistakenly, we make reference to cross-bearing. Disease and suffering lay their heavy hands upon us; we are called upon to minister day after day to a helpless invalid; we are troubled by a wayward child or an antagonistic spouse—and we declare, "Oh well, that is my cross. I will bear it as best I can." All of these things may be burdens, but they are not crosses. Cross-bearing is not the acceptance of something unavoidable that is laid upon us; it is something that we willingly accept: we take up the cross. Jesus' cross was taken up voluntarily, willingly, and in full awareness of the cost to Himself.

The call "take up thy cross" is heard five times in this same contextual setting (Matt. 16:24; Mark 8:34; Luke 9:23; Matt. 10:38; Luke 14:27). In all of these contexts some kind of denial is demanded: self, family, or one's own life. The cross is not just a beautiful ornament, or symbol, or burden: it is a place of death. When you elect to take up your cross you are ready to die—yet it is a death which leads to life which is life indeed. Is this not what Paul meant when he reminded the brethren in Colossae, "For ye died, and your life is hid with Christ in God" (Col. 3:3)?

The meaning of the cross to the Christian ought be dependent upon the meaning of the cross to Jesus. His cross meant death. Our cross should then be a symbol of death to sin. Paul plead with the saints at Rome that they continue not in sin: "Or are ye ignorant that all we who were baptized into Christ Jesus were baptized into his death? We were buried therefore with him through baptism into death: that like as Christ was raised from the dead through the glory of the Father, so we also might walk in newness of life" (Rom. 6:3-4). Paul never forgot the cross upon which he had been crucified, the watery grave where he had been buried, nor the tomb from which he had arisen.

No man ever carried a cross without suffering. Our Example endured agony beneath the burden of His cross. Bearing our cross identifies us with Jesus. In our cult of comfort and contentment, we are prone to attempt to evade the cross, or to search for a painless cross, yet it costs something to follow Jesus, and the cutting edge of the Master's requirements must never be dulled. In the words of W. S. Lilley, "Every high mission means the cross." If there is to be any blessing, there must be some bleeding. The symbol of the followers of the Nazarene is a cross, not a cushion. We appeal to comfort; Jesus appeals to Calvary. Yes, it costs something to follow Jesus, but the best and most heroic in man will answer the challenge.

AND FOLLOW ME. Having denied self, and taken up our cross, we are ready to follow ("keep on following") the One Who leads the way. Dr. Luke adds a significant word to the Master's summons which indicates that cross-bearing is much more than a one-time activity: *daily* - "let him deny himself, and take up his cross daily, and follow me" (Luke 9:23).

As we shoulder our cross and walk down that dusty road in the footsteps of the Master, we experience a precious bond with the One Who carried the cross for us. We are linked to the crucified Christ on one hand, and to the risen Christ on the other. This means that we bear His cross as well as His yoke. We experience the suffering of the former, as well as the partnership of the latter. He has a right to call for followers. He is our Creator, our Redeemer, our Savior, our King—and He wants to be our Lord.

> "Take up thy cross and follow Me."
> I hear the blessed Savior call;
> How can I make a lesser sacrifice,
> When Jesus gave His all.[5]

Concerning a Grain of Wheat

Immediately following the call to cross-bearing, Jesus points out one of the most important reasons as to why men

---

5. A. H. Ackley, "Take Up Thy Cross."

ought respond to this call: "*For* whosoever would save his life shall lose it: and whosoever shall lose his life for my sake shall find it" (Matt. 16:25. Italics are the author's). Here is the only place where it is possible to gain through losing: We save our lives as we lose them for Christ. Our minds immediately go back to those immortal words of Jim Elliott: "He is no fool who gives that which he cannot keep to gain that which he cannot lose."

It was immediately following Jesus' triumphal entry into Jerusalem that "certain Greeks" came to one of Jesus' disciples, saying, "Sirs, we would see Jesus." Tradition has it that these seeking Greeks were looking for one who was worthy to be king of their nation. What a strange response the disciples received when they brought the Greeks' request to Jesus: "Verily, verily, I say unto you, Except a grain of wheat fall into the earth and die, it abideth by itself alone; but if it die, it beareth much fruit. He that loveth his life loseth it; and he that hateth his life in this world shall keep it unto life eternal" (John 12:24-25). He is saying that life is received through life that is given.

There are many yet living who can remember how the farmer once "broadcast" his grain, and will be able to relate to the following illustration. We visualize two farmers, each of whom has a bushel of grain. Farmer number one says, "I will keep my bushel of grain," so he stores it securely in his barn, and a world which does not understand observes and says, "There is a wise man: he is saving his grain."

Farmer number two says, "I believe that I will use my bushel of grain," so he prepares his field, hangs his grain sack on his shoulder, and scatters his grain upon the waiting soil. A world which does not understand observes and says, "Look at that foolish farmer: he is out there, throwing away his grain!"

229

And so the seasons pass. The "wise" farmer who has saved his grain goes out to his barn, only to find that the elements, and the passing of time, have taken their toll. He finds his grain mildewed, ruined, useless. The world had styled him a "wise" man.

But what is this which is appearing in the field of the "foolish" farmer? Blades of green pushing their way out of the soil, growing, ripening, their golden heads waving in the summer breeze. As the season rolls around, the "foolish" farmer thrusts in the sickle and reaps: thirty, sixty, a hundredfold. And we hear again the divine declaration of the Master: "Whosoever would save his life shall lose it: and whosoever shall lose his life for my sake shall find it."

The life which is lost in the Master's service is, in the fullest sense, the *saved* life.

When a Cross Is Not a Cross

We have seen how Jesus transformed the cross by dying on it—willingly, vicariously, and triumphantly, so that the cross became a symbol of glory, rather than a symbol of suffering and shame. Is it not possible that those who have willingly taken up their crosses may also transform them into objects of beauty and devotion?

1. By bearing them patiently.

We know so very little about the man named Simon, other than that he was from Cyrene, yet it was Simon who carried the cross after Jesus. Some of the greatest blessings which have enriched this writer's life have been imparted from saints who were suffering beneath the burden of the cross, yet were bearing it patiently and gladly.

As I write, I think of Margie, a dear saint of God whose body is being eaten away by cancer. She has become so very weak and frail. She can tolerate no solid food. Blockages occur in her intestines. She must now decide whether to have further surgery to give her a few more days of life. Yet, through it all, she is radiant. Her life is a benediction to all she touches. The cancer is not her cross. Long ago she took up her cross and, by bearing it patiently, she now glorifies God in her suffering.

The cross beckons—and frequently we turn aside in fear. It may well be that the crosses we fear are heavier than the crosses we bear.

When you have determined that you will be a Simon, and bear the cross after Jesus, bear it gladly, and bear it faithfully. Never forget that it is much easier to carry your cross than it is to drag it.

2. By glorying in them.

We recall that the great sufferer, Paul, shared with the saints in Galatia how he "gloried" in the cross of Christ. How difficult, but how beautiful, to come to the place in discipleship that we, too, can glory in the cross.

One of the perennial debates which rages among the foresters and the loggers of the Pacific Northwest has to do with varied approaches to logging. "Selective logging," as the name suggests, means to cut only those trees which are mature enough for harvest. Opponents of this logging style believe that this is so time-consuming and costly and that it wastes so much unmarketable timber, that it is better to clear the land completely, re-seed, and start a brand new crop of timber.

The second style of logging is known as "clear-cutting." In this approach, all timber is cut, and that which is not marketable is burned. The clear-cut does not leave a very beautiful hillside: it is stark, black, and ugly. But not many months pass until there is a radical transformation: the green of seedling trees and grass begins to appear. Shrubs and brush once more decorate the hillside. With the coming of the first frosts of autumn, the leaves of the vining maple and dogwood present a riot of gold and flaming crimson. The once ugly clear-cut is transformed into a thing of beauty. God transforms suffering into beauty; so may His disciples.

3. By dying on them.

As Paul speaks of glorying in the cross, he adds, "through which the world hath been crucified unto me, and I unto the world" (Gal. 6:14). A crucified man is a dead man, and thus it is that he can remind the saints and faithful brethren at Colossae: "For ye died, and your life is his with Christ in God" (Col. 3:3). The only way to get rid of your cross is to die on it. The cross is no longer a cross if there is no self to suffer under it.

Cross-bearing involves the complete Lordship of Jesus. It means the submission of the human will to the divine will. A loving father was attempting to explain to his small daughter the meaning of the cross. He took two small sticks and laid one across the other in the form of a cross. "Now," said the wise father, "let's name one of these sticks 'God's will,' and the other stick 'our will'. When God's will points one way and our will points the other way, that makes a cross, but when our will points the same way as God's will there is no longer a cross." When self dies on the cross, when stubborn self-will surrenders to the Divine will, the cross is transformed.

4. By making them emblems of service.

At the time of Christ, crucifixion was a public demonstration of servitude to the powerful government of Rome. May not our cross-bearing be a demonstration of our servitude to Christ? The Red Cross has transformed the cross by making it an emblem which is recognized all around the world as the symbol of service.

It was our Lord's last night upon earth, and He was eating a farewell meal with His dearest friends. The Son of God, knowing full well that He had come from God and was going home to God, arose from the table, lay aside His outer garments, girded Himself with a towel, and tenderly washed the dusty feet of His disciples: the appearance of a servant—the labor of a servant. It is probable that it was following this labor of love that He declared, "I am in the midst of you as he that serveth" (Luke 22:27).

Following this example of the greatness which comes through humble service, Jesus remarked, "I have given you an example, that ye also should do as I have done to you" (John 13:15). What a debt we owe Him! And our debt to God is payable to man. May we bear one another's burdens, and so fulfill the law of Christ (Gal. 6:2).

5. By sharing the Christ of the cross.

Following his encounter with the living Christ on the Damascus road, Saul of Tarsus gave his life to the sharing of the One who had transformed his life. His hunger for souls was so intense that he cried out, "Woe is me, if I preach not the gospel" (I Cor. 9:16), and again, "I could wish that I myself were anathema from Christ for my brethren's sake" (Rom. 9:3). The born-again child of God can never become accustomed to the thud of Christless feet on that broad road which leads to destruction.

Jesus gave His life to save others. If I "follow in his steps," I, too, must give my life to save others. Eugene Storjohann wrote a beautiful article on the Biblical meaning of cross-bearing. As he approaches the conclusion of this appealing presentation, he writes as follows:

> As Christians, we need voluntarily to take it upon ourselves to sit and visit with "the woman at the well." We need to lunch with all sorts of "publicans and sinners" or go call in the home of a "Zacchaeus"—not that we become like them but that we share the good news of how they, too, can have new life.
>
> When is the last time that we have made ourselves vulnerable to criticism in order to witness to the degraded or base segments of our society? Or to go one step further, how much of yourself have you given to save another, to bring him to the foot of the cross?[6]

As Jesus transformed His cross, may He grant us the grace to transform ours.

The Ultimate Transformation

> Just a few more days to be filled with praise,
> And to tell the old, old story;
> Then, when twilight falls, and my Savior calls,
> I shall go to Him in glory.

---

6. Eugene Storjohann, "The Biblical Meaning of Taking up Your Cross," *Christian Standard* (Cincinnati: The Standard Publishing Co., October 21, 1973), p. 10.

Just a few more years with their toil and tears,
And the journey will be ended;
Then I'll be with Him, where the tide of time
With eternity is blended.

Tho' the hills be steep and the valleys deep,
With no flow'rs my way adorning;
Tho' the night be lone and my rest a stone,
Joy awaits me in the morning.

What a joy 'twill be when I wake to see
Him for whom my heart is burning!
Nevermore to sigh, nevermore to die—
For that day my heart is yearning.

I'll exchange my cross for a starry crown,
Where the gates swing outward never;
At His feet I'll lay ev'ry burden down,
And with Jesus reign forever.[7]

Throughout the pages of this book we have been investigating the ramifications of what the Bible has to say about suffering. We have found that "all that would live godly in Christ Jesus shall suffer persecution," and that the Master's call is to daily cross-bearing. The "bottom line" of it all is that, having carried the cross faithfully and patiently to the end, we shall, one glad day, exchange the cross for a crown.

We are challenged and encouraged while cross-bearing by looking unto Jesus "who *for the joy that was set before him,* endured the cross, despising shame, and hath sat down at the right hand of the throne of God" (Heb. 12:2. Italics are the author's). The apostle to the Gentiles picks up this refrain as he addresses the heirs of God in Rome: "If so be that we suffer with him, that we may also be glorified with

---

7. Charles H. Gabriel, "Where the Gates Swing Outward Never."

him. For I reckon that the sufferings of this present time are not worthy to be compared with the glory which shall be revealed to us-ward" (Rom. 8:17-18).

Paul's song of faith, and his vision of the ultimate transformation of his cross, is continued in his second letter to the church in Corinth: "For our light affliction, which is for the moment, worketh for us more and more exceedingly an eternal weight of glory" (II Cor. 4:17).

Cross-bearing saints are sustained by the long look. They know that "the grave is not the goal." In the north woods, a human skeleton was found, propped up against a tree and, just above the grinning skull, some morbid soul had carved in the bark of the tree the words, "The end of the trail." Those who follow in the steps of the Victorious Christ know that the inscription engraved on the tree in the north woods is a lie. The trail goes on. After the cross, the crown.

There were three crosses lifted up on Calvary on that dark crucifixion day, and on these crosses three figures were suspended. All three of the sufferers were there because of sin. Two hung there because of their own sin; one was there for the sins of others. Someone has observed that as these three expired one died *in* sin; one died *to* sin, and one died *for* sin. Fulton J. Sheen, commenting on the crucifixion scene, has written, "Everyone is on a cross. Some ask to be taken down, like the thief on the left; others ask to be taken up, like the thief on the right."

How satisfying it is to rest in the assurance that the trail does not end at the cross. Beyond every cross there lies an Easter morning and, if we will but have it so, we can transform our Calvaries into Easters. The cross raises questions: the resurrection answers them. The agony of Christ's cross

236

was forgotten in the glory of the resurrection. If we but have the grace to fit our shoulder to the cross, we shall, some glorious morning, find our brow fitted for the crown.

> So I'll cherish the old rugged cross,
> Till my trophies at last I lay down;
> I will cling to the old rugged cross,
> And exchange it some day for a crown.[8]

Yes, if you wish, you can avoid the cross. It is really quite simple: all you have to do is to say "no." To reject the cross is to reject Jesus, salvation, discipleship, service, abiding joy, peace, and wealth untold. Dale Evans Rogers once testified, "All my life I searched for the pot of gold at the foot of the rainbow; now I've found it at the foot of the cross."

Peace after pain is an experience that none but those who have suffered can appreciate. In Chapter Fourteen of this book, I expect to share with you the testimony of Eric, my eleven-year-old grandson, who lost his three-year-long battle with leukemia, but emerged the Victor. It was while his only son was lying on a hospital bed in a coma, that Eric's father, in agony of soul, but with an unfaltering trust, wrote this testimony of the faith which transforms crosses.

> I walk through the shadows of death;
>   My eyes can see no light.
> "Oh Lord, my God," I cry out in pain,
>   How can this be right?"
> In anger and question my soul cries out,
>   "Why hast thou forsaken me?"
> Oh God, I beg upon my knees,
>   From this cup to be set free.

---

8. George Bennard, "The Old Rugged Cross."

I heard a voice, so sweet, so strong;
    It fell as from above.
I heard these words come forth in song,
    So full of strength and love,
"Fear thou not, for I am with thee;
    My Son has set you free.
Lift the burdens from your weary back
    And leave them at Calvary."

I said, "I've tried to find the cross,
    But I cannot find that tree."
He said, "I am the way, the truth, the life;
    You have but to follow me."
I lifted my eyes from earth's dim view
    That had offered pain and loss,
And there, on a hill, I found my peace,
    In the glory of a cross.[9]

---

9. Bill White, "Searching."

Chapter Thirteen

GOING HOME

The old farm house was quiet. It had once resounded with the shouts of children and the shared laughter of a happy family. The children had all grown up and left home. Only father and mother remained on the farm, and it was becoming too much of a burden for them, but they were determined to continue as long as possible, for this was home—and it was wrapped in beautiful memory.

The house was large, but mother never permitted those rooms where her children had slept to be disturbed. Each morning, as she did her housework, she stopped for a moment in each of the vacant bedrooms, patted the pillows, and breathed a prayer for the success and safety of each of the children whom she had once tucked in.

Thanksgiving Day was at hand, and the children had agreed that they would surprise Mother and Dad by all coming home for Thanksgiving. They arranged for a mutual friend to visit the parents for a few days prior to Thanksgiving. The friend helped to clean the house and to prepare for the Thanksgiving dinner. The old folks must have wondered why they were making such ample preparation.

The night before the big day, the friend got up in the middle of the night and unlocked the front door. All of the children came in and went quietly to their old rooms. When morning came, the mother started on her accustomed rounds. She entered the first room and saw, buried in the pillow, the head of her oldest boy. With a cry of delight, she rush to him, threw her arms about him, and kissed him. Then the next room—and the next—laughing and rejoicing because all of the children had come home.

What a day of rejoicing it will be when all of God's children get home!

C. S. Lewis fittingly concludes his splendid book on *The Problem of Pain* with a chapter on Heaven. He introduces this thought-provoking chapter with the following statement:

> "I reckon," said St. Paul, "that the sufferings of this present time are not worthy to be compared with the glory that shall be revealed in us." If this is so, a book on suffering which says nothing of heaven, is leaving out almost the whole of one side of the account. Scripture and tradition habitually put the joys of heaven into the scale against the sufferings of earth, and no solution of the problem of pain which does not do so can be called a Christian one.[1]

Some of us recall quite well the name of Florence Chadwick, the famous woman swimmer who, a few years ago, gained world renown by swimming the English Channel. Sometime prior to this successful venture she had made an unsuccessful attempt. The fog had settled in so thickly over the channel that it was impossible for her to see her destination, and she gave up less than a mile from her goal. As she later commented on this failure, she said, "I could have made it if I could have seen the shore." The writer of the Hebrew letter speaks in a similar vein as he portrays "the author and perfecter of our faith, who for the joy that was set before him endured the cross, despising shame, and hath sat down at the right hand of the throne of God" (Heb. 12:2). He made it! He persevered! He saw the shore!

If we need see the shore in order to complete our journey . . . if it is for the joy set before us that we endure suffering and pain and scorn . . . we would do well to take a careful look at the land toward which we journey. What will it be

---

1. C. S. Lewis, *The Problem of Pain* (New York: Macmillan Publishing Co., 1962), p. 144.

when all of God's children get home? What does the Bible say about heaven, our "Home Sweet Home"?

I. HEAVEN IS A PLACE.

It was Jesus' last night upon this earth. Just ahead lay Gethsemane and betrayal, Pilate's hall and the scourge, the thorn crown and the mockery, the spittle and the shame— and the cross. No one knew better than did the Lamb of God the agony which was at hand. Yet His thoughts, that dark night, were not for Himself, but for the little band which He was leaving as lambs among wolves. On that sorrowful night He attempted to share with His disciples the long look. It is John, the beloved, who records for us the Master's cure for heart trouble which He shared with His closest friends on betrayal night.

> Let not your hearts be troubled: believe in God, believe also in me. In my Father's house are many mansions; if it were not so, I would have told you; for I go to prepare a place for you. And if I go and prepare a place for you, I come again, and will receive you unto myself; that where I am, there ye may be also. And whither I go, ye know the way. Thomas saith unto him, Lord, we know not whither thou goest; how know we the way? Jesus saith unto him, I am the way, and the truth, and the life: no one cometh unto the Father, but by me (John 14:1-6).

Cannon Farrar once declared, "Heaven is to be something rather than to go somewhere," but the Man Who never told a lie promised, "I go to prepare *a place*."

The skeptical scientist may search the heavens with his telescope, then turn to us with a supercillious smile and declare, "There is no heaven, for I can't find it with my

241

telescope." I am quite sure that heaven is not the kind of place which can be seen through a telescope. In that glory land we shall dwell in spiritual bodies (I Cor. 15:44), but, even if it were a material place, there is ample room for such a place in a universe such as ours.

We dwell in a mighty roomy old universe. Every night on Mount Palomar, in Southern California, capable and dedicated astronomers use the five-hundred-ton Hale telescope with the 200-inch lens (40,000 times more powerful than the human eye) to photograph galaxies which they declare to be one billion light years from planet earth. That boggles my mind! We accept the fact that light travels at the speed of 186,000 miles per second, but how can I grasp the concept that there are galaxies so far removed from planet earth that the light from these heavenly bodies must travel 186,000 miles per second for one billion years to shine upon our planet tonight! And, to further add to my confusion, Marten Schmidt has now discovered a quasar which may be from four to eight billion light years from the earth!

These learned men turn their telescopes upon our milky way system, with its forty billion blazing suns and trillions of wonder worlds, and then look beyond that to hundreds of millions of milky way systems like our own. Men who claim to know declare that the universe as they can now see it is twelve sextillion miles across!

. . . and then a little infinitestimal speck on a speck will stand up and shake a pusillanimous fist in the face of the One Who made it all and shout, "There is no heaven, for I can't find it with my telescope."

Jesus said, "I go to prepare a place."

242

II. *HEAVEN IS A PREPARED PLACE.*

What assurance to hear our Savior say, "*I go to prepare.*" He has always been the Carpenter, the Builder. As a young man, He must have spent many long hours in the carpenter shop of Nazareth. I am sure that from His mallet and saw and plane there came nothing that was cheap or shoddy. He just wasn't that kind of a workman.

Throughout that brief ministry He was constantly building. He built faith, and hope, and courage, and character, and eternity in the hearts of those who met Him. How appropriate that in the last lessons He taught He should speak of building. How beautiful and how well constructed heaven must be; the Carpenter has been working on it now for nineteen and one-half centuries.

And what materials does He have with which to build those "many mansions"? We have been oft reminded that He has only those building materials which we send on ahead. In the judgment scene, as recorded in the twenty-fifth chapter of the Gospel of Matthew, the King shall say, "come . . . inherit . . . you fed the hungry; you gave drink to the thirsty; you were host to the stranger; you clothed the naked; you ministered to the sick and visited the prisoner." These are mighty good building materials!

The legend of the society matron's dream has been so oft-repeated that it has become a classic. The story goes something like this: A wealthy woman, who had little time for God or for her fellowman, dreamed that she died, ascended the golden staircase, and was ushered through the pearly gates. As the escorting angel led her down the golden streets, they passed many beautiful and costly mansions. One of the most beautiful caught the eye of the matron, and she inquired as to whose home this might be. "That,"

243

replied the angel, "is the home of your cleaning lady." "My cleaning lady," she thought, "in a house like that? Then how wonderful my mansion must be."

The old legend says that as they traveled on down the street the houses became smaller and less ornate and at last they stopped in front of a little shack. "This," announced the angel, "is your home." "But surely I should have something better than this," she objected. "I'm sorry," said the angel, "but, you see, we had only those materials with which to build which you sent us during your time upon the earth."

My friend, what kind of an abiding place is the Carpenter building for you? Is it a mansion—or is it a shack? I am sure that I would willingly settle for just a cabin in the corner of Glory Land, but I want to be sure that I have sent plenty of materials to my Carpenter.

III. *HEAVEN IS A BEAUTIFUL PLACE.*

John, the beloved, was a little nearer the Lord than were any of the other disciples. He was with Him on the Mount of Transfiguration. He leaned back on the Master's breast at the Last Supper. He went into the court of the High Priest as the Lord was brought to trial. He was standing, with breaking heart, at the foot of the cross. It was John who, at the cross, was entrusted with the mother of our Lord. It was John who left us those beautiful epistles of love. John never wavered; He was faithful unto death.

John, the aged, was in the isle called Patmos, for the word of God and the testimony of Jesus. It was there that the curtain of the centuries was drawn aside, and John was permitted to behold the holy city which his Lord had gone to prepare. As John struggled to find words to describe the city which he had beheld, he said that it had streets of gold, gates of pearl, foundations of precious stones, and was lighted by the glory of the Lamb. I am sure that this vivid description is not to be taken literally (some of us would not feel very much at ease walking on actual gold and dazzled by brilliant gems), but when John describes heaven he uses the most beautiful and most precious words that man has ever coined. As James Earl Ladd wrote concerning the final destiny of the children of God, he observed, "The sacred writers are beggared for metaphors and staggered for superlatives when it comes to the description of the home of the redeemed."[2]

The little blind girl had been to the famous surgeon for an operation which they hoped might give sight to those blinded eyes. The moment of truth had arrived—the time of testing when the bandages were to be removed. As loved ones stood by breathlessly, the last of the pads were removed. The little one who had spent those long years in darkness got slowly to her feet, walked to a window and looked out, then to an open doorway and looked out, then sped back to mother's waiting arms, crying out, "Oh, mother, why didn't you tell me it was like this? Why didn't you tell me it was so beautiful?" And the mother replied, through tears of joy, "I tried to dear, but I couldn't." I think that some bright morning we shall meet John on the streets of glory, and we will call out, "Hey, John. Why didn't you tell us it was like this?" And John will reply, "I tried to, but I couldn't."

God is a lover of beauty. If He were not, He would never have made the world so beautiful. He put the red on the

---

2. James Earl Ladd, *As Much As In Me Is* (Portland: Beattie and Company, 1951), p. 200.

robin's breast. He arranged the colors in the rainbow. He painted the wings of the butterfly—and He wipes out His paintbrush on the Oregon hills in autumn. If God were not a lover of beauty, He would never have made our Pacific Northwest.

I have been sitting here at my desk this morning, turning the pages of memory's picture album, and looking again at some of the precious scenes which God has privileged me to view over the span of some seventy years:

The panorama of the Cascade Mountains, spread out below a Forest Service lookout, perched high upon a rugged mountain peak—the delicacy of a maidenhair fern in a mossy glen—a frozen waterfall in mid-winter—the awe-inspiring Redwoods of California—the purple majesties of the Grand Canyon—the soft green pastures of the Emerald Isle—the rollicking fields of Tulips near Amsterdam—the rugged, glistening peaks of the Swiss Alps—stately castles, clinging precariously to the steep slopes overlooking the River Rhine—the cold, soft glow of the crown jewels in the Tower of London—a gleaming white city on an island in the blue Mediterranean—the Avenue of 100 Fountains in Tivoli—the sparkling blue water lapping the golden sand on the coast of southern Australia—the pink and purple mists, rising from the Sea of Galilee at dawning—a golden sunset, framed by the waving palm trees on the banks of the Nile at Luxor . . . breath-taking! Magnificent! But they all fade into drab grey when placed alongside the glories of heaven.

As I review with humble gratitude these glorious scenes, there is one page which seems to stand out above all the rest, and its setting is right here, in my beloved home state of Oregon. I had left camp before daylight, had climbed a mountain ridge, and, at the breaking of day, was seated on a hillside beneath a mountain Juniper. In the canyon below were dozens of deer, foraging among the shrubs for their morning meal. As I sat there in the chill of the October morning, I looked up to the head of the canyon, to see a massive outcropping of rock, etched against the dazzling white frost that lay like snow upon the ground. As I looked breathlessly upon that majestic setting, a huge buck deer walked out from beneath the rock and stood there, silhouetted against the skyline: erect, proud, head up, master of all he surveyed, the first rays of the morning sun glistening like gold from those massive antlers. Thank you, Lord, for permitting me to witness such beauty and majesty!

. . . Beautiful! Beautiful! But not to be compared with the beauty of heaven. Perhaps the words which Paul penned as he exulted over the wisdom of God might also be applied to the beautiful city: "Things which eye saw not, and ear heard not, and which entered not into the heart of man, Whatsoever things God prepared for them that love him" (I Cor. 2:9).

IV. HEAVEN IS A COMFORTABLE PLACE.

There is nothing there to cause discomfort. As John strives to help us to see the glories of heaven, he explains that there will be no more sickness, sorrow, pain, nor death. There will be no "blue Monday" in heaven. No more grinding toil. No more heavy burdens for tired shoulders. A suffering saint, asked of his concept of heaven, replied, "Heaven is rest." I once heard a dear old Christian say, with a sparkle in his eye, "When I get to heaven I'm going to pull the old rocking chair out on the front porch, and

247

for the first hundred years I'm just going to sit—and then I'm going to start rocking—real slow!"

In his first epistle, John writes to his beloved children: "Beloved, now are we children of God, and it is not yet made manifest what we shall be. We know that if he shall be manifested, *we shall be like him*; for we shall see him even as he is" (I John 3:2. Italics are the author's). Like Jesus! Think of it! Our bodies transformed into the likeness of His glorious body. No more arthritic fingers wrapped about the spine. No more sightless eyes or deaf ears. No more twisted limbs. No more cancer-eaten bodies. No more tormented minds. Like Jesus in body—and in soul. The devil's power broken at last—the victory won—a comfortable home with Jesus and our beloved.

> They say I shall some day be like Him,
> My cross and my burdens lay down.
> 'til then, I shall ever be faithful
> In gathering gems for His crown.

We have long been told that the great soul-winner, Dwight L. Moody, was not a highly-educated man, but he was eloquent in simplicity as he expounded the great truths of the Word of God. Perhaps this eloquence is nowhere more evident than when he lifted his hearers toward the Pearly Gates, as he spoke on Revelation 21:4: "And he shall wipe away every tear from their eyes."

A city without tears—God wipes away all tears up yonder. This is a time of weeping, but by and by there will be a time when God shall call us where there will be no tears. A City without pain, a City without sorrow, without sickness, without death . . . Think of a place where temptation can not come. Think of a place where we shall be free from sin . . .

248

and where the righteous shall reign forever. Think of a City that is not built with hands, where the buildings do not grow old with time; a City whose inhabitants are numbered by no census, except the Book of Life . . . Think of a City . . . where no hearses with their nodding plumes creep slowly with their sad burdens to the cemetery; a City without griefs or graves, without sins or sorrows, without marriages or mourning, without births or burials; a City which glories in having Jesus for its King, angels for its guards, and whose citizens are saints.[3]

I can not think of the sufferings of earth transformed into the comforts of heaven without thinking of Everett Lee. The son of Everett and Mary Lee Payton was born blind, with hydrocephalus and cerebral palsy. One leg always dragged, one hand and arm never functioned properly, and he was dependent for life upon a shunt pump in his skull.

Everett Lee brought joy to every life he touched. He loved to make people laugh. He was fascinated by the discovery that his name meant "strong and brave." He was careful to let people know that his name was Everett, that he was strong and brave, and that he was "tough."

As the loving father paid tribute to the memory of his son, he told how Mary Lee had purchased a copy of the popular song, "Hallelujah Square," and was seated at the piano, singing quietly of the blind man, the cripple, and the aged, looking forward to the wonderful time in Hallelujah Square. Everett Lee was listening intently, then walked over and tugged at his mother's arm—"Mommy, is that true? Do you mean, Mommy, that I won't be blind when

---

3. Dwight L. Moody, *When Loved Ones Are Called Home*, by Herbert H. Wernecke (Grand Rapids: Baker Book House, 1972).

I get to heaven?" Upon being assured that this was indeed true, Everett Lee exulted, "That's really neat. I won't be crippled when I see Jesus."

Everett Lee died the Victor at age nine. The overflow audience at the funeral was an eloquent testimony to the contribution that one small crippled boy had made to this earth. But he wasn't crippled when he saw Jesus. As the father wrote, "When God took Everett Lee from our house to his, he perfected all of our son's imperfections."[4]

Thirty years ago we were ministering to a happy, vibrant congregation in Eugene, Oregon. In the splendid youth group there was a lad who was spastic. He longed so very much to be able to do everything that his friends could do. Although he could not keep up with them, his young friends were thoughtful and helpful. One Sunday night we were including in the service a time for testimonial. LeRoy struggled to his feet and declared in his faltering voice: "There are four things that I want in heaven: First, I want to be there. Second, I want to see Him. Third, I want to be able to talk, and, fourth, I want to be able to run." How LeRoy will run and shout along those peaceful streets of Glory— It is a comfortable place!

V. HEAVEN IS A ROOMY PLACE.

In the precious promise before us, as the Carpenter declared that He was going on ahead to prepare a place for those who love and serve Him, He pointed out that in His Father's house there were *many* mansions. There is no housing shortage in heaven. There is a mansion for you if you will but claim the title.

---

4. Everett J. Payton, *I Won't Be Crippled When I See Jesus* (Minneapolis: Augsburg Publishing House, 1979), p. 10.

As John stands enthralled before the splendor of the holy city, he is granted a vision of a surveying angel. The one speaking with John held in his hand a golden reed with which to measure the city, the gates, and the wall. The city was foursquare, and it was found to measure twelve thousand furlongs. That translates to about 1,500 miles in our scale—and that is a city which is even larger than our megalopolis of Los Angeles!

But "the length and the breadth and the height thereof are equal" (Rev. 21:16). Think of it: a cubical city—a city in the third dimension! Even if heaven were a material place, and even if this were a literal measurement, which it is not, this gives us some concept of the extent of heaven: a city containing almost 497 quintillion cubic feet!

According to the report of the surveying angel, just how commodious is heaven? Just how much room is there in 497 quintillion feet? Let's put it this way: If this old world stood for 100,000 years (which it won't), and if there were an average of one billion people in each generation (which there are not), that would make only 33 quadrillion people, and if they all got to heaven (which they won't), a city of this size would be large enough to provide every person who ever lived with a room eight feet high and 43 feet square—and anyone who could not be content with that much room doesn't deserve to go there!

"Many mansions"—be sure, friend, that you make the down payment on yours.

VI. *HEAVEN IS A CLEAN PLACE.*

"And there shall in no wise enter into it anything unclean, or he that maketh an abomination and a lie: but only they that are written in the Lamb's book of life" (Rev. 21:27). Our neighbors in heaven will be clean people, and clean people make a clean city. There will be no unkempt slums, no unsightly litter, no polluted atmosphere.

Some of our cities wouldn't be bad places in which to live were it not for some of the things with which we have to contend. We are called upon to face much in this life with which we will not have to contend in heaven. We will not be pestered by the weasel-eyed gossip in heaven. We will not be compelled to breathe air that is fouled with tobacco smoke and liquor fumes in heaven. It is doubtful if we would be able to find a spittoon or an ash tray in heaven.

Following the "sealing" of the 144,000, John saw a great throng of the redeemed, arrayed in white robes, and palms in their hands. One of the elders asked, "John, who are these in the white robes?" and then he answered his own question: "These are they that come out of the great tribulation, and they washed their robes, and made them white in the blood of the Lamb" (Rev. 7:14). Heaven is a clean place: wouldn't it be a good idea to start getting ready for a place like this in the here and now?

In 1972, Robert Brown wrote with great discernment of the environment which awaits in heaven.

The last chapters of God's revelation through John give the best description of the surroundings we will experience. It will be the garden of Eden restored and magnified. What is rare, sought by all, and possessed by few, will be common, sought by none and possessed by all. What most men die for and never possess, his men will live among but care less. God was doing his best to describe it when He put it in physical terms. A City of Gold, surrounded by walls of Jasper, illuminated by the light of His presence, cooled

252

by the river of Living Water, fed by the tree of life; it is just too much for us to comprehend right now.[5]

VII. *HEAVEN IS A BUSY PLACE.*

After John had looked upon that blood-washed throng of saints, the "elder" revealed to him that these who had washed their robes were privileged to stand before the throne of God; and that they "serve him day and night." There won't be any unemployment in heaven, nor any "freeloaders." All of His children will be happily employed throughout eternity.

We shall be busy, but busy doing what? Some have engaged in wishful thinking, and have opined that in the life to come we will be privileged to do those things we most enjoyed during this life (witness the Indians' "Happy Hunting Ground"). If this be true, in heaven there will be an abundance of available pulpits and eager and responsive congregations, the hills of heaven will teem with the most beautiful deer and elk that you have ever seen, and, flowing downward from the hills, there will be some well-stocked trout streams!

In *Christian Standard,* dated April 15, 1967, Wilbur Reid, Jr., paid tribute to an old country preacher, Dr. L. C. Young. Dr. Young had invested 57 years in the gospel ministry, 42 of those years devoted to one congregation. During this more than one-half century of faithful service, Dr. Young had led 22 revivals for his home church, conducted 1,500 weddings, officiated at 2,500 funerals, and baptized more than 5,000 people—quite an impressive record for a "country preacher."

---

5. Robert A. Brown, "A Worthy Environment," *The Divine Purpose,* edited by W. Carl Ketcherside (St. Louis: Mission Messenger, 1972).

After these long years of dedicated ministry, the old gentleman finally went to a doctor to determine why he had not been feeling as "chipper" as usual. The doctor examined the elderly minister, diagnosed the problem, and told him that he had but a short while to live. His son, L. Palmer Young, who was with him at the time, reported that his father never flinched or seemed upset; he just stood up and said, "Well, I guess I'll just go back to Casey County and preach some more, baptize some more, and go to heaven."

Dr. Young was ready to go home, and, if he is still doing what he enjoyed most, he is doubless still glorifying Jesus Christ. Whatever his occupation, he will be busy—and so will you—and so will I.

VIII. *HEAVEN IS A HAPPY PLACE.*

And why shouldn't it be? There is nothing there which could possibly cause unhappiness. John tells us that God will be there, that He shall wipe away every tear, and that there shall be no more mourning, crying, or pain.

I shall always cherish the memory of the most unusual church service that I ever conducted—it was held for just one man. We had been called to lead an evangelistic meeting for a small church in a small town. We found there a dear saint of God who had lived out his life for Christ and the church. He would have liked so very much to be able to attend, but he could not. He was on his sick-bed for the last time. One night he sent a request: Would you mind coming down and holding a service for me?

What a delight to minister by the bedside of this dying saint. The young couple who traveled with me as musicians played and sang, "There's no disappointment in heaven, no weariness, sorrow, or pain; no hearts that are bleeding and broken, no song with a minor refrain." I opened the Book of Books and read, "Yea, though I walk through the valley of the shadow of death . . . ." It was joy unspeakable and full of glory!

Not the least of the joys of heaven will be the reunion with dear friends and loved ones who have gone on before. The writings of F. B. Meyer have challenged, rebuked, and comforted a great host of people. Just a few days before his death, Meyer wrote to a friend: "I have just heard, to my surprise, that I have only a few more days to live. It may be that before this reaches you, I shall have entered the Palace. Don't trouble to write. We shall meet in the morning." What consolation in the assurance that children of God never see one another for the last time.

There was a time that heaven seemed far away and filled with strangers, but not so today. Heaven is just a step away and many dear ones are awaiting me there. Besides that great host of friends whom we have loved and lost for a season, there is a father, a mother, two dear little grandchildren, and now a loving wife. What a happy time it will be when we all meet up there!

I have in my library a little booklet of beautiful, heart-sprung verse. This book is doubly precious to me because of the inscription on the flyleaf: "From an Australian Mum. To Mr. Willie White. God bless you and keep you. Best wishes, from Mary Lewis nee Spicer."

It was several years ago that I was privileged to lead two brief evangelistic crusades in the "Land Down-under." One afternoon I was entertained in a simple little cottage by one of God's special saints. The house was somewhat a-clutter, but, wherever you looked, there were books and writing materials. This elderly saint gave little thought to earthly things: her citizenship was in heaven. As I reluctantly concluded my delightful visit, this "Australian Mum" inscribed one of her books of poetry and handed me a copy of *Poems, Past and Present.* Tucked away among these folksy verses concerning her life and her community, is a precious little jewel in which she shares her concept of the land toward which she journeyed:

GLORY FOR ME

I know there's a beautiful city
Where our loved ones are singing with glee
They sing with the Angels in Heaven
Oh that will be Glory for me.

Glory for me, Glory for me
Oh that will be Glory for me
When by his Grace I shall look on his face
That will be Glory, be Glory for me.

The River in that beautiful city
Flows way down to the sea
And sweet voices are singing so happy
Oh that will be Glory for me.

Pretty flowers bloom in that city
The rose and the old lilac tree
And you can hear the chimes of the music
Oh that will be Glory for me.

There's no pain in that beautiful city
And everyone's singing with glee
And the smile on their face tells the story
Oh that will be Glory for me.

There's all love in that beautiful city
No hatred or anger we'll see
As we mix with the loved ones in Heaven
Singing that will be Glory for me.

But the price of that beautiful city
Cost our Saviour his life on the tree
That we should be ever singing
Oh that will be Glory for me.

So let us try to love one another
And make love and kindness our plea
And then we shall know why they're singing
Oh that will be Glory for me.

IX. *HEAVEN IS AN ETERNAL PLACE.*

There were many times that Paul grew homesick for heaven and desired to depart and be "at home with the Lord." He gives vent to this longing in the fifth chapter of Second Corinthians, introducing the chapter with a cry of confidence: "For we know that if the earthly house of our tabernacle be dissolved, we have a building from God, a house not made with hands, *eternal,* in the heavens." Every illustration I have read or heard used in an attempt to explain eternity is pitifully inadequate, but I am sure of this: If every individual could but grasp the meaning of eternity, there would not be a non-christian in your fair city.

We hurry and we bustle and we rush about. There are so many things which we would like to do that never get done. For years, the standing joke around our house was what we were going to do when the rush was over. When time has ended, and eternity has begun, what opportunity to do that for which we never found time during this life.

WHAT THE BIBLE SAYS ABOUT SUFFERING

What do you expect to do when you have crossed the Sea of Time and stepped out onto the shores of Eternity? I think that when time shall be no more for me one of the first things I would like to do is to stand for a few thousand years and just look into the face of Jesus—and then I shall realize fully that "It will be worth it all when we see Christ."

I would like to see Mother and Dad. That little shy Irish mother, rejoicing now in the company of the saints. And I would like to see Dad as he is now—with two good eyes and a strong right arm. I think that we would shoulder our packs, hike off into the hills of heaven, build a cheery fire, and sit around it and talk, as we did so long ago.

What a delight to hold a little grandson on my lap and to gather Eric close to me—free from the weaknesses and the pain which so wracked that frail body.

But the very first to greet me will be the one who was my dearest friend and companion for almost one-half century— and when she puts loving arms about me, that will be heaven. We can sit down in the shade of a great Douglas fir tree (please, God, let there be fir trees in heaven) and talk over old times and, looking back, can finally see clearly how God worked all things together for good. Then, after we have experienced this sweet fellowship for a few million years, we can take our suitcases, locate our little white cottage, unpack, and set about enjoying eternity.

Oh, what abounding joy to experience a family reunion which will know no ending! How concerned we ought be that the life of every dear one be ordered in such a way that the circle will be unbroken.

ARE ALL THE CHILDREN IN?

I think oftimes as the night draws nigh
Of an old house on the hill,
Of a yard all wide and blossom-starred

Where the children played at will.
And when the night at last came down,
Hushing the merry din,
Mother would look around and ask,
"Are all the children in?"

'Tis many and many a year since then,
And the old house on the hill
No longer echoes to childish feet,
And the yard is still, so still.
But I see it all, as the shadows creep,
And though many the years have been
Since then, I can still hear mother ask,
"Are all the children in?"

I wonder if when the shadows fall
On the last short, earthly day,
When we say good-bye to the world outside,
All tired with our childish play,
When we step out into that Other Land
Where mother so long has been,
Will we hear her ask, just as of old,
"Are all the children in?"

(Author unknown)

X. *HEAVEN IS AN ACCESSIBLE PLACE.*

As the Unfailing One pledged His word to go and prepare a place, He declared, "And whither I go, ye know the way." Then, in response to the question of Thomas, He drew a well-defined map: "I am the way, and the truth, and the life: no one cometh unto the Father, but by me." The way heavenward is the way of a Person: Jesus of Nazareth—the Christ—the son of the living God.

The way to heaven is not discovered by accident nor without effort. Jesus said that the gate is narrow, the way straitened, and that few find it, whereas the way that leads to destruction has a wide gate, a broad way, and many travelers.

It has been many years since I read Harold Bell Wright's *Shepherd of the Hills* but, as I recall that beautiful old story, it opens and closes with the picture of the two ways. As the pilgrim travels life's pathway, he comes to a parting of the ways. One of the roads is broad and well traveled. It is the easy way. It wends its way on around the hillside, but it leads ever downward to the shadow of the valley of where the laughter is stilled and the vision has dimmed.

The other way is a little narrow pathway. It is steep and rough and not so well traveled, but it leads ever upward until it comes at last to the eternal home on the mountain top, where all is sunshine, and peace, and joy.

If you will but pause for a moment at the crossroads of life, you will notice that there is a marker. It is the old rugged cross, and the cross-bar points out the narrow pathway. If you will examine this signpost carefully, you will note on the cross-bar the inscription, "The Way of the Cross Leads Home." As you stand at the crossroads of life, will you listen intently for the loving Voice which rings like a clarion call: "This is the way, walk ye in it."

Incidentally, there is no mile you must run, no mountain you must climb to fulfill the requirements for admission to such a place. There is no creed written or unwritten that you must adopt to place your feet on the right and your name in the Book of Life. There is just one thing that separates you and me from all that can fulfill and it's not a thing inanimate, it's a life-giving, life-possessing person, Jesus the Christ, the Messiah, and the Atonement for your sins. You are only asked to appropriate His death, accept by faith his Lordship over your life, be covered and raised in water in the likeness of his life and death and follow him. The promise is to all that love his reappearing.[6]

How interested are you in heaven? Are you so enthralled with your glamorous friends, your glittering baubles, your transient dollars, and your selfish pleasures that you are giving it no thought? Why wear glass beads when you can have diamonds? Why play mud pies when you can be building cathedrals? Heaven can get along without us, but we can't very well get along without heaven.

One of the most beautiful home-going stories that I have ever heard is the story of H. C. Morrison. Morrison went as a missionary to Africa. His sole purpose was to lead precious souls to the Savior, and, as a missionary, he gave himself in sacrificial service for Christ on that dark continent. As Morrison embarked on his return journey from the mission field, Teddy Roosevelt was on the same ship. Roosevelt, also, had been in Africa—hunting lions. As the ship steamed into New York harbor, it seemed that all of New York had turned out to welcome Teddy Roosevelt. Horns were blowing; bells were ringing; whistles were tooting; bands were playing; the mayor was there.

H. C. Morrison said, "Broken in body, I stood on board that ship, the loneliest man in all the world. Here, I had been in Africa, slaving for Jesus Christ, and not a person in that whole crowd to welcome me home." Then he said, "Suddenly that scene in New York faded, and I said to myself, 'Why should I be worried? I'm not home yet!'"

---

6. Brown, *op. cit.*, pp. 265-266.

In his imagination, he saw the pearly white city. He heard the trumpets blow, the bands play, and the angelic choir. He saw the gates of pearl, and Gabriel shouted, "Open the gates, H. C. Morrison is coming home!"

The angels put new robes on him and together they walked down the golden streets of glory. Then Morrison came to the great white throne where the King of Kings was seated, and the Lord stepped down from His throne and greeted him with open arms, saying, "Welcome home, Henry, we've been waiting a long time for you."

Is heaven your home tonight?

> When the saints go marching in,
> When the saints go marching in;
> O Lord I want to be in that number
> When the saints go marching in.

William J. Kirkpartrick was a hymn writer. We have all been blessed as we have lifted our voices in his songs: "Jesus Saves," and " 'Tis So Sweet to Trust in Jesus." One night as Mrs. Kirkpatrick was preparing to retire, her husband said that he was going to his study. He frequently worked late at night. It was after midnight when Mrs. Kirkpatrick awoke to find the study light still burning. She found her beloved's body at his desk, pencil still in hand, and, on the paper before him, the words of his last hymn:

> Coming home, coming home,
> Never more to roam.
> Open wide, Thine arms of love,
> Lord, I'm coming home.

Eric

263

Chapter Fourteen

ERIC

May 3, 1966 - April 19, 1978

Occasionally, when God has a few minutes of spare time, just to show His love and His majesty and His beauty, He puts together an extra special package. He reaches down and scoops up a handful of stardust, adds the impish smile of a cherub, the winsome spirit of an angel, and a small portion of the wisdom of the Infinite. He puts it all together, wraps it beautifully, and sends it down to planet earth: a "special" child. And thoughtful parents to whom this special care package is entrusted receive it with gratitude—and pride—and awe—and reverence—and an overwhelming sense of responsibility.

Eric was a gifted child. He could talk before he could walk. At nine months of age he was forming sentences. He memorized a child's story book before he was two, and if Judi (his mother) missed a word while reading the story to him, little Eric would correct her. When he was two he chose books over toys. At the age of four he had memorized the entire fifty-two verses of the second chapter of the Gospel of Luke. He took guitar and piano lessons and taught himself to play the harmonica. After being enrolled in school, despite many illnesses, he was placed in advanced learning classes.

Eric was a normal boy in his fondness for comic books, but he was just as much at home with the newspapers or encyclopedias. He was particularly enthralled with books of astronomy. His greatest problem at age nine was whether to become a minister, a doctor, or a scientist—or all three! As a very young lad he had accepted Jesus as his Lord, had been baptized into Him, and was a dedicated little Christian.

264

It was a happy little family group: the father, Bill, who was minister of the First Christian Church in Pasco, Washington; Judi, the capable and caring mother; Eric, and his mischievous little sister, Misti. They had a beautiful home, a fulfilling ministry, and a rosy future—and then the bottom dropped out . . . .

It was on Mother's Day, just after Eric had celebrated his ninth birthday. Judi was leading a Sunday evening youth group, and her children were with her. Eric was enjoying himself, eating popcorn and endeavoring to win the Bible game which he was playing with the older children. Judi noticed that his face appeared flushed, and, as any caring mother would do, she laid her hand upon his warm forehead. Sensing that he might be coming down with some illness, the parents excused themselves from the evening service and asked the congregation to remember them in prayer. When they arrived at home and took Eric's temperature, it stood at 103 degrees: he must be coming down with the "bug" from which Misti had so recently recovered.

The next day the temperature remained at 103, and Eric was taken to the family doctor. The doctor found that his blood count was low and that he seemed to be anemic.

For several days Eric's temperature hovered between 101 and 103. He was unusually pale and weak. His skin bruised easily. His lymph glands were swollen, and his blood count was extremely low. Judi had always feared leukemia and had read extensively concerning this disease. Recognizing the indications in her son, she informed the doctor that these were symptoms of leukemia. He agreed, and suggested that Eric be taken to the local hospital for a bone marrow test.

The following morning found Eric and his parents at the hospital at 9:00 o'clock. The painful bone marrow tests were taken and the family went home for a long day of uncertainty and prayer. At 7:00 p.m. the phone rang, and the lab reported that they had been unable to discover any leukemia cells. What glad news! Yet the fever persisted, and, after three weeks, the concerned doctor sent the family to the Children's Orthopedic Hospital and Medical Center in Seattle, where they had better equipment to diagnose Eric's problem.

COHMC is one of the outstanding medical centers on the West Coast. It is a large, well-equipped facility, staffed by some of the most competent and caring personnel to be found. This hospital cares for any children, regardless of the family's ability to pay. The care extended is competent, personal, and selfless.

It was five months after Eric was taken to COHMC that Judi sat down and poured out her heart in a mother's perspective of this hospital experience.

As we settled Eric into the hospital bed, Bill assured him that the doctors would find the "infection" and we would be home in a couple of days. We stayed with Eric until he was asleep and then went to a local motel.

The next morning we found Eric sitting up in bed, watching cartoons on T. V. He told me that he wanted a "surprise" from the gift shop, and so off I went.

When I returned with a silly stuffed snake in a sack, I found the room empty, with my husband standing in the doorway. "Where's Eric?" I asked. "They wanted to take some tests," he replied. "What kind of tests?" I demanded. He knew that he couldn't keep it from me, so he told me that the doctors had looked at the slide we had brought with us and thought that they saw leukemia. They wanted to take another bone marrow to make sure.

What did we do as we waited for the results? I remember crying on my knees in the hospital chapel, promising God anything and everything if He would just make some kind of "deal" with me. I also remember putting powder around my eyes so that Eric would not be able to tell that I had been crying. Later, as we sat in Eric's room playing games, a nurse came in and said that the doctor would like to talk to us down the hall.

It was a little room. Bill and I sat on one side, the doctor on the other. He asked if we knew what they were looking for. We replied, "Yes." He said that they had found leukemia cells and proceeded to explain the disease and the new medical procedures and treatment. My heart was pounding in my head and I remember looking out the window and wondering why the sky was so blue. "This must be some kind of nightmare. After all, things like this just don't happen to people like us."

I remember starting to cry and not being able to control myself. The doctor asked if we would like to continue talking later. I remember telling him how very special Eric is. Such a wonderful, bright little boy. Children with so much to offer the world just couldn't get leukemia. Not my son— not Eric. I'm sure that he must have tried to reassure me, but I couldn't make my mind work right. I remember the doctor patting Bill on the shoulder as he left us alone in the room. We sat and talked and cried . . . .

Bill didn't want to leave me alone, but felt that he must go to be with Eric because the doctor had gone to tell him what they had found. We have been honest with Eric from the beginning. This way he knows that he can believe us— good or bad.

As I was alone in the room, I thought back to that day when Eric was born. I watched Eric being born. I had very much wanted a little girl, so when he was born the doctor held him up and said, "Ha, ha, look what you got." He was a beautiful little boy, who seemed to glow a silver color (the doctor later explained that he was covered with an unusual amount of vernix). They laid him on my stomach and I thought how very warm he was. In my mind I can still feel that warmth.

Eric had always wanted love for everyone in this world. When he was little, and overheard his father and I having a "disagreement," he would push us together with all of the strength of his little hands and say, "Don't argue." Oh, how I love that child! How could I even imagine living without him? As I sat there and cried, I felt a sudden peace come over me. You may choose to think what you like. I choose to know that it was God . . . .[1]

With Eric's problem diagnosed as acute lymphoblastic leukemia, the series of painful tests and treatments was begun—and how concerned and believing Christians prayed! Loved ones prayed. Dear friends bowed their kees before the Throne. Prayer chains in several states were activated. Congregations, large and small, assembled to pray. More than one-thousand men, gathered together in convention session in Los Angeles, prayed. And God answered, as He always answers sincere, heart-sprung prayer. But, for some reason that we shall never fully understand until that day when we can ask Him in person, He tenderly answered, "No."

It was July 3rd. The family had just returned from one of their many trips to the Seattle hospital and was eagerly looking forward to a happy 4th of July picnic together. Judi's parents had come from out of state to be with them. Grandma Frances had arisen early and prepared breakfast for Eric (the medication had given him a gargantuan appetite). Grandmother and grandson talked for awhile, then

1. Written by Judi White, October, 1975.

Eric said that he was tired and wanted to go back to sleep. Just before he fell asleep he asked his grandmother when his testing would be over. He felt, as have many older sufferers, that God was testing him, but he was determined to pass the test.

At 9:00 a.m. Judi was sitting at the table, wondering why Bill was taking so much time in telling Eric goodbye. He would be late getting to the office. Then the father called, "Judi, come talk to Eric." Judi hurried to the bedside and asked, "Eric, what's wrong?" Eric looked up and responded, "you guys," then lapsed into a jumble of unattached words. Eric was delirious.

Again he was rushed to the hospital. The attending physician directed, "Eric, raise your hand." Eric raised his foot, and the mother dissolved in tears: "Oh God, no! Not his mind. Please, God, not his beautiful mind!"

Family and friends and elders from the church and two sisters from the local hospital gathered in the chapel for fervent, intercessory prayer. Dear friends from the church lined the halls outside the emergency room. Eric's condition was critical, and a head nurse stated, "You will never get him to Seattle alive."

An ambulance plane was prepared and Eric was loaded aboard. He could neither see nor hear his loved ones: Eric was in a coma. Saliva drooled from his mouth and he had lost control of his bladder. The chartered plane sped through a raging thunder storm, and a distraught mother sat near her son and prayed as she had never prayed before until "the peace of God which passeth all understanding" settled softly upon her. She turned and squeezed Eric's foot, as he lay on the seat behind her, and Eric looked up at his mother and smiled.

The head nurse was mistaken: Eric did arrive at COHMC alive. The doctors determined that he now had spinal meningitis and a blood staph infection. They were united in their opinion that he would not recover from this on-slaught, and, that if he did, he would remain a mental vegetable. Again Eric and God proved them to be wrong!

Bill and Judi celebrated the 4th of July (also their tenth wedding anniversary) in the hospital, but the family was together, and they received the thrilling news that the leu-kemia was now in remission.

There were several trips to the hospital that summer: once with pneumonia, once with a bowel impactment. The medication caused Eric to lose his hair. His face became puffed and moonshaped and he had a pudgy tummy. A few thoughtless school children laughed at him, but, with a maturity far beyond his years, he just smiled and under-stood.

He never lost his smile, the sparkle from his eyes, nor his keen sense of humor. He was visited in his home by a newspaper columnist, to whom Eric remarked, "I look like Alfred Hitchcock," as he postured to form on the wall be-hind him a shadow image of the famous mystery director.

One of the compensations to Eric for his frequent and painful trips to the hospital was the celebrities whom he met and the autographs which he proudly obtained. The entire basketball team of Puget Sound College of the Bible visited him in his hospital room. Among those he was privi-leged to meet during his illness were Pat Boone, Anita Bryant, the Imperials, the Beach Boys, Tom Netherton, Mike Farrell, and astronaut Jim Irwin. The thoughtful visits by these whom the world calls "famous" helped to ease Eric's days of suffering, and his life, in turn, enriched the lives of all who met him.

Eric's deep faith and maturity and unquenchable spirit pierced the heart of every person with whom he came in contact. It was his habit to leave funny little gifts for his nurses. In response to one of these gifts, the recipient wrote him this note: "Thank you for being such a kind, sensitive person. You have touched my heart and given me some sunshine. You belong to a very special family."

Eric kept the faith. His deepest desires were to please his family and to please his God. He was obsessed with heaven. He wanted to see all of those saints of old—and Jesus. His faith was infectious. When the Hospital Chaplain needed a bit of encouragement and cheer, he visited Eric, bringing with him a list of patients for whom Eric might pray.

Just down the hall from Eric's room lay Stephen, who was a bit older than Eric. Stephen was dying with cancer, and Eric prayed earnestly for his recovery. One day, as Bill and Judi visited in a waiting room near Stephen, the mother came out of her son's room, crying out that Stephen was gone. Her long hospital vigil was ended at last. How could Judi tell her son that his friend was gone? but she must. When she entered Eric's room, he looked into her face and said, "It's Stephen, isn't it? He's dead, isn't he?" The mother nodded her head.

After a few moments of silence, Eric spoke: "You know, mother, I feel kind of guilty."

"Guilty, Eric? Guilty about what?"

"Because I feel so happy for Stephen. Now he has all of his hair. He is not sick any more. He can play ball, and he can run." Eric had caught a glimpse of that eternal city which is "full of boys and girls playing in the streets."

FAREWELL TO A LITTLE BOY

Honey, there will be a hoop
and hills to roll it down.

271

(God couldn't give a little boy
the burden of a crown.)

He'll show you lots of trees to climb
and where He keeps the swings.
(God, let him have a ball and bat
instead of shining wings.)

And will He let you fly a kite
up where the sky is clear,
Without tall buildings stooping down?
Of course He will, my dear.

Now close your eyes, I'll kiss them tight,
the way I always do.
(I must not, I must not cry, dear God,
until he's safe with you.)

— *Helen Welshimer.*

Eric was again released from the hospital. The months that followed were tense and painful and difficult. Eric was in and out of the hospital many times. He underwent painful tests and shots. Twice the doctors were able to bring the disease into remission. Through it all, Eric remained patient and trustful.

One of the happy memories of my grandson which is etched upon memory's wall, and that I shall always cherish, was granted me when we were on our annual elk hunting trip. Bill, Judi, Eric, and Misti came to visit us in our hunting camp. Eric was terribly weak, but he wanted to go hunting. Bill, Eric, Misti, and I climbed into our little Ford Bronco and started up the mountain. Deer were plentiful, and Eric's eyes were sharp. He was thrilled and excited as he pointed out large numbers of deer, standing in the brush or bounding through the timber. When we reached the mountain top we left the car and walked slowly against an icy wind to the shelter of an outcropping of rock from whence we could glass the hillsides for elk. We found no elk that day, but Eric looked with fascination across that vast, rugged Minam River gorge, and, as I looked into my grandson's face, I received the distinct impression that he was seeing far beyond that which any of us were seeing with mortal eyes.

The weeks and the months slipped by. It was now more than two years since loving parents had heard that dread diagnosis: leukemia. Eric had passed his eleventh birthday, and was receiving his shots regularly. One day Judi took Eric to the doctor for one of his regular shots. Shortly after returning home, the phone rang. It was the nurse's voice: "The doctor is afraid that he did not give Eric enough medication." Judi replied, "But there was medication in that bottle for four shots." "Oh, no," replied the nurse. "That was just for one shot. Let me check with the doctor."

It was but a moment until the doctor was on the line. Judi repeated the information: the bottle contained medication for four shots. The doctor dropped the phone and hurried to the trash basket to check the discarded bottle. He rushed back to the phone and, with anguished voice, asked Judi to call her husband while he got in touch with the hospital in Seattle.

Again, an ambulance plane was chartered, and a very sick boy was rushed to the Seattle hospital. The overdose had brought on a stroke. The doctors took a brain scan and deliberated whether to attempt brain surgery. Their decision was that it was inoperable and that the situation was hopeless. Again they were wrong.

Little Eric was again in intensive care, in a coma, and on life-support systems. Again, there were agonizing days of waiting, with no response from the quiet figure on the cot. One day, as the mother stood by the bedside, holding the emaciated hand of her son, she begged, "Eric, if you can hear mama, squeeze my hand." The little fingers slowly tightened as the son softly squeezed the loving hand of the mother . . . .

The lad for whose life the specialists had so often despaired was again released from the hospital and was doing quite well. Bill was now involved in gospel music and was promoting concerts for some of the nation's "top flight" gospel singers. It was November 29, and the family was on tour with the Imperials and the Gospelites, when Eric's condition suddenly worsened. His body was covered with bruises. He was rushed to the emergency room of the Sacred Heart Hospital in Eugene, Oregon, and, as soon as possible, was transferred for the last time to COHMC in Seattle. Judi accompanied her son and, with the exception of a few brief visits to her home, never left the hospital for the remaining four months.

Eric had many Bible verses which were "favorites." Perhaps the verse which was his "very own" was I John 4:4: ". . . greater is he that is in you than he that is in the world." He repeated it often with his parents, and leaned heavily upon this assurance. As the little body finally surrendered to three rough years of suffering and disease, Judi bent low over her son and said softly, "Eric, remember your verse: 'greater is he that is in you than he that is in the world.'" Eric smiled, He knew, now at last, that he had won the victory. Judi went to the phone to again request special prayer, leaving Bill in the room with the son he loved. When Judi returned to the room Eric had gone home with Jesus.

Hundreds wept—and blessed God for the transformation of life and the renewal of faith which had been wrought by the life and the trust of one small boy.

Dr. Ronald Chard, Associate Director of the Division of Hematology/Oncology at COHMC, was not frequently involved with the personal care of his patients, but he formed an attachment to Eric, and frequently attended him personally. He was with him when he died. When death inexorably laid its hand upon the suffering body, Dr. Chard sent the others out of the room while he tenderly removed the needles and ministered for the last time to a boy whom he had come to love.

It was one week after Eric's death that Dr. Chard paid tribute to Eric's memory, as he wrote a personal letter of comfort to the parents. This beautiful outpouring of soul contained the following incisive paragraph:

> One would never expect all of the pain and emptiness to completely go away, because what each of us contributes no one else can exactly duplicate; however, all the strength he showed to all of us through his very difficult illness should give those of us whom he loved, particuarly you, his family, continued strength to carry on as he would have wished.[2]

The victory service was conducted at the Buell Chapel in Springfield, Oregon. The funeral director testified that the overflow crowd was the largest ever seen at the chapel. Ten ministers were in attendance. Music consisted of taped gospel solos by Doug Oldham, a friend of the family. As Pat Boone expressed it, it was a moment "etched in time and bathed in tears." Bill preached the funeral sermon for his son, and the frail house, which Eric had inhabited for almost twelve years, found rest beneath the green grass near an oak tree, on a hillside in East Springfield. The marker bears the simple inscription, "Our Son - Eric Christopher White."

---

2. Portion of a letter from Dr. Ronald Chard, dated April 27, 1978.

Following the funeral came the avalanche of cards and letters from those whose lives Eric had touched. Doctors and nurses testified freely that their lives would never be the same because of meeting Eric. Barbara Clark, who was one of Eric's doctors, wrote, "Eric's special spirit touched many lives and taught us all a great deal about courage and faith . . . . Knowing all of you has affected my life for the better."

Ellen Walton, who was Eric's "favorite" nurse, penned the following testimony to the parents:

> I hardly know what to say . . . . They say that losing a patient becomes easier as you gain experience. I guess with Eric that isn't so because he was more of a friend to me than a patient. What a blessing it was to have known him! He handled his illness the way most kids react to a bad cold— it was always hard for me to look at his lab results—then at him and know that I was dealing with the same person! . . . Last night I sat in his room for awhile and was torn between grief and warm thoughts of such a beautiful person.

God used a little boy, just as he used common people so long ago, to touch lives and bring them to Jesus, one of whom was his own maternal grandfather who, since that time, has gone to be with Eric.

Pat Boone met Eric just a short while before he became ill, and was impressed by the faith and dedication of a little boy. Bill had promoted a concert for the Boone family, and they became long-distance friends. Upon hearing of Eric's illness, Pat frequently prayed with Bill and Judi over the phone. A few months after Eric had gone back home with Jesus Pat wrote a book in which he testified to the influence that one small boy had exerted upon his own life.

276

ERIC

I met Eric when he was seven—and he died at ten (sic)—but I've met few people in any walk of life who've had more of a lasting influence on me than Eric.

I told Bill and Judy later, "You know, there won't be a whole lot of people who, after living seventy or more years, and stand before the Lord and say, *'I've brought you a hundred others.'* Yet little Eric, who only lived ten (sic) years, will be able to say that."[3]

God used one frail little boy, his body wracked with pain and disease, to lead multitudes to the foot of the cross. God help us to follow in his train!

God scooped up a bit of stardust, the impish smile of a cherub, the winsome spirit of an angel, and a small portion of the wisdom of the Infinite, wrapped it in a special package, and loaned it to the world for twelve brief years.

> "I'll lend you for a little while
>   A child of mine," He said.
> "For you to love the while he lives
>   And mourn for when he's dead.
> It may be one day or seven years,
>   Or twenty-two or three.
> But will you, 'til I call him back,
>   Take care of him for Me?
> He'll bring his charms to gladden you,
>   And should his stay be brief,
> You'll have his lovely memories
>   As solace for your grief."
>
> "I cannot promise he will stay,
>   Since all from earth return,
> But there are lessons taught down there
>   I want this child to learn.

---

3. Pat Boone, *Pray to Win* (New York: G. P. Putnam's Sons), p. 193.

I've looked the wide world over
   In my search for teachers true
And from the throngs that crowd life's
   lanes, I have selected you.
Now will you give him all your love,
   Nor think the labor vain,
Nor hate Me when I come to call
   To take him back again?"

I fancied that I heard them say,
   "Dear Lord, Thy will be done,
For all the joy Thy child shall bring
   The risk of grief we'll run.
We'll shelter him with tenderness,
   We'll love him while we may,
And for the happiness we've known,
   Forever grateful stay;
But should the angels call for him
   Much sooner than we've planned,
We'll brave the bitter grief that comes
   And try to understand."[4]

At Dartmouth College there is a building known as Dick Hall's House, built in memory of a lad who died in 1917. In the house is a book with a famous inscription, written by another father who had also lost a boy. The other father was Calvin Coolidge, who wrote in the house book: "To Edward K. Hall: In recollection of his son and my son, who have the privilege, by the grace of God, to be boys through all eternity."

From the time he was just a toddler Eric had been fascinated by rainbows. In a children's Sunday School class he

---

4. "To You Who Loved Him," author unknown (imprinted in the Memorial Brochure by Buell Chapel).

had learned how God had set His bow in the clouds as a token of His covenant-promise to Noah. How exciting to be able to look upon the beauty of the rainbow and to remember that the God Who had made it all had promised that the world would never again be destroyed by raging floods.

When he was three he showed a rainbow to his grandmother and carefully explained, "That is God's promise that everything is going to be all right."

As the plane was speeding its mercy flight from Pasco to Seattle, and was being buffeted by a raging thunder storm, God again hung His bow of promise against the black bank of clouds.

Following Eric's death, the family was making that long trip from Seattle to Eugene—but all the way through the State of Washington, across the mighty Columbia, and up the Willamette Valley, they followed a brilliant, double-rainbow. There were scores of friends who testified that they, too, looked that day upon the rainbow—and remembered Eric. Perhaps some thoughtful ones realized that the soul would have no rainbow if the eyes had no tears, and that where there is a rainbow, somewhere the sun is shining.

The long procession slowly made its sorrowing way to God's Little Acre, and as they arrived to place a little body in mother earth, the rain ceased. They looked up, and there, in the East—a rainbow.

"That is God's promise—Everything is going to be all right."

Chapter Fifteen

WHAT THE BIBLE SAYS ABOUT SUFFERING

(summary)

1. *Suffering is the common lot of man.*

> But man is born unto trouble, as the sparks fly upward (Job 5:7).

> For we know that the whole creation groaneth and travaileth in pain together until now (Rom. 8:22).

2. *Suffering came to mankind as a result of sin.*

> Unto the woman he said, I will greatly multiply thy pain and thy conception; in pain thou shalt bring forth children; and thy desire shall be to thy husband, and he shall rule over thee. And unto Adam he said, Because thou hast hearkened unto the voice of thy wife, and hast eaten of the tree, of which I commanded thee, saying, Thou shalt not eat of it: cursed is the ground for thy sake; in toil shalt thou eat of it all the days of thy life; thorns also and thistles shall it bring forth to thee; and thou shalt eat the herb of the field; in the sweat of thy face shalt thou eat bread, till thou return unto the ground; for out of it wast thou taken: from dust thou art, and unto dust shalt thou return (Gen. 3:16-19).

> Therefore, as through one man sin entered into the world, and death through sin; and so death passed unto all men, for that all sinned (Rom. 5:12).

3. *Suffering is not a penalty for the sufferer's sins.*

> Now there were some present at that very season who told him of the Galilaeans, whose blood Pilate had mingled with their sacrifices. And he answered and said unto them, Think ye that these Galilaeans were sinners above

all the Galilaeans, because they have suffered these things? I tell you, Nay: but except ye repent, ye shall all in like manner perish. Or those eighteen upon whom the tower in Siloam fell, and killed them, think ye that they were offenders above all the men that dwell in Jerusalem? I tell you, Nay: but, except ye repent, ye shall all likewise perish (Luke 13:1-5).

And as he passed by, he saw a man blind from his birth. And his disciples asked him, saying, Rabbi, who sinned, this man, or his parents, that he should be born blind? Jesus answered, Neither did this man sin, nor his parents: but that the works of God should be made manifest in him (John 9:1-3).

4. *Our suffering may be caused by the sins of others.*

And they stoned Stephen, calling upon the Lord, and saying, Lord Jesus, receive my spirit. And he kneeled down, and cried with a loud voice, Lord, lay not this sin to their charge (Acts 7:59-60).

Him who knew no sin he made to be sin on our behalf; that we might become the righteousness of God in him (II Cor. 5:21).

Of the Jews five times received I forty stripes save one. Thrice was I beaten with rods, once was I stoned, thrice I suffered shipwreck, a night and a day have I been in the deep; in journeyings often, in perils of rivers, in perils of robbers, in perils from my countrymen, in perils from the Gentiles, in perils in the city, in perils in the wilderness, in perils in the sea, in perils among false brethren; in labor and travail, in watchings often, in hunger and thirst, in fastings often, in cold and nakedness. Besides those things that are without, there is that which presseth upon me daily, anxiety for all the churches. Who is weak, and I am not weak? Who is caused to stumble, and I burn not (II Cor. 11:24-29)?

5. *Christians are not immune to suffering.*

> Yea, and all that would live godly in Christ Jesus shall suffer persecution (II Tim. 3:12).

> Then said Jesus unto his disciples, If any man would come after me, let him deny himself, and take up his cross, and follow me (Matt. 16:24).

> Because to you it hath been granted in the behalf of Christ, not only to believe on him, but also to suffer in his behalf: having the same conflict which ye saw in me, and now hear to be in me (Phil. 1:29-30).

6. *God cares when we suffer.*

> Casting all your anxiety upon him, because he careth for you (I Peter 5:7).

> For the Lord will not cast off for ever. For though he cause grief, yet will he have compassion according to the multitude of his lovingkindnesses (Lam. 3:31-32).

7. *God is with us in suffering.*

> But now thus saith Jehovah that created thee, O Jacob, and he that formed thee, O Israel: Fear not, for I have redeemed thee; I have called thee by thy name, thou art mine. When thou passest through the waters, I will be with thee; and through the rivers, they shall not overflow thee: when thou walkest through the fire, thou shalt not be burned, neither shall the flame kindle upon thee. For I am Jehovah thy God, the Holy One of Israel, thy Saviour; I have given Egypt as thy ransom, Ethiopia and Seba in thy stead (Isa. 43:1-3).

> God is our refuge and strength, a very present help in trouble. Therefore will we not fear, though the earth do

change, and though the mountains be shaken into the heart of the seas: though the waters thereof roar and be troubled, though the mountains tremble with the swelling thereof (Psalm 46:1-3).

Who shall separate us from the love of Christ? shall tribulation, or anguish, or persecution, or famine, or nakedness, or peril, or sword? Even as it is written,

For thy sake we are killed all the day long; we were accounted as sheep for the slaughter.

Nay, in all these things we are more than conquerors through him that loved us. For I am persuaded, that neither death, nor life, nor angels, nor principalities, nor things present, nor things to come, nor powers, nor height, nor depth, nor any other creature, shall be able to separate us from the love of God, which is in Christ Jesus our Lord (Rom. 8:35-39).

Be ye free from the love of money; content with such things as ye have: for himself hath said, I will in no wise fail thee, neither will I in any wise forsake thee. So that with good courage we say,

The Lord is my helper; I will not fear: what shall man do unto me (Heb. 13:5-6)?

8. *God does not cause suffering: God PERMITS suffering.*

There was a man in the land of Uz, whose name was Job; and that man was perfect and upright, and one that feared God, and turned away from evil . . . And Jehovah said unto Satan, Behold, all that he hath is in thy power; only upon himself put not forth thy hand . . . And Jehovah said unto Satan, Behold, *he is in thy hand*; only spare his life (Job 1:1, 12; 2:6).

283

9. *God permits suffering for the good of the sufferer.*

   a) To bring us back when we stray.

   Before I was afflicted I went astray; but now I observe thy word . . . . It is good for me that I have been afflicted; that I may learn thy statutes (Psalm 119:67, 71).

   b) To purify our lives.

   Behold, I have refined thee, but not as silver; I have chosen thee in the furnace of affliction (Isa. 48:10).

   c) To make us stedfast.

   And not only so, but we also rejoice in our tribulations: knowing that tribulation worketh stedfastness; and stedfastness, approvedness; and approvedness, hope: and hope putteth not to shame; because the love of God hath been shed abroad in our hearts through the Holy Spirit which was given unto us (Rom. 5:3-5).

   d) To make our lives complete.

   And the God of all grace, who called you unto his eternal glory in Christ, after that ye have suffered a little while, shall himself perfect, establish, strengthen you (I Peter 5:10).

   e) To equip us for heaven.

   But insomuch as ye are partakers of Christ's sufferings, rejoice; that at the revelation of his glory also ye may rejoice with exceeding joy (I Peter 4:13).

10. *God permits suffering for the good of others.*

   Blessed be the God and Father of our Lord Jesus Christ, the Father of mercies and God of all comfort;

who comforteth us in all our affliction, that we may be able to comfort them that are in any affliction, through the comfort wherewith we ourselves are comforted of God. For as the sufferings of Christ abound unto us, even so our comfort also aboundeth through Christ. But whether we are afflicted, it is for your comfort and salvation; or whether we are comforted, it is for your comfort, which worketh in the patient enduring of the same sufferings which we also suffer: and our hope for you is stedfast; knowing that, as ye are partakers of the sufferings, so also are ye of the comfort (II Cor. 1:3-7).

We are pressed on every side, yet not straitened; perplexed, yet not unto despair; pursued, yet not forsaken; smitten down, yet not destroyed; always bearing about in the body the dying of Jesus, that the life also of Jesus may be manifested in our body. For we who live are always delivered unto death for Jesus' sake, that the life also of Jesus may be manifested in our mortal flesh . . . . For all things are for your sakes (II Cor. 4:7-11, 15).

11. *God permits suffering that He might be glorified.*

And as he passed by, he saw a man blind from his birth. And his disciples asked him, saying, Rabbi, who sinned, this man or his parents, that he should be born blind? Jesus answered, Neither did this man sin, nor his parents: but that the works of God should be made manifest in him (John 9:1-3).

Verily, verily, I say unto thee, When thou wast young, thou girdest thyself, and walkedst whither thou wouldest: but when thou shalt be old, thou shalt stretch forth thy hands, and another shall gird thee, and carry thee whither thou wouldest not. Now this he spake, signifying by what manner of death he should glorify God . . . (John 21:18-19).

Beloved, think it not strange concerning the fiery trial among you, which cometh upon you to prove you, as though a strange thing happened unto you: but insomuch as ye are partakers of Christ's sufferings, rejoice; that at the revelation of his glory also ye may rejoice with exceeding joy. If ye are reproached for the name of Christ, blessed are ye; because the Spirit of glory and the Spirit of God resteth upon you. For let none of you suffer as a murderer, or as a thief, or an evildoer, or as a meddler in other men's matters: but if a man suffer as a Christian, let him not be ashamed; but let him glorify God in this name (I Peter 4:12-16).

12. *Jesus was made perfect (complete) through suffering.*

But we behold him who hath been made a little lower than the angels, even Jesus, because of the suffering of death crowned with glory and honor, that by the grace of God he should taste of death for every man. For it became him, for whom are all things, and through whom are all things, in bringing many sons unto glory, to make the author of their salvation perfect through sufferings (Heb. 2:9-10).

13. *Jesus is our example in suffering.*

For hereunto were ye called: because Christ also suffered for you, leaving you an example, that ye should follow his steps: who did no sin, neither was guile found in his mouth: who, when he was reviled, reviled not again, when he suffered, threatened not; but committed himself to him that judgeth righteously: who his own self bare our sins in his body upon the tree, that we, having died unto sins, might live unto righteousness; by whose stripes ye were healed. For ye were going astray like sheep; but are now returned

286

unto the Shepherd and Bishop of your souls (I Peter 2:21-25).

14. *Because Jesus suffered He understands our suffering.*

Wherefore it behooved him in all things to be made like unto his brethren, that he might become a merciful and faithful high priest in things pertaining to God, to make propitiation for the sins of the people. For in that he himself hath suffered being tempted, he is able to succor them that are tempted (Heb. 2:17-18).

Having then a great high priest, who hath passed through the heavens, Jesus the Son of God, let us hold fast our confession. For we have not a high priest that cannot be touched with the feeling of our infirmities; but one that hath been in all points tempted like as we are, yet without sin. Let us therefore draw near with boldness unto the throne of grace, that we may receive mercy, and may find grace to help us in time of need (Heb. 4:14-16).

15. *Christians should rejoice in spite of suffering.*

Blessed are they that have been persecuted for righteousness' sake: for theirs is the kingdom of heaven. Blessed are ye when men shall reproach you, and persecute you, and say all manner of evil against you falsely, for my sake. Rejoice, and be exceedingly glad: for great is your reward in heaven: for so persecuted they the prophets that were before you (Matt. 5:10-12).

And to him they agreed: and when they had called the apostles unto them, they beat them and charged them not to speak in the name of Jesus, and let them go. They therefore departed from the presence of the council, rejoicing that they were counted worthy to suffer dishonor for the Name (Acts 5:40-41).

And when they had laid many stripes upon them, they cast them into prison, and made their feet fast in the stocks. But about midnight Paul and Silas were praying and singing hymns unto God, and the prisoners were listening to them . . . (Acts 16:23-25).

Being therefore justified by faith, we have peace with God through our Lord Jesus Christ; through whom also we have had our access by faith into this grace wherein we stand; and we rejoice in hope of the glory of God. And not only so, but we rejoice in our tribulations . . . (Rom. 5:1-3).

16. *Present sufferings are not comparable with future glory.*

The Spirit himself beareth witness with our spirit, that we are children of God: and if children, then heirs; heirs of God, and joint-heirs with Christ; if so be that we suffer with him, that we may be also glorified with him. For I reckon that the sufferings of this present time are not worthy to be compared with the glory which shall be revealed to us-ward (Rom. 8:16-18).

17. *Jesus invites us to suffering - and to fellowship - and to joy.*

And he said unto all, If any man would come after me, let him deny himself, and take up his cross daily, and follow me. For whosoever would save his life shall lose it; but whosoever shall lose his life for my sake, the same shall save it (Luke 9:23-24).

Only let your manner of life be worthy of the gospel of Christ: that, whether I come and see you or be absent, I may hear of your state, that ye stand fast in one spirit, with one soul striving for the faith of the gospel; and in nothing affrighted by the adversaries: which is for them an evident token of perdition, but

WHAT THE BIBLE SAYS ABOUT SUFFERING

of your salvation, and that from God; because to you it hath been granted in the behalf of Christ, not only to believe on him, but also to suffer in his behalf: having the same conflict which ye saw in me, and now hear to be in me (Phil. 1:27-30).

For his anger is but for a moment; His favor is for a lifetime: Weeping may tarry for the night, but joy cometh in the morning (Psalm 30:5).

18. *With God, we are more than conquerors.*

Nay, in all these things we are more than conquerors through him that loved us (Rom. 8:37).

Many are the afflictions of the righteous; but Jehovah delivereth him out of them all (Psalm 34:19).

I can do all things in him that strengtheneth me (Phil. 4:13).

19. *A crown awaits the victor.*

Fear not the things which thou art about to suffer; behold, the devil is about to cast some of you into prison, that ye may be tried; and ye shall have tribulation ten days. Be thou faithful unto death, and I will give thee the crown of life (Rev. 2:10).

. . . if so be that we suffer with him, that we may be also glorified with him (Rom. 8:17).

And one of the elders answered, saying unto me, These that are arrayed in the white robes, who are they, and whence came they? And I say unto him, My lord, thou knowest. And he said to me, These are they that come out of the great tribulation, and they washed their robes, and made them white in the blood of the Lamb. Therefore are they before the throne of God; and they serve him day and night in his temple: and he that sitteth

289

on the throne shall spread his tabernacle over them. They shall hunger no more, neither thirst any more; neither shall the sun strike upon them, nor any heat: for the Lamb that is in the midst of the throne shall be their shepherd, and shall guide them unto fountains of waters of life: and God shall wipe away every tear from their eyes (Rev. 7:13-17).

20. The last word on suffering.

And I saw a new heaven and a new earth: for the first heaven and the first earth are passed away; and the sea is no more. And I saw the holy city, new Jerusalem, coming down out of heaven from God, made ready as a bride adorned for her husband. And I heard a great voice out of the throne saying, Behold, the tabernacle of God is with men, and he shall dwell with them, and be their God: and he shall wipe away every tear from their eyes; and death shall be no more; neither shall there be mourning, nor crying, nor pain, any more: the first things are passed away. And he that sitteth on the throne said, Behold, I make all things new. And he saith, Write: for these words are faithful and true. And he said unto me, They are come to pass. I am the Alpha and the Omega, the beginning and the end. I will give unto him that is athirst of the fountain of the water of life freely. He that overcometh shall inherit these things; and I will be his God, and he shall be my son (Rev. 21:1-7).

Addenda

WHERE ARE YOU, GOD?

A meditation from a hospital bed - by Willie W. White
(as published in the Christian Standard, September 30, 1979)

WHERE ARE YOU, GOD?

These boils are so painful . . . and I am covered from the
sole of my foot to my crown.

The oxen are gone. The asses are gone. The sheep are
gone. The camels are gone. My sons and daughters are
gone. There is none remaining.

My friends attribute my suffering to my sin. Miserable
comforters are they all.

My own beloved begs me to renounce God and die . . . .
God, where are You?

*I am here, Job, permitting Satan's testing, knowing that
when you have been tried, you shall come forth as gold.*

*Your latter end, Job, shall be more blessed than your
beginning.*

  Acquaint now thyself with me, and be at peace.

WHERE ARE YOU, GOD?

I have been very jealous for Jehovah, the God of hosts.
The children of Israel have broken Your covenant.
They have thrown down Your altars. They have slain
Your prophets. I, only, am left, and they seek my life
to take it away . . . .

  God, where are you?

*I am here, Elijah, and I leave seven thousand in Israel
that have not bowed unto Baal.*

*No, Elijah, I am not in the wind, nor in the earthquake,
nor in the fire—but in the still small voice.*

  I am here, Elijah; listen for me.

291

WHERE ARE YOU, GOD?

God, a stone just crushed my shoulder. And the cruel stones are falling from the hands of Your people—the priests and the council.

God, You know that I tried to be Your man. I accepted Jesus of Nazareth as the Lord of my life. I was selected to serve tables in His name because they said I was a man full of faith and of the Holy Spirit.

I testified for You before the high court. I spoke a good word for Jesus—and now I lay down my life . . . .

God, where are You?

I am here, Stephen, in the home I have prepared for you. My Son is standing at my right hand, ready to welcome home the spirit of His first martyr.

I am here, Stephen; rest in me.

WHERE ARE YOU, GOD?

God, You know that I have always been religious: a Hebrew of the Hebrews, a Pharisee of the Pharisees. As touching zeal, persecuting the church; as touching righteousness, found blameless.

And You called me to be a chosen vessel, to bear Your name before Gentiles and kings, and the children of Israel.

Five times I have received forty stripes save one. Three times I was beaten with rods. Once I was stoned. Three times I suffered shipwreck. I have been in journeyings and perils and labor and travail . . . and now, God, this thorn in the flesh . . . .

God, where are You?

I am here, Paul, to strengthen, sustain and comfort. My grace is sufficient for you, Paul, for my power is made

292

perfect in weakness. Take pleasure in that weakness,
for when you are weak then are you strong in me.
I am here, Paul; lean hard on me.

WHERE ARE YOU, GOD?

The island is lonely, and the cave cold and dreary. The
restless sea is beautiful, but it bars me from my loved
ones.

I left nets to follow the Nazarene. I was closest to Him.
I was "the disciple He loved." I was with Him on the
mount of transfiguration, in the garden, and at the
cross. I took His mother into my own home. I have
ever been faithful.

And now I am in the isle that is called Patmos, for the
Word of God and the testimony of Jesus . . . .
God, where are You?

I am here, John, in the city not made with hands — the
city that knows no sickness, sorrow, pain, or death —
eternal in the heavens.

I am waiting for you, John. Lift up your head; your re-
demption draweth nigh.

WHERE ARE YOU, GOD?

The thorns pierced deeply. The soldiers struck me and
spit in my face. The scourge lacerated my back until it
was a raw mass of bloody pulp. And the cross! The
cross was so heavy; and it was laid upon my bruised
and bleeding back.

The spikes are agonizing, as I press against them, striving for breath.

The religious leaders mock me. I who knew no sin am
ready to become sin on their behalf — and You, my

Father, will hide Your face . . . . My God, my God, why has Thou forsaken me?

God, where are You?

I am here, Son, in the home which You had with me from the beginning. I shared Your pain. I felt every blow. I heard every word. My heart, too, is breaking. But daylight lies just beyond the darkness . . . joy lies just beyond the grief . . . home lies just beyond the exile.

I am here, Son; welcome home.

WHERE ARE YOU, GOD?

God, it has been such a difficult year!

We love You. We trust You. We strive to serve You. But this year we have known suffering. We have said good-bye to loved ones. Those who are dearest to us have been in the valley of affliction.

That to which we looked for "security" has melted away. The "golden years" are becoming tarnished . . . .

God, where are You?

I am here, my child; standing here in the shadow, keeping watch over my own.

I am here where I was when I lost my own son . . . when He left the courts of glory for the darkness of a sin-cursed world, a man of sorrows and acquainted with grief, having nowhere to lay His head, and not owning six feet of ground, in which to be buried.

I am here. I understand. I care. Cast all your care upon me, and someday you, too, will understand that all things work together for good . . . .

I am here, my child; trust me.

294

THE END OF THE MATTER

More than a year has now passed since I set out upon the quest to rediscover what the Bible really says about suffering. Our journey has taken us over ground that has been watered with tears and stained with bloody footprints.

There remains much that is yet to be discovered in the land of human suffering. We have found that suffering contains within it much which may be used for the glory of God and the good of man. Suffering has within it these *possible* values, but not these *inevitable* values. The value of suffering is left for you to determine.

If you will but recognize suffering for what it is—accept it —use it—throw nothing away—and see it through with God, you will have begun to comprehend the meaning . . . the value . . . the beauty . . . and the joy of suffering.

This is the end of the matter; all hath been heard: Fear God, and keep his commandments; for this is the whole duty of man (Eccl. 12:13).

295

Bibliography

Applebury, T. R. *Studies in Second Corinthians.* Joplin, MO: College Press, 1966.

Archer, Gleason L. Jr. *The Book of Job.* Grand Rapids: Baker Book House, 1982.

Beeman, June. "Where Are You When It Hurts?" *Christian Standard.* Cincinnati: Standard Pub.Co. (Oct. 2, 1983).

Boone, Pat. *Pray To Win.* New York: G. P. Putman's Sons.

Boatman, Don Earl, ed. *Out Of My Treasure.* Vol. II. Joplin: College Press, 1965.

Brown, Robert A. "A Worthy Environment," *The Divine Purpose,* edited by W. Carl Ketcherside. St. Louis: Mission Messenger, 1972.

Church World Press, Inc. The Fellowship of Suffering, *Be Assured.* Cleveland.

Doty, Brant Lee. "Job—The Problem of Suffering," *Christian Standard.* Cincinnati: Standard Pub. Co. (Dec. 14, 1967).

Forbush, William Byron, D.D. *Fox's Book of Martyrs.* Philadelphia: Universal Book & Bible House, 1926.

Fowler, Harold. *The Gospel of Matthew.* Volume Three. Joplin: College Press, 1978.

Gaither, William & Gloria. "Joy Comes In The Morning." Alexandria: Alexandria House, 1974.

Halley, Henry H. *Halley's Bible Handbook.* Grand Rapids: Zondervan Pub. House, 1965.

Johnson, B. W. & Don DeWelt. *The Gospel of Mark.* Joplin: College Press, 1965.

Jones, E. Stanley. *Christ and Human Suffering.* New York, Nashville: Abingdon-Cokesbury Press, 1933.

Ketcherside, W. Carl. *Talks To Jews and Non Jews.* Cincinnati: Standard Pub. Co.

Ladd, James Earl. *As Much As In Me Is.* Portland: Beattie & Co., 1951.

Lewis, C. S. *The Problem of Pain.* New York: MacMillan Pub. Co., 1962.

Lutzer, H. Erwin. *How To Say No To A Stubborn Habit.* Wheaton: Victor Books, 1979.

Maclaren, A. *A Homiletic Commentary on the Book of Psalms,* by W. L. Watkingson. N.Y./London: Funk & Wagnalls Co.

Maxwell, C. Merwyn. *Man, What a God!* Mountain View: Pacific Press Publishing Assn., 1970.

McConkey, James H. *The Surrendered Life.* Pittsburgh: Silver Pub. Society, 1902.

McMillen, S. I., M.D. *None of These Diseases.* Westwood Fleming H. Revell Co., 1963.

Moody, Dwight L. *When Loved Ones Are Called Home,* by Herbert H. Wernecke. Grand Rapids: Baker Book House, 1972.

Morgan, Anna Rose. *The A, B, Cs of My Dying.* Bend: Maverick Publications, 1980.

Morgan, Anna Rose. *Until That Day.* Bend: Maverick Publications, 1982.

Orr, William W. *Does God Heal Today?* Los Angeles: Bible Institute of Los Angeles.

Paton, Everett J. *I Won't Be Crippled When I See Jesus.* Minneapolis: Augsburg Publishing House, 1979.

Robertson, A. T. *Word Pictures In The New Testament.* Vol. 5. Nashville, 1933.

Spurgeon, C. H. *Treasury of David,* condensed by David Otis Fuller. Grand Rapids: Zondervan Pub. House, 1940.

Sternberg, Brian with John Poppy. "My Search for Faith," *Look.* (March 10, 1964).

Storjohann, Eugene. "The Biblical Meaning of Taking Up Your Cross," *Christian Standard.* Cincinnati: Standard Pub. Co. (Oct. 21, 1973).

Strauss, James D. *Shattering of Silence — Job.* Joplin: College Press, 1976.

212 Victory Poems, compiled & written by Clifford Lewis. Grand Rapids: Zondervan Pub. House, 1941.

Weatherhead, Leslie D. *Why Do Men Suffer?* New York, Nashville: Abington Press, 1936.

White, W. W., ed. *Out Of My Treasure.* Vol. I. Joplin: College Press, 1964.

Yancey, Philip. *Where Is God When It Hurts?* Grand Rapids: Zondervan Pub. House, 1977.

Index of Topics and Authors

Index of Scriptures

INDEX OF SCRIPTURES